The Next 40 Days to Enlightened Eating:

Transformation Through Yoga and *Ayurveda*

ELISE CANTRELL

Shining Lotus Publishing books may be ordered through booksellers or by contacting:

Shining Lotus Publishing

524 Sir Howard Circle

Kohler, WI 53044

www.shininglotusyoga@gmail.com

www.40DaystoEnlightenedEating.com

1(920) 287-7302

1(920) 917-8562

ISBN-:978-0-9963624-4-3
ISBN-:978-0-9963624-5-0

Cover image/photography is a copyright of Ella Gamba Photography.

Billie Edmonds, Editor

Sharon Smith-Carter, Assistant Editor

Christine Hitchcock, Designer

Printed in the United States of America

Acknowledgements

I would like to express my heartfelt gratitude and appreciation to Billie Edmonds, my editor, and mother, for her sharp eye for language, grammar, and syntax. I am grateful for the professional editing job done by my dear yoga instructor/editor friend, Sharon Smith-Carter, whose suggestions helped this book come together in perfection. I deeply thank friend and professional photographer, Ella Gamba for her creative and professional book cover photography. I would like to thank friend and graphic artist, Christine Hitchcock for the beautiful book interior and cover design. I thank my longtime friend Shannon Schomberg for helping me develop, design and revise the Daily Food Journal.

The book would not be possible without the insights, inspirations and enthusiasm of my students, clients and friends. I want to thank you from the bottom of my heart. Most of all I want to thank my precious family for their support, sacrifice and for enduring the writing and publishing process. Without your love and support, I would not be sharing my passion with others! I want to thank God for writing this book through me, for the credit belongs to God alone! Thank you to the masters, gurus, teachers, scientists, philosophers and dreamers who developed and passed on the amazing sciences of Yoga and *Ayurveda*. What was truth then, is truth today. It is my prayer that the truth behind human health is rediscovered here in the 21st century.

Namaste,

Elise Cantrell

In Dedication and Appreciation

This book/material is possible because of the wisdom of my guides, teachers, numerous authors, and experts in the field of Yoga and *Ayurveda* as well as my students, clients, family and friends. I have been especially and deeply influenced by my studies at the White Lotus Institute, Kripalu institute of Yoga and health, The American Institute of Vedic Studies, numerous *Ayurvedic* textbooks by Dr. David Frawley and Dr. Vasant Lad as well as each and every writer mentioned in the bibliography and more.

I am a student for life and I am continually reading, studying and learning. There are so many insights and inspirations that I have expressed in this book which have come from my own personal journey. My ideas have developed and evolved over a period of years from countless observations and experiences with students, clients and myself. It is impossible for me to acknowledge or remember the source from which every idea came. Oftentimes, it seemed to me as if my hands were typing, but the book was writing itself!

If I have inadvertently herein articulated a concept as my own, as if from my own thoughts, but if in fact they are someone else's, I express my sincere apology. I am deeply appreciative of the transmission of this wisdom, and will happily correct any misperception to honor authentic authorship. It is my pure intention to help lead others to better health and a better life.

To all who have played a role in the creation of this book, I honor the light and the teacher *within you*, which has inspired the light and the teacher *within me*.

Namaste,

Elise Cantrell

Table of Contents

PART 3 Eating for the Spirit

Introduction

Let us be together,

Let us eat together,

Let us be vital together,

Let us be radiating truth,

radiating the light of life. ~The Upanishads

Deep down we all know that eating the way we were designed to eat is the way to perfect health, energy and longevity, but knowing that isn't enough. If you are reading this book, then you have been divinely guided to make changes in your eating and in your life to honor your mind, body and soul. You have been inspired to practice the "yoga of eating."

In this book, I will show you a path. I have walked this path myself for many years. However, information does not lead to transformation; you have to "walk the walk." I cannot walk it for you. Each day is another step moving you forward. What I do promise is that if you walk this path, you will not turn back. You will not look back. You will never long for the old you. What I promise is transformation. Wellness is our true nature. When we eat in alignment with wellness, we default to our natural state of health and vitality.

For decades now we have entrusted the food industry with our diet and with our health. Modern processed food, convenience food and fast-food has allowed us to live a fast-paced life. However, we have lost quality of our food along with quality of our life! Our trust in the food industry has been misplaced as they have put profit above safety and health of the consumer. The food industry has failed us by feeding us toxin laden artificial foods that have made our culture sick, depressed and fat. If it could be determined how many deaths are direct results of the foods we eat, it would surpass our greatest fears. We deserve better! For the highest good of humankind, it is essential that we slow down, simplify our lives and return to the sacred act of preparing our meals with natural wholesome ingredients which grow on bushes, plants, vines and trees. It is essential to reestablish the harmony that once existed between man and nature. This harmony existed because we are nature.

When it comes to diet, the laws of health are constantly being broken. Most people dig their own graves with their knives and forks. The animals in the zoo are fed more scientifically than the average human being. ~Parmahansa Yogananda

What is Yogic Eating?

- Yogic eating is about cultivating *sattva* or harmony and purity in our diet to support harmony and purity in our body, mind and soul.

- It is about eating in balance, with mindfulness, in alignment with the mind, body and soul.

- Yoga means unity, oneness or to "yoke" or "unite." Yoga is a practice of cultivating oneness, oneness with your authentic self, with others, with nature and with all that is. It is about uniting the body, mind and soul. Eating is also a practice of oneness. After all, you become one with everything you eat. You become one with the food, and it becomes one with you. What you eat, you become. Who and what you are now is a direct reflection of the foods you have eaten. What you eat *now* determines who you are to become.

- Yogic eating has been traditionally connected to its sister science *Ayurveda*. *Ayurveda* is a complex healing science of eternal truths, timeless wisdom and common sense. *Ayurveda* is built upon basic principles, which operate within the innate intelligence of nature. It teaches that we create rhythm, order and harmony within ourselves when we operate in balance and harmony with nature at large. *Ayurveda* assumes that humans themselves are part of the natural world. Nature mirrors the inner workings of our bodies and minds. We are a microcosm of the macrocosm. We are nature! It is only when we become at odds and out of harmony with nature, that our body-mind system falls prey to chaos, imbalance and *disease*. *Ayurveda* is quite simply common sense that we have lost in the modern age.

- *Ayurveda* is considered the "mother" of all healing systems. It is full of common sense and age-old wisdom just like a mom! When I need trustworthy advice, I always turn to my own mother. For wellness, health and healing it makes sense to consult the mother of healing and health, *Ayurveda*.

- *Ayurveda* literally translates as the "science of life" or the "science of longevity." Modern medicine has over-complicated things, and has "surgically" separated the body from the mind and spirit. It is impossible to heal the body without healing the mind too. Most importantly, the soul cannot thrive in an atmosphere of disharmony and disease. Now more than ever this world needs your soul to thrive!

It is important to note that in *Ayurveda*, the lack of disease does not equate to good health. Symptoms of illness only begin to present themselves at stage 4 of imbalance. Stage 5 indicates full-blown disease, and stage 6 denotes chronic disease. According to the Buddha "Our body is precious. It is our vehicle for awakening. Treat it with care." One of my deepest intentions for this book is to inspire people to the best version of themselves body, mind and soul. The sister sciences of yoga and *Ayurveda* together provide a powerful alchemy which results in overall wellbeing. I have experienced this myself first hand, and time and time again, I have witnessed it in my students. I have done my best to make the health and eating principles of these timeless healing sciences practical, easy to follow and understandable to all.

An "Enlightened" Approach to Weight Loss The biggest surprise? A more "Zen" approach really works! People lose weight, come off of medications, and discover the best versions of themselves. The skin begins to glow, inches melt away, thinking becomes clear, and energy is awakened. A harmonious approach to weight and health enlivens on every level! Extreme eating and exercise regimes never work for the long term. They result in fatigue, frustration and injury. Hard-core regimes are not the only way, and are not sustainable for life. With an "enlightened" approach, you can re-set appetite, cravings and metabolism while restoring health, harmony and balance for a lifetime. The book, *40 Days to Enlightened Eating* is a "Zen" approach to exercise, eating and food which sharply contrasts with conventional thinking about weight loss and health. It realigns the body, mind and spirit into harmony instead of warring against each other. The natural side effect of eating and exercising in a balanced way is ideal weight and perfect health! This holistic approach allows the healthy, fit and energetic person that was always hidden inside to finally be revealed.

Changing your eating is a journey and a practice just like yoga. With effort and discipline, just one day at a time, transformation is not only possible, it is inevitable!

> It takes 40 days to break a habit;
> 90 days to gain the new habit;
> 120 days and you are the habit;
> 1,000 days you are Master of it. ~Yogi Bhajan

It is said that God's work does itself. Perhaps that is why this book wrote itself as easily as the first 40 Days was written. So many life lessons can be learned from eating to nurture and nourish the mind, body and spirit. It is from these lessons that transformation occurs on all levels.

The Buddha told his disciples, "Do not believe a word I say, go and find out for yourself." I agree completely! I am not here to convince you that this is how to eat, but I am encouraging you to try "enlightened eating" for 40 Days and see for yourself!

Changing your eating alters you at the *cellular level*! The science of epigenetics has discovered that foods directly affect our DNA. Certain foods can turn specific genes "on" or "off." Just because you have a genetic predisposition for a condition that "runs in the family," does not mean it has to come about! You have the power to create change in the very fabric of your DNA through diet and lifestyle changes. Certain food turn on the aging genes, and other foods shut them off! Food and lifestyle choices are the miracle medicine of the future. Pharmaceutical medicines frequently don't heal the root cause, but instead they mask and suppress symptoms, while allowing the body to fall further and further into imbalance without signs or awareness. Symptoms are the body's way of imploring you to make healthy lifestyle changes. By covering up symptoms with the latest pill, we continue to support the lifestyle choices that are making us sick in the first place. This is why I encourage everyone to choose diet over drugs!

Top ways I and my students have transformed with eating alone!

- Better sleep
- No longer need medicine, as food is your medicine now
- Increased energy
- Balanced and uplifted moods
- Lower blood pressure, cholesterol, and blood sugar
- Nourishes the body back from chemotherapy
- Aches and pains disappear
- Reduced headaches
- Better metabolism
- Look and feel more youthful
- Increased clarity and positive thinking-the clouds of the mind diminish
- Lower BMI index
- Weight-loss
- Improved mood
- Reduced bloating
- Clearer, more radiant skin
- Shinier, thicker and stronger hair and nails
- Improved digestion
- Improved overall sense of wellbeing and health
- Healthy weight

If you try just a few of the suggestions I give you over the 40 Days, you will change! If you do many of the suggestions, you will transform!

If you Change nothing, nothing will change. ~unknown

Why 40 Days? Beyond the spiritual implications of the 40 Day time period discussed in *40 Days to Enlightened Eating,* changing your diet and lifestyle is not something most people can do overnight! The science of *Ayurveda* teaches that the mind is also an instrument of digestion. The mind must digest new ideas and information in manageable "bite-sized" nuggets. If the mind is fed too much information at once, not everything will be digested or absorbed, just like overeating food causes indigestion! It is my desire to make these new eating and lifestyle changes palatable, digestible and a lasting habit.

Ayurveda can be a complex science, but it is my intention to make it understandable, applicable and doable for everyone! It has been said that, "You can do everything you want, but not at the same time." Learning and teaching the sciences of Yoga and *Ayurveda* have taught me that it is best to absorb a little bit every day! Making a few small changes daily add up to huge transformation over time! Too much at once can lead to feelings of being overwhelmed and frustrated. For the next 40 Days, take just one day at a time. Just a few changes each day over 40 days, constructs a whole new lifestyle and a whole new you! With these changes, you can't help but transform your body, mind and soul! By combining the changes in *40 Days to Enlightened Eating* followed by *The Next 40 Days to Enlightened Eating: Deepening the Journey* in succession for 80 days, you will climb to the summit of your existence to meet the best version of you!

To journey without being changed is to be a nomad. To change without journeying is to be a chameleon. To journey and be transformed by the journey is to be a pilgrim.

~Mark Nepo

The best version of you is already there waiting to be liberated. The world needs that YOU to show up . . . to serve the highest good of yourself and all creation. If not now, when?

40 Days to "ENLIGHTENED" Eating means:

E–Easy: Recipes are stress-free and hassle free.

N–No deprivation: Never go hungry. Never sacrifice taste.

L–Life-force: Foods are full of vitality-nutrient dense

I–Intelligent: Foods containing the intelligence of nature

G–Get slimmer: Return to your optimal weight.

H–Healing for mind, body and soul.

T–Time friendly: Quick and convenient recipes for busy lives

E–Eating with intention and mindfulness

N–Natural foods: Whole foods, chemical-free, non-GMO

E–Earth friendly: Organic and non-GMO

D–Delicious: Food must taste great!

Body, Mind and Spirit

This book is divided into 3 parts: Eating for the body, the mind and the spirit. First it is important to understand how food and the physical body interact. Here we will focus more on the physical. In *Ayurveda*, the physical body is referred to as the "food body" or *annamaya kosha,* because it is composed entirely of the foods we eat! Once the physical body is reaping the benefits of right eating, the "mental body" or *manomaya kosha* (the thinking and emotional part of our being) begins to reap the rewards. Once our thoughts and emotions are stable and harmonious, and the physical body is functioning at its optimum, the spirit, the part of us that is infinite and eternal, is able to thrive. A thriving spirit is essential for a blossoming soul. It is here that we have access to our greatest and highest self. It is here that we show up in the world in the way we are designed.

Often people ask me what food has to do with our spirit or our soul. The answer is this:

As above, so below. As within, so without. As the universe, so the soul. ~Hermes Trismegistus

Whatever is going on inside of your body, mind or soul, is what will manifest in your outward life. The *external* will mirror the *internal*. When you make changes at the very building block level or your existence, at the DNA level (and you can with your diet) the small things come together inside of you, and allow the bigger things to begin to fall into place. It is just that simple. I have seen it happen over and over, with myself and with my students and clients who have taken this journey with me. When we begin to intentionally create health and harmony in our bodies, it begins to show up in our lives.

It is my greatest hope and fervent prayer that this book becomes obsolete. It is my hope there will be no more GMO tainted foods, and no more harmful artificial and chemical ingredients. It is my prayer that foods will not be doused in pesticides, herbicides, antibiotics, growth hormones and chemical fertilizers, and that diet related death and disease will become a thing of the past. After all, "The food you eat can be the safest form of medicine, or the slowest form of poison." ~Ann Wigmore

It is my intention that humankind will return to harmony with its true nature, which is wellness, ease and balance. It is my intention that cancers, autoimmune disease, heart disease, diabetes, stroke, autism, ADD, ADHD, Alzheimer's, and the many other diseases that plague our times, will become but a distant memory! This journey begins with each of us individually. This journey begins with YOU!

Part 1
Eating for the Body

Day 1

Reboot

Welcome to today. Another day. Another chance. Feel free to change. ~unknown

When the computer gets slow and sluggish or even stuck, what do we do? We reboot! After rebooting it is amazing how much better, faster and more efficiently it runs! The body, mind and soul are the same. By resetting the body, you also reset the mind. By uplifting and clarifying the mind, you enliven the soul. True wellbeing, optimal energy and health, must encompass all three components of who we really are body, mind and soul.

The reason most eating plans fail is that they are only focused on the external appearance of the physical body. They are not a lifestyle change, only a means to an end! Our culture focuses on a "bikini body," "6-pack abs," and "getting ripped" and places a culturally idealized version of the physical frame on a pedestal above the mind and the soul. To obtain a flawless body on the outside; we often end up doing great damage on the inside. We place the body, mind and soul in competition and opposition rather than in alignment. In order to obtain this cultural ideal, the body, mind and soul are often undernourished and underfed. They are punished, overworked, under-rested and whipped into shape.

You will never arrive at the optimal version of you or your best and highest self by taking a path of abuse, misuse and deprivation. These 40 days are about nourishing, and nurturing the body, mind, and soul by returning to alignment with the foods they were designed to consume and embracing a lifestyle of health, wholeness and wellbeing. It is only when we do these things, that we are empowered to live the life we were meant to live.

We have been tempted, betrayed and deceived by the diet industry, the food industry and the pharmaceutical industry to give away our personal power and control over the energy, health and vitality that is our birthright. We were created to be vibrant, happy, healthy and whole. Now is the time to reclaim our bodies, retrieve our minds and awaken our souls so we can become the greatest contribution and serve the greatest and highest good.

It is empowering to know that each of us has everything we need to heal and transform within our reach and within ourselves. We often get so ingrained in the habits and lifestyle choices we have been making, that we forget that we ourselves are the keys to change. Transformation begins with taking back control in your own life and making new empowered choices.

There is no looking backwards and lamenting about what you should have done, could have done or used to do. The power to change lies in the "now." Staying focused on making conscious lifestyle changes in the present moment, on an on-going basis, is the path to transformation. Taking one day at a time, will allow us to become the architect and the builder of the best version of ourselves over the next 40 Days.

To rebuild and renew, the architect and builder begin with a clear, well thought out design and plan. Then the ground is cleared so the foundation can be laid. Beginning today we will follow a 40 day plan to rebuild the body, renew the mind and enliven the soul from the inside out using the very basic building materials humans are composed of: food.

> I decided to start anew, to strip away what I had been taught.
>
> ~Georgia O'Keefe

Digestion: The Cornerstone of Weight and Health

Ayurvedic physicians have known for millennia that optimal weight and health begin with digestion. When I have clients or students come to me and tell me that they have healthy eating habits, and a regular healthy exercise regime, yet still seem to gain weight or are unable to lose excess weight, the most likely culprit is digestion on some level! Once we improve digestion and eliminate *ama* (toxic sludge) from the channels, tissues and cells, then healthy eating and exercise begins to do its work. However, if digestion is poor and *ama* is present, no amount of exercise, healthy eating or calorie cutting will do the trick to help you obtain optimal weight and health. Everything always boils down to healthy digestion.

The single most important factor in overall health, weight, energy and vitality is digestion. In the healing science of *Ayurveda*, digestion occurs not only in the belly. The seven tissues of the body (plasma, blood, muscle, fat, bone, nerve and marrow, and reproductive tissues) digest food material that is given to them. The cells themselves must also digest and assimilate the nutrients at a cellular level. Over time, with less than optimal eating habits, all levels of digestion weaken and we begin to build up a post-digestive residue in the tissues, channels and cells, as well as in the space around the cells. It can be compared to the clogs that happen in the engine of a car when routine maintenance is not followed. This sludge slows down and prevents the proper digestion and absorption of nutrients. *Ayurveda* refers to this slimy substance as *ama*.

As we age, digestion can slow down and become less efficient. Many women find that around menopause the metabolism seems to slow down and weight begins to accumulate, even if they are exercising and eating the same way they always have. When the metabolic process slows, it is always due to inefficient digestion and the accumulation of heavy, toxic *ama*. *Ama* blocks nutrients from flowing through the channels and being absorbed into the cells, tissues, organs, and brain. To "reboot" the metabolism, energy, vibrancy and vitality that comes along with an optimal digestion, we must clear away *ama* and restore digestion its ideal state. The big question is how do we eliminate *ama*?

Ayurvedic Cleanse/Detox

Ayurveda implements a periodic cleanse/detoxification process, to help eliminate *ama* from the channels, tissues and cells and to give the digestion process a boost. A detox or cleanse is like getting an oil change and a "tune-up" for your car. The murky, thick sludge is removed from the engine to keep it from clogging things up. When the engine is clear, it can run more efficiently. The car can "rev" and go at FULL THROTTLE! And so, it is with the body and metabolism!

When spark plugs become corroded, they can't spark. When our channels, tissues and cells become over-run with muck of *ama*, we lose our spark and radiance! A deep cleanse is recommended with the change of the seasons, particularly in the fall and the spring. Since *Ayurveda*'s purpose and goal is to bring the body back to its natural state of balance, it does so in a way that is never harsh or extreme. There is never any starvation, depletion or removal of vital energy and nutrients, but only the removal of waste and toxins. As we remove waste and toxins, the natural outcome is improved energy, metabolism, digestion and weight loss. Contrary to what we have been conditioned to believe, we don't have to go hungry to lose weight!

Modern medicine can no longer dismiss the fact that clearing toxins and subsequently refueling the body with nutrient dense food not only prevents disease, but can reverse it! Studies have shown that diseases such as Diabetes, Heart Disease, Fibromyalgia, Alzheimer's, Lupus, Rheumatoid Arthritis and even cancers have shown an astonishing response to detoxifying the system and revamping the diet by focusing on nutrient dense foods and eliminating foods containing or causing toxicity in the body. Often, with diet alone, the disease process can be reversed and prevented without the need for medicine. (Please do not discontinue medications without consulting with your physician.) In *Ayurveda*, the healing process almost always begins with detoxifying and cleansing so that the body can better absorb healing nutrients. How can you tell if you need to detoxify?

The following are signs and symptoms that your channels, cells and tissues are clogged with toxins *(ama)***:**

- Difficulty losing weight even with healthy diet and regular exercise.
- Weight gain despite healthy diet and exercise.
- Low or unpredictable energy levels. Ongoing fatigue.
- Cravings for sweets, alcohol or junk foods.
- Forgetful, muddled or cloudy thinking. Feeling "foggy."
- Low mood or mood swings.
- Ongoing postnasal drip and throat congestion.
- Unexplained aches and pains.
- Difficulty sleeping or restless sleep.
- Feeling bloated, water retention.
- Burping or gassiness.
- Inflammation.
- Nutritional (vitamin and mineral) deficiencies despite having a healthy diet.
- Hormonal imbalance.
- Low immunity.
- Pasty coating on the tongue, white, brownish or yellowish in color.
- Constipation or irregular bowel movements.
- Bad breath and body odor.
- Negative thoughts, self-doubt, fear, and insecurity.

Surprising Causes of *Ama*:

- Overeating (even healthy foods).
- Eating heavy meals in the evening.
- Eating late at night or during the night.
- Grazing, munching or eating within less than 3-4 hours of the last meal.
- Eating a diet heavy in meat.
- Overdoing raw foods.
- Overdoing bread, pasta or refined grains.
- Over doing heavy foods such as fried foods, dairy and cheese.
- Overly strenuous or excessive exercise.
- Sporadic or lack of exercise.
- Irregular eating times.

- Not eating when hungry. Extreme dieting.
- Eating same foods regularly. Getting stuck in a food rut.
- Consuming ice-cold beverages with or between meals.

Indications of being *ama*-free:

- Naturally awakening in the morning refreshed and energized.
- Elevated, uplifted mood.
- Sound sleep.
- Good memory and clear thinking.
- Positive thoughts, enthusiasm, creativity, inspiration.
- Disappearance of bloating, aches and pains.
- Lustrous youthful skin, hair and nails.
- Pink, healthy tongue, clear of any coating.
- Bright clear eyes, with no redness, yellowing or graying of the whites.
- Improved metabolism.
- Vibrant energy.
- Strong immune system.

Why cleanse or detox?

- Remove *ama* and toxins from tissues, channels, and cells.
- Rev up metabolism.
- Bolster immune system.
- Remove excess *dosha* and bring the *doshas* back to their natural healthy balance in the body.
- Eliminate cravings for the wrong foods
- Enhance the body's natural self-healing capabilities.
- Reverse pre-mature aging, and slow the aging process.
- Reduce menopausal symptoms.
- Return to optimal state of energy, vitality and aliveness.
- Improve overall health.
- Recover emotional balance.
- Reduce inflammation.

How to Remove *Ama* from the tissues channels and cells?

In order to reboot the metabolism, and clear away *ama* we will undertake an *Ayurvedic* cleanse. The healing science of *Ayurveda* recommends a mono-diet of *Kitchari* for optimal detoxification results. *Kitchari* is an *Ayurvedic* detox meal, which rebalances the body and the *doshas* as it encourages detoxification. Read on to discover all the great benefits of a *Kitchari* cleanse!

Benefits of *Kitchari*

Kitchari is known as "the chicken soup" of *Ayurveda*. Every ingredient has detoxifying properties. Not only does it work to detoxify the organs, channels, blood and cells, but it is known to flush out excess or toxic *vata, pitta* or *kapha dosha*. (To learn more about the *doshas,* read *40 Days to Enlightened Eating*.) *Kitchari* is a "go-to" *Ayurvedic* detox dish. It is unique from other methods of cleansing and detoxification in that it keeps the body in balance, and supports the body as it cleanses. Many detox methods distress the mind-body system. *Kitchari* is harmonizing, helping to balance the *doshas* while it cleanses. *Kitchari* also helps reduce hunger and cravings. Mung beans, an important ingredient in *Kitchari*, are a legume with powerful detoxifying properties. Mixing together equal portions of rice and beans creates a full protein causing the meal to stick with you longer and help you feel satiated, helping keep hunger hormones at bay. Juice fasts and fruit fasts do not have this balancing effect and cause blood sugar levels to surge, acidity levels to rise, and hunger hormones to soar. *Kitchari* keeps the body perfectly supported and balanced as it cleanses, and it is delicious! You never feel deprived. A *Kitchari* cleanse usually lasts from 3-7 days as needed. *Ayurveda* teaches that in order to remove the buildup of *ama* or toxins from the channels, organs and cells, it is important to detoxify the body two to three times a year.

Kitchari with mung beans vs. red lentils:

Mung beans: These legumes are considered a nutritional "powerhouse" and considered highly *sattvic* (pure and harmonious.) They are packed full of nutrients, high in fiber, and easy to digest. Mung beans are an astringent bean with powerful detoxifying properties. Mung beans are balancing for all the *doshas*. They help the body eliminate any excess *doshas* as they pass through the digestive tract. When served along with brown rice, a complete protein is formed. This allows the belly to stay full longer, and keeps hunger at bay. Mung beans are the preferred bean for *Ayurvedic Kitchari*.

Red lentils: These legumes are highly nutritive, but more difficult to digest than mung beans, and slightly more *vata* aggravating. However, they are an acceptable if mung beans are not available. Please note that some *pitta* types may not do well digesting lentils.

Adzuki Beans: Adzuki beans are another good detoxifying option for Kitchari, and tend to be a good choice for diabetics due to their insulin regulating properties. These beans are a nutritional powerhouse, and have been long known for their medicinal properties in Traditional Chinese Medicine. Adzuki beans contain a high concentration of the mineral molybdenum, which assists in liver detoxification.

Ayurvedic Detox/Cleanse — 4 Options:

Depending on your own needs and your present state of energy and health, choose from the following three *Ayurvedic* cleanse options. If you're already a healthy eater, three days can be a great reset. If your diet could stand a bit of improvement, then opt for the seven-day regime. Although people typically notice immediate improvement after detoxing, it is important to note that you cannot detox 40 years of diet and lifestyle indiscretions in 3 or 7 days! The cleanse is simply a "kick start" to a 40 day journey towards a new way of living and being clean and clear.

Option 1 — 3-7 Day *Kitchari* cleanse: This option is a deep cleanse. Choose 3-7 days depending on your previous lifestyle and eating habits. The full seven-day cleanse is recommended for those who previously have had poor eating habits, such as a diet of processed food, junk food, heavy meat or fast food. For those who already have healthy habits, 3-4 days is adequate. Personally, after completing this *Ayurvedic* cleanse for just 4 days, I told my students I felt my vision had improved. Indeed, my eyesight was better! At my yearly visit to the optometrist a month later, it was confirmed that my vision had improved 2 steps!

Morning: Hot lemon water first thing in the morning before eating. Squeeze and then drop a small wedge of fresh organic lemon into hot water. (Water should not be microwaved.) I use a teakettle to heat my water. Lemon should be fresh and organic, no pesticide residue on the peel. Just a small wedge of lemon will do. The taste should be pleasant and refreshing, not make your mouth pucker.

Breakfast: *Ayurvedic* stewed fruit (recipe at end of chapter) It is not necessary to give up coffee if it is organic and used in moderation. Optionally, you can substitute organic green tea for your coffee due to its powerful detoxifying properties. Organic coffee is fine in moderation.

How does stewed fruit help with detoxification? Not only does stewed fruit taste great, it has some cleansing properties. The spices of cinnamon and ginger help to liquefy *ama* and improve digestion. The fiber from the stewed fruit will help remove toxins through the digestive channel by promoting elimination. My students describe this dish as tasting like apple pie without the crust!

Sip throughout the day: *Ayurvedic* Detox tea. This tea recipe is known to promote the secretion of digestive enzymes, heal the gut lining, boost *agni's* digestive powers and clear *ama* from the channels. (Recipe at end of chapter.)

Between Meals:

- Leave 3-4 hours between every meal and snack. If you cannot wait 3-4 hours, you are either not eating enough or you are in a habit of grazing. After several days of this practice, you can reset your gut to eliminate munching and craving between meals. In *Ayurveda*, it is important for optimal digestion to let your food completely digest before eating again. Combining undigested food with partially digested food impedes optimal digestion and is a recipe for *ama*, sluggish metabolism, and weight gain.

- It is important to eat adequate portions at meals to prevent hunger. *Ayurvedic* detoxing is not about deprivation.

- The amount you can cup in your hands with your palms placed together side-by-side, is said to be the amount of food your body is able to fully digest at one sitting without creating *ama* according to *Ayurveda*.

- Sip *Ayurvedic* Detox tea throughout the day to liquefy *ama*. (recipe at end of chapter)

- Hot lemon water or detox tea helps when cravings hit. And as the body detoxifies, cravings are likely to arise. Be prepared to counter cravings when they arise!

- If hunger occurs, eat fresh organic fruit, nuts, seeds, veggies and hummus, dark chocolate if needed between meals. Be sure at least 3 hours have passed between every eating experience! This helps optimize digestion and clear away *ama*.

Lunch: Kitchari served over organic brown basmati rice (50% bean and spice mixture /50% rice) for lunch and dinner meals for 7 full days. (recipe at end of chapter) You will be eating kitchari for 2 meals a day during the cleanse. Serving size should be no larger than the palms of both hands cupped together made of equal portions of beans and rice. Eat lunch between 10 am and 2 pm.

Dinner: Kitchari over rice 50/50 or "kitchari cakes" cooked in ghee served over a bed of greens. (Recipe at end of chapter.) Dinner should be eaten by 7pm.

Evening: Eliminate alcohol entirely during the cleanse. Calming tea is a nice substitute for wine or alcohol. Begin to cultivate new strategies for dealing with stress other than having alcohol. Try a warm aromatherapy bath, meditation, yoga nidra, conscious breathing, time in nature, relaxing music or another coping strategy rather than turning to the "spirits!" Alcohol is "empty calories" and stresses the liver, which is a critical organ of detoxification.

Option 2 — 7-Day Cleanse Alternative: 3 days of the Kitchari cleanse as specified above, and on **Day 4** transition to the original cleanse in *40 Days to Enlightened Eating* for the next 4 days. (A quick guide is following.)

Option 3 — 7-Day Cleanse Alternative 2: Stay on the original 3-Day cleanse from *40 Days to Enlightened Eating* for 7 days. (See quick guide following for details.)

Tips:

- It is best to only drink warm water or hot tea during a meal to optimize digestion and avoid production of *ama*. Sipping warm liquids throughout the day is also encouraged, particularly the detox tea or hot water. No iced beverages! These dampen digestion and promote *ama*. Hot water is preferable because it is easier for the body to assimilate than cold or ice water, hydrating the tissues and mucous membranes. The heat helps to loosen and liquefy the sticky *ama* in your tissues, channels and cells so it can be flushed from the body.

- *Ayurveda* considers a serving size to be no larger than the palms of both hands cupped together. (2 *anjali*) This is the measurable amount of food the body is able to digest at one sitting.

- *Kitchari* should be served with an equal portion of beans and rice. Aim for a 50/50 ratio. This combination helps to form a full protein and keeps you satiated longer. My students are always amazed by how satisfied they are from a kitchari meal. It truly staves away hunger for hours!

- Do not leave a meal feeling hungry and do not leave a meal feeling too full. Moderation is the key! Over-eating and under-eating both lower the power of *agni* and thus slow the metabolism.

- Intense, excessive or extreme exercise is not recommended during a detoxification or cleansing regime. Intense exercise is known to create toxins or *ama*. It is important not to work against the cleansing process. During the duration of the cleanse, it is best to engage in light to moderate activity such as gentle to moderate yoga, walking, or other forms of non-strenuous movement. It is also encouraged to take time off from activity and let the body rest and restore during the detoxifying process.

- A suggestion is to begin "the cleanse" over a weekend for even greater results. We tend to eat more unwholesome foods and throw caution to the wind on a weekend more so than during the week. Therefore, if we break ourselves out of that pattern, and detox instead, the cleanse will have an even greater impact.

- For enhanced detoxifying effects, you can opt to add the *Ayurvedic* herb *Triphala* at bedtime. This herb, enhances digestion and absorption, improves intestinal motility, and assists with the elimination of excess *ama* and *dosha* through the digestive channel. This herb is safe to take throughout the entire 40 Days and beyond, and is one of the most widely used herbs in *Ayurveda*.

- Some people find that constipation can be an issue as their bodies adjust to a new way of eating. Take care not to eat too many raw foods, which tend to aggravate constipation. If constipation is ever an issue, a teaspoon of organic psyllium husk stirred into a glass of warm water right before bed, helps encourage regular morning bowel movements and the elimination of toxins. You can continue this practice throughout the 40 Days and even beyond if you find it helpful.

- Do not eat late in the evening or wake up in the night to eat. This is a recipe for *ama*, poor metabolism and weight gain.

*Note: Depending on the number of toxins stored up in the tissues, channels and cells, it is possible for a cleanse have a few side-effects as the toxins are released and dispelled from the body. Side effects can include headaches, loose bowel movements, more frequent urination, fatigue, and strong cravings for unhealthy foods, particularly sugar cravings. For these reasons, *Ayurveda* suggest doing a cleanse during a time where you are able to rest more than usual.

If you really want to change your life, start immediately.

~Osho

Easy Guide to the 3-Day Cleanse

Good Foods	Foods to Avoid	Shopping List
Coffee (organic)	Alcohol	Ghee (or make your own -
Dairy (organic) - butter,	Artificial colors	see Recipe)
cheese, yogurt	Artificial flavors	Organic lemons
Dark chocolate (70% or	Artificial sweeteners	Organic apples and/or pears
higher) (organic)	Candy	Organic berries, fresh or
Fresh fruits (organic)	Canned foods	frozen
Fresh veggies (organic)	Chewing gum	Fresh berries
Nuts (peanuts, cashews,	Desserts	Organic steel-cut oats (op-
and pistachios should be	Eggs	tional gluten-free)
organic)	Fast foods	Raw honey
Oatmeal (organic)	Fried foods	Organic green tea
Oils - coconut, extra virgin	Frozen dinners	Organic detox tea
olive, flaxseed, grape seed,	High fructose corn syrup	Relaxing/calming teas (as
hempseed, pumpkin seed,	Hydrogenated fats	substitute for alcohol)
walnut, sesame seed, sun-	Junk food	Organic mung beans
flower seed	Leftovers after 24 hours	Organic carrots
Snacks - nuts, seeds, KIND	Meat	Fresh ginger and garlic
Bars, LARABARs, PRO-	Non-organic foods (as pos-	Organic brown rice or
BARs	sible)	quinoa
Soups (using organic veggie	Preservatives	Nuts and nut butters (pref-
stock)	Processed foods	erably organic)
Spices and herbs	Soft drinks	Organic 70% dark chocolate
Sweeteners - honey, agave	White flour	Organic dairy
nectar, molasses, raw sugar	White sugar	Organic fruits and veg-
Teas (organic), detoxifying		etables
teas		Organic sesame oil
Whole grains - barley, black		Organic kale, spinach or
rice, bulgur, faro, millet,		Swiss chard
quinoa, whole oats, whole		Cinnamon, fennel seed,
wheat		cumin, cilantro, turmeric,
		cardamom, coriander, bay
		leaf

Recommended Recipes - Ayurvedic Detoxifying Tea, *Ayurvedic* Stewed Fruit, Elise's Simple *Kitchari*, *Kitchari* Cakes, Oven-Baked Brown Rice

What is your BMI-Body Mass Index?

Body mass index (BMI) is a simple ratio of weight to height that is commonly used to classify overweight and obesity in adults. It is defined as a person's weight divided by the square of his height. (lbs/In²). The BMI index is not necessarily a foolproof indicator of health, but it can help you determine whether or not you are at a healthy weight. Today you can determine your beginning or baseline BMI before you begin the 40 Days. At the end, we will measure it again as evidence that changing your eating has a measurable effect. Please remember that the BMI is a measuring index to help determine healthy body mass. Keep in mind the BMI does not measure who you are! Also, it is possible that someone with a healthy *kapha* constitution may not fit the "healthy weight" category specifications enumerated below. The BMI index is being presented just as a guideline to move you away from focusing so much on scales and weight! *Ayurveda* teaches that human beings are not one size fits all!

Calculate and record your BMI Index:

U.S.	Metric
$\dfrac{703 \times \text{weight (lb)}}{\text{height (in)}}$	$\dfrac{\text{weight (kg)}}{\text{height (m)}}$

Body Mass Index:

Underweight = <18.5

Healthy weight = 18.5–24.9

Overweight = 25–29.9

Obesity = BMI of 30 or greater

The Healthy Weight Paradox:

Not being overweight is not necessarily a sign of good health. There are many people who are normal or underweight and poorly nourished due to bad eating habits and poor lifestyle choices. There are some folks who have an ideal BMI, but smoke, drink heavily and subsist on a junk food diet. BMI alone does not determine your state of health. Poor nutrition may not always be evident on the outside, but is always evident on the inside! People who are not overweight and eating foods that do not contain health and vitality are not the "lucky ones." It is they who may not be getting the warning signs and motivation to change the way they are eating in order to preserve long term health, energy and vitality. It may not show up in the short term, but there is little doubt these habits will accumulate in the long term.

Shopping list for 3-Day Cleanse:

Ghee (or make your own-recipe page 38 of *40 Days to Enlightened Eating*)

Organic lemons

Organic apples/pears

Organic berries fresh or frozen

Organic steel cut oats (optional gluten-free)

Raw honey

Organic coconut milk

Organic green tea

Organic detox tea

Relaxing/calming teas (as substitute for alcohol)

Organic Mung beans

Organic carrots

Fresh ginger and garlic

Organic brown rice or quinoa

Fresh berries

Nuts and nut butters-preferably organic

Organic 70% dark chocolate

Organic dairy

Organic fruits and vegetables

Organic sesame oil

Organic kale, spinach or Swiss chard

Spices: cinnamon, fennel seed, cumin, cilantro, turmeric cardamom, coriander, bay leaf. Cumin, coriander and fennel are the ingredients in the *Ayurvedic* Detox Tea recipe.

Some other good detoxifiers to incorporate into a cleanse:

1. **Fresh organic juicy fruits**, berries, pomegranate, figs, and prunes.

2. **Organic vegetables**, especially celery, artichokes, asparagus

3. **Whole grains**, especially quinoa.

4. *Ayurvedic* **Detox tea:** Do not underestimate the effects of this powerful tea made of cumin, coriander and fennel, often referred to as CCF tea. (Recipe at end of chapter) This tea helps the body release toxins as well as excess fat by speeding up the breakdown of fat and then assisting the body to flush it out. This tea is known to increase the metabolic "fire", *agni*, according to *Ayurveda*.

5. **Pure water.** Water is nature's most potent detoxifier. Drinking plenty of pure fresh water, allows your body to eliminate toxins though the urinary tract, sweat, and the digestive system. Keep in mind that warm or hot water is known to dilate the channels and help to move and flush out *ama* keeping the channels free of blockages and build-up. Cold or ice water weakens digestion and constricts the channels while coagulating *ama* making it more difficult to flush. We can compare the effects of ice in nature to the effects of ice water in our system. Ice water slows and stagnates the flow in creeks, rivers and streams and can create blockages. This same effect is reflected in our bodies by the drinking of iced water as it creates blockages in the flow though our own internal channels. Nature is a mirror for our bodies, for we are a part of nature.

6. **Daily yoga practice.** Yoga practice cultivates regular detoxification in the body by moving the lymph through the lymphatic system, improving digestion and elimination, stimulating the kidneys and the liver (two organs involved in detoxifying the body), circulating fresh blood to the tissues, and promoting sweat.

Enlightened Food of the Day: Mung Beans

- Easy bean to digest
- Nutritional powerhouse
- Has powerful detoxifying properties
- Balancing for all the *doshas*
- Inhibits growth of tumors and cancer cells
- Low glycemic
- Lowers cholesterol
- Balancing to hormones
- High in plant protein
- A "superfood"

Affirmation: It is OK to start over and today is a GREAT day to begin anew! Today I restart making the best food choices to restore and nourish my body, mind and health!

Success journal: Record all the things you did today to make "enlightened eating" a success. Do not focus on the negative, focus on the positive!

Food for thought: Reboot! Seize this day as the first day on 40-Day journey of transformation. Very seldom is transformation sudden and instantaneous. It is a one day at a time, one step at a time process beginning with the *intention* to change for the better. Do not look back and judge yourself on what you have been doing "wrong." Stay focused on what you are doing differently now beginning today!

Recipes for the 3-Day Cleanse

Ayurvedic Detoxifying Tea (Known in *Ayurveda* as CCF Tea)

This recipe for is from The Council of Maharishi Ayurveda Physicians. Make a new batch every morning and sip throughout the day.

2 quarts of water

¼ tsp. cumin seed

½ tsp. coriander seed

½ tsp. fennel seed

Boil water in the morning. Add the spices to the water, and let steep for 10 minutes with the lid on. Strain out the spices, and pour the tea into a thermos. Sip throughout the day. This tea may also be made overnight in a crockpot.

Detox Tea #2 Good for Winter

2 Quarts filtered water

1 large piece of fresh ginger, roughly chopped

1 organic lemon, sliced into circles

2 cinnamon sticks

Raw unfiltered honey, optional

Bring ingredients to a boil. Simmer for 20 minutes. Strain and place tea into a thermos, sip throughout the day. Mix in honey to taste upon drinking. Do not boil honey, or you will lose its many healing and detoxifying properties. I also do this tea overnight in a crockpot.

Detox Tea #3 Good for Winter

FRESH turmeric, sliced (or powdered if not available)

Fresh ginger, peeled and sliced

1 Fresh lemon, sliced

1 Cinnamon stick

5 Cardamom pods

½ tsp Black peppercorns,

1 tsp Coriander seeds

2 quarts Filtered water

Bring ingredients to a boil. Simmer for 20 minutes. Strain and place tea into a thermos, sip throughout the day. Mix in honey to taste upon drinking. I also do this tea in a crockpot over night to have it ready the next day. Honey to taste to sweeten. Do not boil honey, or you will lose its many healing and detoxifying properties.

Summer Detox Tea #4

2 quarts filtered water

1 cucumber, sliced

1 lemon, sliced

1 lime, sliced

1 orange, sliced

5-10 fresh mint leaves or 2 drops peppermint essential oil

Place mixture in fridge overnight. Remove from fridge and sip throughout the day.

Ayurvedic Stewed Fruit

Eat this detoxifying fruit dish for your breakfast every day for 3 days. In Ayurveda, fruit should be eaten alone for optimal digestion.

1 organic apple or pear, unpeeled and chopped

½ cup organic fresh or frozen berries

½ cup coconut milk, full fat

½ tsp ginger powder

½ tsp cinnamon

Simmer together in a pot on the stovetop until well softened. Enjoy warm.

Elise's Simple Kitchari Recipe

This is a traditional Ayurvedic cleansing dish. Use organic ingredients. Most of the ingredients have cleansing properties. It is traditionally served over basmati rice. When served, kitchari should be combined with an equal amount of rice. Your serving size should be no larger than the palms of both hands cupped together. The rice and beans combine to make a full protein, and this combination keeps the appetite satiated. I sometimes enjoy kitchari with quinoa. It can be made in the Crockpot on low, but I prefer it made on stove top. This recipe makes enough kitchari to be eaten for lunch and dinner for 3 days.

1 cup split mung beans *(Or red lentils – see Note below.)*

1-2 carrots, finely chopped

3 ½ to 4 cups water *(I use filtered water.)*

2 Tbsp extra virgin olive oil, sesame oil or *ghee*

2 tsp turmeric

1 tsp cardamom

1 tsp coriander

1 tsp fresh ginger, peeled and finely chopped, or ½ tsp ground ginger

Large handful of fresh cilantro, chopped

1 tsp cumin

1 small bay leaf

3 cloves garlic minced

2 cups fresh organic spinach, chard or kale (bitter greens)

Juice of ½ lemon

Sea salt and black pepper to taste

Note: Red lentils can be substituted for the mung beans, however mung beans have powerful detoxifying properties and are balancing for all constitutions, while lentils are not.

First, heat the dry spices in the oil or ghee until fragrant. Stir in the carrots, garlic, and ginger, and allow to soften. Add mung beans and water to the mixture. Reduce heat and allow to thicken so that it is no longer watery, which will take about 45 minutes. Add the cilantro, greens, and lemon juice, and cook until spinach and cilantro are wilted. Salt and pepper to taste.

*Serve over organic brown basmati rice or organic quinoa.

Kitchari Cakes
I usually make kitchari cakes with the remaining kitchari and rice on the final night of my cleanse. These are great served over a bed of fresh salad greens.

Kitchari, prepared *(See "Elise's Simple Kitchari Recipe.")*

Brown rice, cooked

2 Tbsp butter, *ghee* or sesame oil

Fresh lemon juice

Blend equal parts kitchari and cooked brown rice together in a blender until a lumpy "batter" forms, like pancake batter. Do not puree, leave a bit of chunky texture from the beans and rice. In a frying pan, add 2 Tbsp of butter, oil or *ghee*. (*Ghee* makes them even more flavorful and is detoxifying!) Let the oil/*ghee* get hot, and then form the batter into several "cakes" about 4 inches in diameter. Cook over medium heat until cakes begin to firm up. They are delicate, so turn over very carefully, to cook both sides. Serve over a bed of salad greens, and drizzle with fresh squeezed lemon juice.

Yogurt Sauce for *Kitchari* Cakes

½ cup organic Greek yogurt

1 clove garlic

2 Tbsp organic oil of your choice

Juice of ½ lemon

Sea salt and pepper to taste

Blend ingredients together in blender and serve with kitchari cakes.

Oven-Baked Brown Rice (by Chef Richard Palm)

This preparation lowers the glycemic level of the rice. You can freeze this and break chunks off for each meal.

1 ½ cups organic brown rice

2 1/3 cups water

1 Tbsp organic butter or *ghee*

½ tsp sea salt

Adjust the oven rack so the rack is in the middle, and preheat oven to 365 degrees.

Place the rice in a 1½-quart casserole dish with a tight-fitting lid. In a separate pot, bring the water and butter to a boil. Once boiling, stir in the sea salt. Pour the water over the rice in the casserole dish, and place the lid on the dish. Place dish in the preheated oven. Bake on the middle rack at 365 degrees for 60 minutes.

Remove from the oven and uncover. Fluff the rice with a dinner fork. Cover with a clean kitchen towel and let rest ad steam for 5 minutes. Uncover and let the rice stand another 5 minutes.

Serve immediately, or cool and store. (You can freeze and break chunks off for each meal.)

Day 2
Setting Intentions

The starting point of any journey is having a clear intention.

~Unknown

By intention alone, great things are accomplished! Mountains are moved, and obstacles are removed! By saying "no" to old unproductive eating patterns and habits, you are saying "yes" to a better version of yourself. We as humans are so fortunate to be able to reconstruct our lives and ourselves simply through the power of intention.

An intention synchronistically organizes its own fulfillment.

~Deepak Chopra

The foods we eat set the intention for how we look, think and feel. In yoga and *Ayurveda*, our physical body is considered the *annamaya kosha or* "food body," and is composed entirely of the foods we eat. With that in mind, we have the power of rebuilding ourselves from the inside out. A house built of poor, cheap materials would have to be torn down and rebuilt completely. We humans can begin to remake ourselves today.

Once you make a decision, the universe conspires to make it happen. ~Ralph Waldo Emmerson

The food industry works diligently to set their own intentions for us with slogans like, "You just can't get enough." "You'll keep coming back for more." "Finger-lickin' good." The food industry spends billions on influencing your own intentions in favor of their profits! Foods are deliberately packaged and marketed in ways that attract and tempt consumers to buy and devour. "Big food" is known to scientifically formulate processed foods to have the perfect taste profile of salt, sugar, fat and crunch to get people to crave more and eat more so they can sell more! Many of these foods are designed to dissolve quickly in the mouth so that the brain is tricked into believing it had less food and fewer calories than it had, so that you will keep on eating! These processed foods are artificially formulated with flavor and taste enhancers because these synthetic foods would be unpalatable to eat if they were not disguised! These artificial foods do not deliver to the body nutritionally what they promise the taste buds. When our taste buds and brain are tricked on a regular basis, the mind-body system becomes confused about food. We no longer crave the foods we were designed to eat. Our palates are disturbed and false cravings are triggered . . . and we do "keep coming back for more." It is important that we are aware of the food industry's intentions, so that we can set our own intentions! Food corporation's intentions are to influence your eating in ways that create more profit. Our own intentions should serve the health of our bodies, minds and souls.

Your intention is the most powerful tool at your disposal.

~Dr. Deepak Chopra

Your body believes everything it's told! The cells in your body respond to everything you think and say. We will begin today to consciously choose thoughts and words as carefully as we choose the foods we eat! We will be harnessing the power of thoughts and words throughout the 40 days, by incorporating our own intentions and daily affirmations to empower our enlightened eating practice.

Our intention creates our reality. ~Dr. Wayne Dyer

Part of rebooting our body-mind system involves "reprogramming" our way of thinking about eating and food. Before beginning the 40 Days, you already have been setting intentions for yourself consciously or unconsciously. We often set negative intentions without even realizing it! The most dangerous intentions we set are the ones we are unaware of! What negative messages have you subtly been telling yourself? Here are some examples: "Healthy food is boring." "I hate to cook." "I have a slow metabolism." "I can't lose weight." "I weigh too much." "I am heavy." "I can't go all day without sugar." "I don't have the energy or the time to exercise." "I am tired." It came into my awareness that I was reinforcing an intention myself that was, "My metabolism has slowed down since I hit my mid-forties."

My words reflect my thoughts . . .

My thoughts reflect my beliefs . . .

My beliefs run my life . . .

Especially the unexamined ones . . . ~Judith Hansen Lasater

Become aware of the unconscious intentions you have been setting up for yourself until now. List the subtle negative messages you have been "feeding" yourself to bring them into conscious awareness: (Don't worry we will be rebooting our intentions too!)

1.

2.

3.

4.

5.

By repeatedly telling yourself these messages, you have been aligning yourself with these intentions unconsciously. How do these messages make you feel? Heavy or light? (Heavy feelings equate to physical heaviness. We will discuss this in more in more depth later in the book.) Any surprises now that you have brought these thoughts and messages into conscious awareness? Has the constant repetition of them made these your reality? Who would you be if you changed these messages?

Let's do some reprogramming! Now change and rewrite these negative messages into a positive intention. Use the same negative intention and write down its equal and opposite positive counterpart. Example: "I have a fast metabolism." "I lose weight with ease." "I am full of energy, and exercise is fun!" Now list yours:

1.

2.

3.

4.

5.

How do these new messages make you feel? Heavy or light? (Light feelings equate to physical lightness. We will discuss this more in depth later in the book.) This second list will become your intentions for the 40 days. By writing these and stating these daily, you are resetting the brain to believe a new truth, a new paradigm. By overwriting the old messages, you change your neurochemistry and build new neural-pathways. Changing your thoughts causes you to change biologically and physically to begin to align with these new intentions!

When setting your intentions, it is important that they are reasonable and believable. For example, "I am losing 2 pounds a week for the next 6 weeks," rather than "I am going to lose 10 pounds by tomorrow morning." "I will lower my cholesterol into the normal range over the next 4 months." If you don't believe your intentions, your body and mind will override them. The body doesn't lie and it can't be tricked. Each and every cell is programmed with generations of wisdom! To keep from being overwhelmed, think of a few small changes you can make. Over time, small things add up to big changes.

> You can fill an entire pitcher with one tiny drop at a time!
>
> ~The Buddha

Write the small changes you plan to make over the 40 Days right here.

> A goal that is not written is not a goal. It only becomes real when you write it down. ~Bryant McGill

1.

2.

3.

4.

5.

What are some other messages you are constantly telling yourself? The mind-body connection is so strong that if you tell yourself a certain food is "bad" for you (like chips or fries for example), and you eat it anyway, the body will respond to that intention! Begin to erase the negative stories you have been telling yourself about eating and food! Most importantly don't stress about eating! This sets an intention too! According to *Ayurveda*, stressing over eating a less than healthy food will do more harm to you than the food itself!

Intend to Practice Yoga:

Set the intention to practice yoga regularly even if it is only for 10 or 15 minutes. Even a few gentle stretches every day make a profound difference in the body-mind system. To empower yourself to keep this commitment, find a place in your home that you can devote to yoga. I keep my yoga mat out in our guest room. I make this a sacred space by surrounding the mat with special items that inspire me. The dimensions of a yoga mat are only 2' x 7', so everyone can find somewhere to place a mat indoors or out. Go to your mat anytime you need to move, stretch, meditate or relax. Let your mat be an open invitation to go within and explore who you are, what you want, and who you are becoming. I block off time on my calendar for my yoga and meditation practice. This is sacred time for me. Life and other people often have other intentions for your time, this is why it is so important to schedule in your daily practice.

Listen to your body when you practice. What is your body-mind asking for today? Some days my body is anxious for strong, vigorous movement, and my yoga practice will reflect that. Other days my body wants to stretch, relax and restore. I honor whatever shows up. My practice may range from yoga nidra, yin yoga, or restorative yoga to a gentle, moderate or even vigorous yoga practice. **As you begin to tune into the intensity of practice that your body is asking for, you learn to listen to your body's signals when it comes to eating and food. Set the intention over the 40 days to really listen and hear what your body is craving, on the mat and at the table!**

Empower: Set the intention to "empower" the body rather than achieving the "perfect" the body. The physical body is a vehicle for the spirit to experience, explore, learn and evolve. The lighter and freer the physical body, the lighter and freer you are able to move through the world on your soul's journey in physical form. Striving towards the "perfect" body keeps you distracted from your true work and keeps you focused only on the physical self, the small Self, and not on the Highest Self, the Big Self, the Soul Self. Focus on NOURISHING your body rather than perfecting your body! Perfection is an illusion, a lie! Perfection is a Soul limiting trap. Eating to empower the body also empowers the Soul.

Perfection is the enemy of the good. ~Gustave Flaubert

Practice: As you observe your eating choices and behavior with attention and awareness, ask yourself, "Does this choice align with my intentions? Does this choice support my best and highest self?" If it does not, then you may want to consider a different choice. If you decide to make a choice that doesn't align with your intentions, at least you are doing it with awareness.

Intention Bracelet: To strengthen your intentions, buy or choose a bracelet you already have, one that feels good on your wrist. Mentally and energetically infuse your intentions into the bracelet. Wear the bracelet for the 40 days. As you notice the bracelet on your wrist, be reminded of the intentions that you have set. When you feel tempted to stray away from your intentions, glance at your wrist to be reminded that those intentions are still with you.

Tip: Let what is inside your fridge and cupboard set the intentions for the inside of your body! Clean out your fridge and cupboards so that they sparkle and shine, filled only with clean foods. Let this symbolize how the inside of your body looks and feels as well!

Make your own "Convenience food!"

Freeze left-overs immediately in several individual portions for quick lunches on the go!

I often make double-batches of recipes with the intent to have a "dinner in waiting" for those days when my schedule is hectic so I don't resort to self-sabotaging fast foods, take-out food, delivery or convenience foods. This keeps me right on track!

Crock-pot cooking: I use the Crock-pot a lot for busy occasions. Most soups, chilies and stews, and even kitchari, do well in the Crock-pot!

I also make Crock-pot oatmeal the night before to enjoy on a busy morning! It takes all of 5 minutes to make, and presto you wake up the next morning with a healthy no-fuss breakfast!

What you vividly IMAGINE, ardently DESIRE, sincerely BE-
LIEVE, and enthusiastically ACT upon MUST inevitably come
to pass. ~Paul J. Meyer

Affirmation: I am ready for transformation, I begin today.

Today's biggest success:

Food for thought: Become aware of the intentions you have been unconsciously
setting in your life. Reboot your intentions too, by giving them a make-over and
creating new intentions that align with how you wish to look, think, and feel.

Journal:

My Intentions for 40 Days to Enlightened Eating

Write your intentions in positive affirming words. Write the intentions
as if they have already happened. Ex. "I feel vibrant and enjoy a steady
stream of energy each day."

Body:

Weight:

Mind:

Spirit:

Health:

Energy:

Mood:

My long-term intentions beyond the 40 days:

Day 3

Positively Positive-
Cultivating *Sattva*

The cells in your body react to everything your mind says.
Negativity brings your immune system down.

~Alexander Groseth

Yogis and sages have known for millennia that positive thoughts contribute to overall health and longevity! It is also known that pure living foods contribute to having positive thoughts, positive moods, and overall wellbeing. One of the principal goals of yoga and *Ayurveda* is to cultivate more *sattva*. *Sattva* is being in the highest state of peace, harmony and bliss. On this 40 Day journey, we will encourage and build more *sattva* though positivity, harmony and purity in body and mind. As we increase *sattva*, we develop and nurture our best and highest self. Ultimately that is what the yoga is really about: finding and uncovering that best version of YOU that has been there all along. Yoga is ultimately about clearing away that which comes in the way of our best and highest self. Here are some ways we will develop more *sattva* over the 40 days.

1. **Consciously choosing your thoughts . . . Affirmation.** On this 40 day journey, we will be harnessing the power intention through affirmations. Affirmations are intentions spoken in the *present* tense, using *positive* language, as if the outcome we desire has already happened.

Intentions compressed into words enfold magical power.

~Deepak Chopra

Words contain knowledge, energy and intent. Affirmations allow us to break out of old habits and limited thinking by the power of their vibration and energy. Using the power of affirmation consistently begins to create new neural pathways in the brain, which redirect our thoughts, energy, and actions in new positive ways. Affirmations enter into the vibrational field of the body-mind system first as an awareness, then as an invitation, and finally as a reality. Affirmations literally change the vibrational frequency of your own field of energy to match that of the words. After all, words and language is vibration and vibrations are energy. Spells and incantations work in the very same way. They harness the energy of words. Affirmations however, use the power of love and positivity to heal and transform. Every invitation you send out into the field of possibility garners a result whether it is conscious or unconscious. Affirmation harnesses the power of conscious awareness, positivity and words to bring about the intended result. Each day of the 40 Days will have a corresponding affirmation for you to speak out loud, in order to bring the intention into your field of awareness.

2. **Law of attraction:** The energy that is in your field of awareness is the very same energy that you will attract. This is called the "Law of Attraction." Become aware of the thoughts and words you are placing into your own vibrational field. By consciously choosing what we wish to attract and being mindful of that which we do not wish to attract, the act of transformation begins.

For example: Don't call it a "work-out." Words are powerful! The word "work" carries the energy of toiling, trudging, and grinding it out to get a job done. There is no JOY! Instead consciously choose physical activities that you enjoy and integrate them into your day: dancing, a brisk walk in nature, rollerblading, yoga, etc. With this shift in energy, movement no longer becomes work; it becomes fun! Move in ways that make you happy and wellness will never feel like WORK! The law of attraction is about becoming a master over your thoughts instead of letting them become the master over you! You can choose thoughts that work in your favor and bring you powerful momentum towards your success.

Are you sending out mixed messages? If you are doing one thing and saying another you are attracting mixed results! When your thoughts, actions and words align, success is guaranteed!

3. **Success.** In this 40 Day journey, we will track and record our successes, not our faults and shortcomings. Noticing and celebrating our successes rather than our failures help us attain victory and transformation! In sports, we keep score of the home runs, slam-dunks, goals, and wins, rather than every mistake and error in the game. Winning is about succeeding over and over, despite setbacks, slip-ups and blunders. In winning, we let go of missteps and keep moving forward. This is how to succeed at any goal and any journey. Placing focus on success builds positive momentum on the path to transformation.

Do not stop trying just because perfection eludes you.

~BKS Iyengar

4. **Attention.** Whatever you focus your attention on, you increase the energy around it. Where the attention goes, energy flows. We are cultured and conditioned to direct our attention to our problems, frustrations, failures, sins, shortcomings and difficulties. On this 40 Day journey, we will applaud our victories and let go of our faults and setbacks in order to keep moving in the right direction. When we obsess about our own flaws, we naturally become preoccupied with the shortcomings and flaws of others. Faults and failures become our focus, our life and our world if we let it. What kind of world do you want to live in? You make your choice simply by where you place your attention.

When we put our attention on the negative, we are increasing the power and energy of these things in our lives. We fail to recognize the progress, beauty and greatness of ourselves and others by only paying attention to the negative. Transformation happens when we learn to direct our attention to the positive end of the spectrum. Instead of staying focused on problems; focus on solutions. Instead of foibles and failures, focus on achievements and successes. Wherever your attention is, you increase that. Many folks spend much time, effort and energy focusing on their dismay about their weight or shape. Many of us criticize and judge parts of our body. Guilt about eating slip-ups consumes us. We bash our lack of willpower and self-control, and lament over perceived slow metabolism.

Stop squandering your time, energy, efforts and thoughts over things you wish to lessen not increase. Obsessing about these things only intensifies them giving them energy and momentum. When you notice yourself defaulting into negative thinking, STOP. Replace the negative thought with its opposite. Instead return your energy and attention to your desired outcome. Appreciate the things you love about yourself. Celebrate your triumphs. Notice your gifts, attributes and your beauty. As you do this, you are already effortlessly moving towards the optimal version of you!

5. *Sattva.* *Sattva* is the state of harmony, balance and purity. It is the energy of love, joy and bliss. *Sattva* is the highest vibration and most powerful energy there is. On this 40 Day journey, we are going to harness the force of *sattva* to provide added momentum, strength and potency to our intentions and ultimately to our journey through life. Increasing *sattva*, the highest state of being in the body, mind and soul is the ultimate goal of yogic eating. Eating natural divinely created whole foods connects us to divine life force or Source energy. This *prana* (spiritually charged energy) governs, directs and supports our actions, thoughts and moods to align with natural law. Simply by eating in harmony, we begin to merge with divine wisdom, creative potential, optimal health and the essence of unity and harmony. We were created to be healthy, joyful, peaceful and harmonious. Our true nature is *Sattva*. It is only lost when we become out of sync with whom we were created to be, how we were created to live, and who we are to become.

Sattva is the state of returning to who we really are. *Sattva* begins with our life-style choices *moment to moment*. Because humans are entirely composed of food, we promote *sattva* when we align with eating the way we were designed to eat: eating with *sattva*.

Delight and joy are the very essence of life-emotions that direct your inner guidance to bring abundance to your life.

~Dr. Christiane Northrup

Fact: According to *Ayurveda*, alcohol is said to work against *sattva*. It promotes the opposite energy from *sattva*: darkness, dullness and inertia. When we over-imbibe, we work against our highest selves.

Why is alcohol called "spirits?" Historically, alcohol was called "spirits" because it sometimes makes people behave out-of-character, as if possessed. They may do things they wouldn't ordinarily do, even inappropriate, shocking things. Often this outrageous behavior can be accompanied by blackouts as if the person's body has been taken over by spirits. Many intuitives, clairvoyants and psychics notice that alcohol creates holes in the aura, which can allow entities, parasites and attachments access to your consciousness. This is also why people do things that are out of character that they regret when under the influence of alcohol. This is also why they have "black-outs" because their consciousness can be taken over by other energy beings. The English word "alcohol" comes from the English word for an entity, "a ghoul" or al-cohol." This English word is derived from the Arabic word "al-kuhl" which was the name of a body-eating spirit. Alcohol is a known depressant, and when used on a regular basis can facilitate negative thinking, self-doubt, low mood, gloomy demeanor, anger and melancholy. In *Ayurveda*, alcohol is considered *tamasic* carrying the energy of darkness, dullness and dispiritedness. This is the opposite energy of *sattva*.

Affirmation: Today, I align myself with my true nature and highest essence; beginning with the foods I eat.

Today's biggest success:

Food for thought: Success is a positive outcome. In order to cultivate success with anything you do, you must stay focused on the positive in order to reinforce it. When we focus on our failures and shortcomings, then it is really those we are strengthening. Where attention goes, energy flows. Stay focused on your positive steps forward on your journey to Enlightened Eating.

Journal: Contemplate today's teaching on positivity. What does this shift for you?

Day 4

Inquiry And Investigation

Don't believe anything I tell you.
Go and find out for yourself. ~The Buddha

It is no wonder that I am a *Kripalu* yoga instructor. Kripalu yoga is all about inquiry and investigation. It is about experimenting with what is right for you in your practice. We give ourselves permission to explore, and with trial and error, we discover new ways of doing things and better ways of being!

I was born with an "inquiring mind". This has been both a blessing and a curse. At the age of three I remember standing in the seat of a chair at the kitchen counter "helping" my mother cook. On the counter was an assortment of colorful peppers. As she left the kitchen for a moment, my mom warned me not to eat them, they were too hot! Well, she barely got out of the room before I had one of the hot peppers in my mouth. Inquiry got the best of me! She returned to shrieks and tears! It was in this moment that I learned that sometimes when you bite into inquiry, it bites back! Undeterred, this was only the beginning of my life of inquiry.

As a kid, my favorite TV show was Leonard Nimoy's, In Search Of . . . As an adult, my inquiry is body, mind and spirit. I am "in search of" the truth at the core of soul, spirit, God and self. At its core, yoga is really about inquiry. In yoga and *Ayurveda* philosophy, it is understood that direct perception alone is the path to truth. Generations of gurus, sages, and rishis spent their days exploring the sensations, benefits, and body/mind enhancing effects of postures, hand *mudras*, poses, pressure points, herbs, breath techniques, and meditation practices. (They had plenty of time on their hands before the dawn of Facebook, Instagram, Google and Pinterest) Some yogis even learned how to stop the heart and still the breath, as if no longer alive. Yoga was born out of inquiry! Yoga itself was developed from direct perception, trial and error. Over millennia of trial and error, yoga has evolved into a powerful practice of inner peace, healing and health. It is also a practice that leads us to our own inner truth.

Little did I know when tasting those hot peppers, that I was already destined for the path of yoga. I cannot imagine life without my inquisitive and curious nature! Where would we be without inquiry? If Galileo had failed to inquire into the solar system, we would still adhere to the notion that the earth was at the center of the universe! If Christopher Columbus hadn't set out to explore the planet, we'd still believe that Earth was flat! Can you imagine what technology would be like without the inquiring mind of Steve Jobs or Mr. Bill Gates? Inquiry leads to discovery, discovery leads to understanding, understanding leads to true knowledge, and true knowledge leads to evolution. Without inquiry, intelligence as we know it would stand still. It is inquiry or direct perception, which keeps moving us forward. Nothing is more "enlightening" than actual experience!

What if we viewed life as more of an experiment rather than something to perform or perfect? Each of us can look back and see that we learned so much more from our own trials and errors, than from following a script. Often we are closed off to trying something new. "What if I don't like it? What if I look stupid? What if it is a waste of time? What if it is a waste of money?" I think that the very worst thing that could happen is to NOT to have tried something new, and NEVER have had the chance to find out that I DID like it, I DIDN'T look stupid, and not only was NOT a waste of time, but it changed my life! What is it that you have been waiting to try, explore, or examine? Inquiring minds want to know!

Get out of your old comfort zone! Experiment with recipes, ingredients, new restaurants and new ways of eating that get you out of the rut! Inquiry, investigation and experimentation is essential in the practice of life and in the practice of eating. Constantly experiment in your kitchen and in your life to find better ways of doing things better ways of being and better ways of living! When it comes to eating, and exercise I am my own Guinea pig, trying new recipes, practices, and ways of doing things. Each time I restart the 40 Days for myself, I set up a new inquiry for myself. At one time or another I have tried dairy-free, coffee-free, alcohol-free, gluten-free, vegan in my quest for ways of eating that worked for me. As I experimented, I was able to decipher how I felt with these changes, mind, body and soul. By experimenting, I was able to discover what was right for me and my body! I invite you to set up your own experiment for these 40 days. Design and create your own inquiry into eating and food.

Possible Inquiries over the 40 days:

- How will I feel if I make a concerted effort at incorporating nutrient dense foods into every meal and snack I take?
- Perhaps 6 weeks of "Meatless Mondays."
- Or if you are ready to make an even bigger splash, how will you feel going meatless for 40 days, or giving up red meat altogether.
- You could experiment with how you feel without wine, gluten, caffeine, or dairy.

- Perhaps you've always wondered how you would feel as a vegan?
- What if you try vegan during the week and vegetarian on the weekend, or vegan during the day and vegetarian for dinner?
- You could try eliminating the microwave for 40 Days!
- Would you love to experiment with not looking at the scales for the whole 40 Days?

Whatever experiment you would like to incorporate into your 40 Days, go for it! As exciting as it seems to make an experiment for yourself, be sure not to bite off more than you can chew. Don't set your sites on too many inquiries at once!

Over the 40 Days, be willing to experiment with new foods. I remember the first time I tried quinoa, kale, black bean pasta, or even kitchari! Experts attest that it can take up to ten tries of a new food to develop a taste for it! Many people think they don't like beans or beets until they have given them several chances! Be open to trying things again that you tried years ago, and didn't care for. Tastes change!!! I used to hate broccoli up to a couple of years ago, and now it is one of my favorite foods! Step out of your routine and out of the box with recipes. Try new things on the menu at restaurants! Let eating and food become an adventure and a journey of exploration. You cannot change if you are unwilling to make changes!

What has NOT been working for you?

As you step into the journey of inquiry, it is equally important to inquire into what hasn't been working for you on your path to optimal weight energy and health. Take a moment and think of the efforts you have previously made when it comes to eating and exercise. Consider whether you may have been doing the following in order to reach your optimal weight and health:

- Obsessing
- Complaining
- Fretting and worrying
- Berating yourself for your "mistakes"
- Denial that there is an issue
- Giving up completely
- Trying harder instead of trying something different
- Forcing yourself to do exercises you hate and to eat bland "diet" foods you dislike

Have any of these things been helpful to you? Inquiry is a practice of letting go of what doesn't work and trying something different. If we keep trying the same things, how can we expect to suddenly begin to get different results?

Choice. Chance. Change. You must make a choice, take a chance, or your life will never change. ~Unknown

Affirmation: When I look at all of life as an experiment, I allow myself to discover what is best for me.

Today's biggest success:

Food for Thought: Devise your own experiment for the 40 Day journey. What would you like to work on? What do you sense would move you closer to the best version of yourself, body, mind and soul?

Journal: Write about your experiment here. Allow your words to help you focus the direction of your inquiry. Why have you chosen this direction for your inquiry?

I am Done with the Cleanse, Now What?

I tell my students that you can't undo 40 years of poor eating choices in just 3 days. The whole 40 Days is a part of the cleansing and resetting process. But studies do show that just 3 days of dietary changes already begin to change us at the cellular level. Just 3 days can reboot the body, metabolism and cravings, to give us a boost in moving forward with a new way of eating.

Many people notice after the 3 day cleanse they no longer crave the foods that used to be their downfall, like cake, cookies, Starbucks, Dorito's, soda, etc. *Ayurveda* teaches that "like" increases "like." This holds true on every level including the food you eat. When you eat junk, you automatically crave more junk. When you eat pure wholesome *sattvic* foods, you automatically crave more of the same! Now that both toxins and unwanted cravings are gone, we don't want to undo what we just did, so here is how to stay the course over the long haul.

Post Cleanse Do's:

1. Drink 8 oz. warm lemon water each morning before anything else is ingested. Make sure you are using fresh organic lemons, not bottled lemon juice. Put the slices into the water, because some of the active enzymes and essential oils are in the peel. The heat releases these into the water. Also, because the lemon is fresh, there are more active properties in the lemon slices. This is an

Ayurvedic daily practice or *dinacharya* for optimal health. It is highly recommended that you continue this practice well beyond the 40 Days. Make this a practice for life! Surprisingly, lemon water is alkalinizing to the body making it less hospitable to disease.

2. Coffee should be organic. Teas should also be organic when possible.

3. Let your breakfast set the intentions for your eating each day by choosing a delicious, nourishing and healthful breakfast.

4. Continue eating a mix of raw and cooked organic fruits and vegetables. Soups, salads, curries, stews and stir-fries are all great options.

5. All breads should be 100% whole grain. Organic sprouted breads are ideal. Use whole grains and nutrient-dense brown rice and whole grain pastas. Since most conventionally grown grains are highly sprayed just prior to harvest, it is best to opt for organic grains to ensure detoxification continues.

6. Chocolate should be organic 70% cocoa. Chocolate is a superfood! It is a great alternative to turn to when cravings arise.

7. Enjoy nuts and nut butters in moderation, organic when possible.

8. Use oils such as sesame, olive, coconut, flaxseed, pumpkin, walnut, sunflower, grape seed, hempseed, organic butter, or "*ghee*", which is clarified butter. *Ghee* is said to be an ideal food and have powerful *Ayurvedic* healing properties. In *Ayurveda*, *ghee* is used as a medicine and it is also mixed with herbs, used as a vehicle to transport the herbs to the bodily tissues. Ghee is a powerful digestive tonic and is said to boost metabolism when used in moderation.

9. Make sure a meal is fully digested before eating again or snacking. Wait 3-4 hours, and avoid eating right before bed. When we add un-digested food to partially digested food, we diminish the digestive fire. This slows the digestive process and creates *ama*. This slows the metabolism and clogs the channels.

10. Portion your plate as follows. A Yogi's plate consists of:

    ¼ protein

    ¼ grains

    ½ fresh vegetables and fruits, cooked or raw.

    *Your entire meal should be able to fit in the palms of both hands cupped together. A quantity of food greater than this will weaken the digestive fire, creating toxins.

11. Dairy is preferably organic. Livestock is often given GMO feed. Chemical sprays on these GMO feeds have been detected in the milk. Hormone and antibiotic-free, grass-fed dairy is in keeping with a healthy *Ayurvedic* diet.

Dairy products coming from farms using these practices are also acceptable. Amish farmers pride themselves in their traditional farming practices. French cheeses and butters for the most part also employ safe traditional dairy farming methods as well. Amish and French cheeses and butters are also good options. My enlightened eating students have been astonished by how quickly skin blemishes and acne disappear simply by switching to organic dairy.

12. Opt for more plant-based proteins. Some suggested non-meat proteins include nuts and beans. I put both on a salad, which is delicious! I recommend sprinkling black beans, black eye peas, cashews, chickpeas, walnuts and sunflower seeds on salads. Organic Greek yogurt is high in protein. I make salad dressings with it, smoothies, and eat it as a snack! Tofu is high in soy protein. Make sure your soy is organic, and non-organic soy is GMO and highly sprayed. You can make salad dressing with tofu, or I will sometimes chop it up and put it on a salad too. I add it to soups and stir-fries. Some people marinate and grill it! Nut butters on toast are great. Try cashew butter or almond butter on toast, drizzle it with raw honey and sprinkle a little cinnamon on top! It is yummy! I make smoothies with nut butters too, and some of those recipes are included in the book. Hummus with veggies is a protein-filled treat! Whole grains have a lot of protein too, such as oatmeal and brown rice. Quinoa has the highest protein levels of all grains because it is actually a seed. Kale, broccoli and spinach are a few sources of "green" protein. You can get plenty of protein without ever eating meat! We will discuss more on this ahead.

13. Desserts should be mostly fruit-based (fresh, cooked or raw), and should not be sweetened with white sugar or artificial sweeteners. Natural sweeteners and spices are fine.

14. Give yourself at least 2-3 hours for your food to digest before you go to sleep.

15. Drink plenty of fresh pure water. This helps your body continue to flush out toxins. Feel free to flavor your water with natural juices, herbs, etc. to make it more enjoyable.

16. Meats should be free-range, grass-fed. Eggs should be cage-free and organic. If you notice that you are not craving meats, do not be in a hurry to add them back. Wait until you really want them. Limit meat and fish to three times a week. Keep in that mind nuts, dairy, soy, whole grains and legumes are also sources of protein. We will discuss food combining to create a full protein ahead.

Post Cleanse Food Don'ts:

1. Do not drink iced beverages. I cannot emphasize this enough! Ice cold drinks cool the digestive fire. Slowing the digestive fire slows the metabolism and causes *ama* or toxins to clog the channels, tissues and cells. Warm beverages

are best, but if you are unable to drink warm, then opt for room temperature. Warm and hot water dilate the channels or *nadis* to help move blockages and keep the channels freely flowing.

2. Do not eat meat more than three times per week. Meat is difficult to digest and creates *ama* in the body as it putrefies during the digestive process. Meat is also higher on the food chain and contains more toxins, especially factory farmed meat. Meat has been shown to contain 14 times the toxic and chemical residue of conventional produce. If you are not craving meat, then wait to add it back into your diet until you are "craving" it. I encourage you to use grass-fed, free-range meat because it contains fewer toxins and more nutrients. Since you are eating less meat, this should not affect your budget. Eat fish and seafood no more than twice weekly, due to toxic contaminates found in fish.

3. Avoid microwaving foods. According to *Ayurveda*, microwaves damage foods' life-force. In studies, more nutrients are destroyed through microwave heating than through other forms of heating. Microwave heating also creates carcinogenic bi-products as it changes the molecular structure of foods.

4. Avoid aluminum cook-ware which is said to impart toxic properties into the food according to *Ayurvedic* texts. It is preferable to cook with copper, stainless steel, tempered glass or clay based cookware. Avoid cookware with non-stick coatings which have been shown to release toxins into the food.

5. Avoid processed food, junk food, fast food, or deep-fried food. These contain *ama*. The 3-day cleanse has begun to rid the system of toxins. In order to optimize the metabolism, it is important to limit toxins entering the system. It is important to understand that when we introduce toxins into the system, the metabolism becomes sluggish as it attempts to process aberrant foods.

6. No artificial sweeteners or white sugar. According to *Ayurveda*, white sugar increases *ama* in the body. White sugar is said to weaken the immune system and feed infections. Sweetness itself is not something to avoid and is not forbidden in the Enlightened Eating plan. Opt for natural sweeteners such as raw honey, stevia, agave, molasses, maple syrup, coconut sugar or raw sugar. If you find that you regularly have strong cravings for sweets, it may be a sign that you are craving for more "sweetness" in your life. To reduce these cravings, add more "sweetness" into your living rather than into your eating. Avoid artificial, flavors, colors and preservatives. These chemical additives have in many cases been found to be probable carcinogens, endocrine disruptors and neurotoxins.

7. No artificial ingredients. Rule of thumb: If it sounds like a chemical or you can't pronounce it, don't eat it. It's not "really" food.

8. Limit alcoholic beverages to red wine, which has beneficial anti-inflammatory and anti-oxidant properties. Women, no more than 1 glass/day; men no more than 2 glasses/day. Overconsumption of alcohol creates *ama*. If you notice that wine creates a toxic effect for you (headache, joint and muscle aches, sudden weight gain after drinking or fatigue) then it should be eliminated entirely. I have found organic and sulfite-free wines have the fewest toxic effects (joint discomfort, puffiness, water-retention, inflammation, fatigue) on my own body. Therefore, I recommend drinking organic wine if alcohol is a must. Personally, I reserve alcohol only for special occasions.

9. Avoid left-overs older than 24 hours, or re-heated foods when possible. These foods have begun to lose *prana* or life-force, and accumulate bacteria and toxins. I recommend freezing left-overs which you do not plan to eat within 24 hours. It then becomes a convenient meal on a busy day. In *Ayurveda*, frozen foods are not ideal, however, frozen meals you have cooked yourself with love and fresh organic ingredients is a much better alternative on a busy night than the drive-thru or take-out.

10. No soft drinks, candy or gum. (Why no gum? The chewing process makes the body feel that food is coming. Digestive juices and enzymes are released without knowing no food will arrive. This confuses the body, mind and digestive system. Since healthy digestion is considered to be the very basis of optimal health, weight, energy and vitality in *Ayurveda*, chewing gum works against this.

11. No margarine, opt for real organic butter, *ghee* or natural oils (nothing hydrogenated).

12. I have provided a "suggested" grocery list in Appendix 1 to help you with ideas to navigate the 40 Days. In no way is this list a must by any means, but is meant to be a resource to help you as you shop. I suggest going to the store when you can really take time to read ingredients and discover new products, which will truly serve you along the 40 Day journey.

13. There is no "blowing it" there is no "giving up". At any time during the 40 Day journey when you find you have strayed from the path to enlightened eating, simply repeat the Cleanse. I find with my students that just about everyone has a point in which they have become derailed from eating the right foods. Simply repeat the cleanse and keep moving ahead! Never get lost, give up or feel left behind.

Easy Guide to 40-Days to Enlightened Eating

Use liberally	In Moderation	Avoid
All fresh fruits (organic) All fresh veggies (organ-ic) All nuts and seeds (pea-nuts, cashews, and pista-chios should be organic) All Superfoods Legumes/beans Soups, broths, stews, stir-fries, curries (organ-ic) Salads Spices and herbs Teas (organic), detoxify-ing teas, calming teas Whole grains - barley, brown & black rice, bul-gur, faro, millet, quinoa, whole oats, whole wheat Hot lemon water-first thing Warm water/beverages Largest Meal at Mid-day	Organic Red Wine Meat no more than 3X week (Grass-fed/free-range/organic) Fish no more than 2X week Coffee (organic) Dairy (organic) - butter, cheese, yogurt, milk: use as a condiment Dark chocolate (70% or higher) (organic) Ghee, coconut oil, olive oil, sesame oil, avocado oil, grape seed oil, etc. hemp seed, pumpkin seed, walnut, sesame seed, sun-flower seed Snacks - nuts, seeds, pop-corn, healthy energy bars Sweeteners - honey, agave nectar, molasses, raw sugar Organic tofu Organic fruit juices Raw local honey, maple syrup, stevia, raw sugar, coconut sugar, brown rice syrup, molasses Organic nut butters Coconut water	Artificial Sweeteners Deep fried foods Crackers, chips Sugary Desserts Candy, Cookies Cakes, etc Chewing gum Mixed drinks Margarine/hydrogenated fats Sodas, sports drinks Fast food, take-out, pro-cessed food Overcooked food Canned food Overly sweetened food Overly salted food Left-overs-more than 24-hours Eating less than 3-4 hours apart. White sugar White flour Iced/cold Beverages Eating after 7pm Eating late at night or in the middle of the night Eating heavy meals at night Microwaving foods and beverages. Non-organic foods GMO foods

*Recommended Recipes at end of each chapter and in the *40 Days to Enlightened Eating Cookbook*!

Could a Vegetarian or Vegan Lifestyle be Right for You?

First, let it be said that I have no judgments whatsoever about those who enjoy and eat meat! As an *Ayurveda* practitioner, I am aware our bodies are individual and unique to us and have differing requirements to keep us healthy and balanced! I am mostly vegetarian, but eat fish once or twice a week to maintain balance.

I have never been a person who particularly liked or craved meat. As a child, I remember spitting it out into my napkin on many occasions, or gagging while trying to chew it! I know that is not everyone's experience! As a young adult, I suddenly realized that I didn't *have* to eat meat, it was my choice, and that being a vegetarian was an option! However, I went about it completely wrong in my early twenties! Naively, I thought all I had to do was eliminate meat, so I left out meat and ignorantly filled in with more junk food! After about a month of this, I felt terrible and decided that being a vegetarian would never work for me. What I failed to recognize was that the word "vegetable" is in the word "vegetarian!" I wasn't eating more vegetables, I was instead eating food that had no nutritional value whatsoever. My body became depleted and let me know quickly. I had low energy and my immune system grew weak.

Thankfully, I gave vegetarianism another shot! I am now a little older and a little wiser, and I realize that being a vegetarian means incorporating a lot of vegetables into my meals. Never have I felt better, and I have not suffered from any deficiency of protein. I do eat fish once or twice a week, but I also consciously increase protein intake through plant sources. I now realize that people who are just avoiding meat and filling their diet with junk instead, are not vegetarians. They are "Junkatarians" and are the ones who end up with protein, vitamin and mineral deficiencies, like I did! This is not a true vegetarian!

A vegetarian or vegan lifestyle is not for everyone! However, as a vegetarian for over 8 years, I am often asked about my energy and health, and how I could possibly be getting enough protein! Many people aren't aware that plants do contain protein! A vegetarian diet includes a large amount of plant protein! It is not JUST about eliminating meat, but it is about consciously obtaining protein from plant sources. I like to remind my students that a 900-lb. gorilla is all muscle but eats nothing but leafy plants! Plant protein is more bioavailable than animal protein, which means we get more protein calorie for calorie by consuming plant protein. Plant protein is more easily digested and readily assimilated than animal protein.

Interestingly, some of the gold medal-winning athletes in recent Olympic games were vegetarians or vegans!

One of the greatest benefits of a vegetarian lifestyle is that it allows me to reap the benefits of many more healthy plant nutrients, micronutrients, antioxidants, fiber and vitamins than I would ingest if I filled up on meat at every meal instead. Current science is proving that it is much more beneficial to receive these vital nutrients from their natural sources rather than from a vitamin pill created in a lab!

Being a vegetarian inspires me to get creative in the kitchen, and gets me out of the meat and potato rut, and challenges me to create something more exciting than the traditional "meat and 3 sides" at every meal! I like to challenge myself to see how many different vegetables I can incorporate into my day, so that I am loaded up on as many nutrients as possible! I am always experimenting with new recipes, flavors, herbs, spices and combinations! I have lots of fun in my kitchen whether it be cooking or eating these new creations!

It is not my objective to turn everyone into a vegetarian or vegan at all. However, most Americans would be healthier if they reduced meat consumption and began getting more health saving plant nutrients and fibers into their diet and body!

One way to reduce animal protein consumption is to use meat more like a condiment by adding it in soups, stews and salads, rather than as the centerpiece of a meal. Fish and chicken are much healthier choices than red meat. Consuming sausages, processed luncheon meats, canned meats, preserved meats and bacon are the least healthy forms of meat and do nothing to bring out the best version of you or your optimal health. Ironically, many commercial meat substitutes are equally health prohibiting as they contain long ingredient lists of artificial and chemical ingredients and may contain GMO soy.

In my book *40 Days to Enlightened Eating*, I recommend eating meat no more than 3 times a week for optimal health. This allows you to ingest more nutrients from plant foods. When eating meat, I recommend always making sure it is hormone-fee, antibiotic free, free-range, grass-fed and not raised on GMO feed. Ultimately, studies consistently show that a vegetarian diet is more optimal for health and longevity.

Nothing will benefit human health and increase the chances for survival of life on earth as much as the evolution to a vegetarian diet ~Albert Einstein

6 reasons to consider a plant based diet: (According to cardiologist Dr. Joel Kahn)

1. Vegetarians and vegans live on average 5 years longer than meat eaters.

2. Vegetarians and vegans have a substantially lower cancer rate. Vegans have by far the lowest.

3. Vegetarians and vegans have significantly lower risk of heart disease. There is a 50% reduction in men who are vegan.

4. Vegetarians and vegans have a considerably lower risk of diabetes.

5. Vegetarians and Vegans much lower blood pressure.

6. Plant proteins are more bioavailable than animal based proteins.

Question: How do Vegetarians and vegans get enough protein in their diet?

Answer: By eating foods which in combination have the 9 amino acids which are the building blocks of a complete protein. It is not necessary to get all 9 of these amino acids at a single meal. When these foods are eaten in variety throughout the day, the body takes what it needs and assimilates it. There is no need to stress about getting adequate protein as long as you are eating a variety of vegetables, nuts, seeds, whole grains, fruits and legumes throughout the day.

According to Dr. Garth Davis, "We eat more protein than any other country in the world, except maybe Iceland. On average, depending on which source you read, we eat 80-120 gm of protein a day, many eat more. The RDA is 44 for females and 52 for males, so we are eating about double the recommendation. Despite the plethora of protein, we consume we have the lowest longevity, highest heart disease, highest rates of obesity, and highest rates of many forms of cancer. Our high protein diet isn't making us very healthy. Now, if we are one of the sickest countries in the world then how about looking at the healthier countries. In fact, the healthiest people in the world eat relatively low levels of protein. The Okinawans and Sardinians average only 7-10% of their calories from protein while we consume 15-20%. This obsession we have with protein is ridiculous. We can only process a certain amount at a time, so all this excess protein in the end is just excess calories."

Food combining to form a complete protein:

Nuts or seeds + whole grains = Complete Protein

Beans/legumes + whole grains = Complete Protein

Nuts and seeds + beans/legumes = Complete Protein

Other vegetarian sources of Complete Protein: quinoa, hempseed, organic soy, Greek yogurt, milk and eggs.

Plant foods also contain plant protein. I like to remind my students that a 900-lb. gorilla is all muscle but eats nothing but leafy plants! Plant protein is more bioavailable than animal protein, which means we get more protein calorie for calorie by consuming plant protein. Plant protein is more easily digested and readily assimilated than animal protein.

Here is a list of the top protein containing plant foods:

- Asparagus
- Avocado
- Broccoli
- Cauliflower
- Chia seeds
- Hemp seeds
- Goji berries
- Kale
- Legumes
- Nuts
- Quinoa
- Potato
- Spinach
- Spirulina
- Sweet potato
- Seeds

Day 5

The *Karma* of Lifestyle

One of the main causes of disease is "intellectual blasphemy," which means not listening to the body's intelligence. Intelligence means the flow of awareness, and that flow tells us what we should and should not do. Even when an action is wrong, we often go ahead and do it anyway. By that action, we are insulting the intelligence of the body. ~Dr. Vasant Lad

Many people mistakenly associate the word *Karma* with retribution, justice, payback or even revenge. On the contrary, *Karma* is simply the law of cause and effect. The word *Karma* means "action." Every action you take is accompanied by an effect of like kind. *Karma* is simply the law of cause and effect as it applies to human experience. There is nothing "voodoo" about it! Every effect you experience has a cause or an action behind it. Cause and effect are always equal and equivalent in force, and of similar nature.

Like cause =Like effect

Peacefulness cannot produce violence. Hate cannot generate love. Peace brings about peace; and love brings about love. This law of cause and effect governs everything in the natural world. Self-neglect cannot produce wellness. Self-care cannot bring about disease. Self-abuse cannot bring about wellbeing.

Whatever our condition, there was a cause behind it. The reason behind the condition is always of the same energy or type. Therefore, we have the power to correct a condition by applying its opposite instead. *Ayurveda* is a science of applying opposites. Just as we have created the effect with an action or cause, we can similarly undo it by taking counteractive courses of action.

Who you are reflects the lifestyle choices you have been making. What you see now is the cumulative effect of these choices over time. I call this "lifestyle *karma*." If you want to change what you see, you need only 2 things: different choices and time. 40 Days can make a huge difference!

Our daily actions, routine and duties carry their own *karma* (cause and effect) without us even being conscious of their profound impact. Seemingly simple patterns of eating, sleeping, drinking, movement, elimination and work have a powerful effect on our wellbeing and overall health. When you perform these actions skillfully and consciously rather than being unaware or unconscious, it is transformational! I tell my students that by consciously integrating yoga, meditation, and healthy eating into your lifestyle, you become the alchemist of your own life, transforming base metal to gold! Now is the time to selectively choose your daily actions, rituals and lifestyle choices, in order to move closer to your best, healthiest and highest self.

Food carries *karma*. Natural whole living foods carry the karma of health, energy and vitality. Unnatural foods lacking nutrients and life bring with them the *karma* of disease and suffering. Eating well maximizes the natural potential for the body to remain in harmony, balance and health. Unnatural foods shift the body out of its natural state of harmony, optimizing the potential for disease. This is a common-sense truth that we have been rediscovering here in the 21st century. Eating the foods our bodies were designed to eat, digest and be fueled by, is following a timeless natural law, one that has been carelessly broken in recent decades.

The eating of mistreated animals carries *karma*. If you are eating animals that were mistreated, you are *karmically* linked to their suffering. By buying and eating them, at some level, you are supporting the very industry that caused them harm. Some sensitive people even respond to the negative energy that the meats of suffering animals contains with symptoms like fear, nightmares, sadness, hopelessness, agitation, anxiety and worry.

The *Karma* of Lifestyle

Every time I return to my hometown, I catch up with old friends and classmates. Unfortunately, over the last several years, this catching up often includes sad stories and tragic losses. What is not surprising is that these sad endings started out with ill-fated beginnings. This is particularly evident in lifestyle choices. In most cases, these former classmates are simply facing their own lifestyle *karma*.

Now don't get me wrong, these are and were good people. *Karma* is not about getting a just punishment or a deserved reward. In every case, what comes about in our lives is due to what we have already set into motion in one way or another. Let me illustrate the *karma* of lifestyle.

We have one classmate who has completely burned out his brains on drugs, so much so, that he can no longer function in society. A couple of others have already died of cirrhosis of the liver, due to excessive drinking. Another classmate died of an obesity-related cancer. Our class beauty queen has been a smoker, heavy drinker and sun-worshipper over the years, and now looks as if she could have graduated with my mom! Although these cases sound extreme, these are not random accidents. These are the causes and effects of lifestyle choices.

Many folks are in the process of causing their own demise through their own lifestyle choices. This includes heavy drinkers, junk-food junkies, workaholics, smokers, drug users, overeaters, diet soda addicts, fast-food enthusiasts, TV dinner connoisseurs, stress magnets, drama queens and couch potatoes.

I'd like to emphasize that the lifestyle choices you are making right now are already in the process of determining your *karma* whether positive or negative. Good *karma* is really about living in a skillful way. We determine our future right now in the present. It is a fact that women who eat poor diets, don't exercise, have high-stress daily lives, and live in overdrive, tend to suffer the most acute symptoms during the transition into menopause. Many types of cancer are born of lifestyle choices such as poor diet, overexposure to the sun, smoking, or living high-stress lifestyles. There is nothing malicious, unjust, or vindictive going on. It is simply cause and effect.

Excessive or overly strenuous exercise and lack of rest also has its own lifestyle *karma* of worn out joints, premature aging, and layers of strain accumulated in the mind-body system.

Take a moment to assess your lifestyle. What future are you currently creating for yourself? Is this the future of your choosing? It is not too late to adjust and change course. Your current state of health is a reflection of your past. You have the power to determine your future. Although we cannot control environmental toxins, genetic predispositions, accidents or the negligence of others, for the most part we have the capacity to pre-select our future state of health. What does your *karma* look like?

What is your state of health?_____

energy level?_____ weight? _____

List the things that you have been doing up until now that have contributed to your condition.

1.

2.

3.

4.

5.

What is your ideal health?_____

energy?_____ weight?_____

Imagine someone at your ideal weight, health and energy. How do they look and feel? What do they do with extra energy? List the lifestyle habits that might have contributed to this ideal weight, health and energy.

1.

2.

3.

4.

5.

How does your lifestyle differ from this other individual's? Visualize yourself as you adopt the lifestyle choices of this person. What are you doing differently now? These are the lifestyle changes you need to make for yourself to align yourself with your ideal future. List what you now know you need to do differently.

1.

2.

3.

4.

5.

Affirmation: If you change nothing, nothing will change. ~Unknown

Today's biggest success:

Food for thought: *Karma* is simply the law of Cause and effect. Who and what you are now is a direct reflection of the lifestyle practices you've followed up until now. What you do now predetermines who you are to become.

Journal: List any lifestyle changes you feel moved to make after today's reading.

Day 6

The Art of Paying Attention

Start with "just this," whatever has bubbled up from the Source, add a pinch of awareness, and you have the recipe for Awakened Presence, which is ready to be enjoyed immediately. Enjoy! ~Unknown

A dear friend of mine broke out into a horrible case of hives. They lasted for months with no resolution, and she had no idea what was the cause of this allergic reaction. These hives got her attention. While she was suffering with these itchy skin patches, she began to scrutinize everything she was eating. She was already an extremely healthy eater. But as she paid close attention, she noticed that anything with sulfites, a common preservative, caused the hives to flare up. As she began to scrutinize ingredients in her foods and avoid sulfites like the plague, her hives began to clear up. Every once in a while, a flare-up would lead to the discovery of a new product in which sulfites were hiding!

Novocain, a drug used when she was fitted with a crown, K-cups for her Keurig coffee machine, sauces, salad dressings and dried fruit were all found to be culprits. In an effort to avoid hives, the awareness that she has developed around her foods was taken to a new level. Her body gave her instant feed-back with every bite she took. "My allergies started at birth, so my survival as a kid, was to learn to listen to my body. I have a good 45 years of learning through my body, back when no one did that and thought you were crazy if you talked about it. So I learned to not talk about it . . . thank God we have grown into a better healthy era. Now we need to share it, so others wake up!" ~Marie Friedlander, Professional Level Baptiste Yoga Instructor.

Marie opted for a vegan diet for a period of 9 months, and then noticed that her body was asking her to add in some additional protein. She felt depleted and began to experience hair loss. She decided to add back a bit of cheese, yogurt, eggs and occasional fish. This helped to bring her back into balance. Many people opt for a way of eating without any wiggle room. They resign themselves to a diet without listening to the body, refusing to make necessary tweaks and changes, and neglect to observe how the mind-body system responds and reacts. They ignore their physical symptoms and their cravings.

I have a family member who has resigned herself to the Atkins' Diet for over a decade. Despite remaining overweight and accumulating a laundry list of physical symptoms, she resists anything else that may improve her life. We don't need to have a case of hives to start paying attention. Our bodies give us constant feedback about the foods we eat! Unfortunately, there are millions of westerners who feel, achy, tired and sluggish, and just assume that this is the norm, or that they "are just getting old." I have seen so many people clean up their diet and recognize that this doesn't have to be *their* norm. They choose a new enlivened, vibrant and healthy norm, by being selective about what they put into their bodies.

Enlightened Eating is about paying attention to your body. Is it really hungry? Do you really need another bite? How did you feel after eating that meal? Were you tired, sluggish and lethargic? Are you waking up with energy and enthusiasm, or is it taking everything you have to get going in the morning? Do your joints ache after eating certain foods? Do some foods create phlegm and congestion? Has something you've eaten caused you to feel bloated with a puffy face and hands? Do you experience blemishes or pimples after eating certain foods?

How do you feel the next day after overeating? How do you feel the next day after imbibing in alcohol? In *Ayurveda*, it is understood that whatever you have done the previous day, affects how you feel today! The *karmic* effects of our eating choices are almost immediate, we just have to learn to pay attention.

Paying attention includes:

1. **Listen to your cravings.** If you crave blueberries, there is something in them that your body needs today. Craving junk is always a sign of imbalance according to *Ayurveda*. If you are craving donuts, let this message tell you that something is out of balance in the mind-body system. Begin to ponder what this might be. Are you overworking? Was your workout overly strenuous? Have you been eating other processed foods, which may have caused imbalance? Like increases like in *Ayurveda*. If you indulge in junk food, you will increase your cravings for more junk. If you are eating healthy foods regularly, you will begin to crave more of the same!

2. **Become aware of what is in your food.** Read labels. Check ingredients. Find out if produce has been chemically sprayed. Are there artificial colors, dyes, flavors or preservatives? Is it GMO? Is it highly processed? Produce labeling numbers starting with 9 are organic, and organic foods cannot be genetically modified. Produce number starting with 4 are conventionally grown, which means they are produced with chemical fertilizers, weed killers, pesticides, etc. Common potential sources of GMOs are canola oil, cereal, corn, corn syrup, edamame, papaya, peanut butter, soy, soybean oil sugar, sugar beets, summer squash, tortilla chips, and tofu. By opting for organic products, you

can minimize exposure to GMO foods. Roundup® spray, deemed a probable carcinogen by the World Health Organization, is heavily used on GMO crops.

3. **Sense when you are beginning to feel satiated.** Notice when your *BODY* is saying you're done, rather than your *tongue*! Are you being distracted from sensing hunger and fullness by eating in a hurry, eating in the car, eating at the computer or eating while watching television? Are your taste buds over-riding your belly?

4. **Pay attention to how you feel immediately after eating.** Do you feel energized or sluggish? Are you stuffed or pleasantly satisfied? Is your stomach gurgling? Are your joints aching? Are you burping or gassy? Does this food serve you or hinder you?

5. **Observe your thoughts and moods after eating.** Do you feel uplifted and positive? Does your mood feel light or heavy? Are the thoughts that follow your eating positive or negative? Do you feel edgy or relaxed? Are you beating yourself up for what you ate, or are you being kind and compassionate? I have noticed that my food choices can immediately and directly affect my moods for better or worse, and my students report observing this as well.

6. **Notice how you sleep.** The things we ingest can have a direct effect on sleep. Over or under eating can also affect sleep. Notice how your eating patterns connect to your sleeping patterns.

7. **Recognize the connection to how you feel the next day.** Are you energized and vibrant, or did you awaken puffy, bloated and sluggish? How is your mood today? Are your joints stiff and achy? Do you want to nap? I even notice my intuition is powerfully affected by the foods I eat. As someone who is used to being highly perceptive, I can immediately sense my intuition become dulled down by ingesting alcohol or less than optimal food choices.

It is through paying attention that we are able to make the right choices and decisions to serve our own body-mind system. If we pay attention when the body-mind system is in harmony, it is quickly apparent when things get out of balance.

Western medicine has us programmed to believe that disease doesn't exist until full-blown symptoms appear. *Ayurveda*, teaches that symptoms don't begin to manifest until Stage 4 out of the 6 stages of disease. Disease is relatively easy to treat if caught in the early stages of imbalance, but difficult or impossible to cure once it reaches Stage 5 or 6. By paying attention, you can perceive an issue early on, possibly even before it may be picked up through medical testing. By paying attention, our bodies will silently speak, providing us an opportunity to make changes early on to keep the mind body system in harmony and out of disorder or *dis*-ease. Let your own observations intelligently guide you forward into making the best choices for your own vibrant health, energy and vitality!

It doesn't matter what kind of diet you decide to begin when your stomach is full—what matters is what you do when you're hungry and you are choosing what food to eat for your meal. The most critical decisions we make that shape our lives are those we make during discomfort or duress. When we are upset, lonely, hungry, etc. we are tempted to succumb to the most expedient path to feeling better rather than the best path. ~Max Strom

Foods most people eat too much of:

- refined grains
- potatoes
- dairy
- sweets
- salt
- red meat
- pasta
- bread

Foods most people eat too little of:

- fresh vegetables
- bitter greens
- legumes
- nuts and seeds
- fresh berries
- water and other fluids

Affirmation: Beginning today, I pay attention to my body's wisdom and honor what it asks of me. When I am tired, I rest; when I am hungry, I eat. I choose foods that help me to feel my best. When I feel complete, I am done eating.

Today's biggest success:

Food for thought: When you start paying attention, you become aware of what is helping you and what is holding you back. You become aware of your relationship with eating and food and how it affects your body, mind and soul. When you learn to bring the light of awareness to your eating, you begin to shine that same light in too many other facets of your life, noticing what is working and what is not working.

Journal: What have you become aware of today through the art of paying attention?

Day 7

Yoga is Eating and Eating is Yoga

Swami Kripalu and Mahatma Gandhi both spoke often about how a real yogi's character can be measured by their mouth. Yes, you heard me, their mouth! Yoga of the mouth. By what goes IN IT, and what comes OUT OF IT. Gandhi said that those who are not in control of what goes in their mouth, and what goes out of their mouth, have no self-control in other areas of their life as well. Your mouth is a measure of your self-discipline and conscious. Your mouth is a mirror for your yoga practice, much more than your mat. Swami Kripalu called the tongue, the body's "mischievous elf," the tail that wags the dog.

~Devarshi Steve Hartman

Eating is yoga. Eating is a spiritual practice to nourish the body, strengthen the mind and enliven the soul. Eating involves the same critical components as a well-composed yoga practice. Think of eating as *asana* (the yoga postures). Yoga literally means "union" or oneness. Eating is yoga because you become one with your food when you eat it. You are what you eat. What you eat you become. When you eat natural whole foods, you become one with nature. Since human beings are also a part of nature, we are reconnected and reunited with who and what we really are. When we eat processed or artificial foods, we become one with that energy as well. We take on the vibration of fakery and phoniness and become disconnected and misaligned from who and what we really are. When we do not eat authentic foods, we lose our own authenticity. We forget who we really are. We lose touch with our true nature. We are no longer aligned with reality and who we are and what we came here to do and be. We lose our sense of oneness and unity. Disharmony and misalignment going into the body equals inner conflict and discord.

Eating and food is simply a practice just as yoga is a practice. How you approach eating and food informs you about countless other areas in your life. Begin to notice how your patterns of eating are really a mirror into other patterns that show up in other areas of your day-to-day life.

How eating is your yoga:

- **Alignment:** (with self and with nature) Are you eating in alignment with how you were created to eat? Are you eating in alignment with your highest good? Are you living in alignment with the laws of nature and with your own highest good? In what ways are your eating and lifestyle choices out of alignment with the best version of you?

- **Balance:** Are you eating in balance with your *dosha*? Are your meals balanced between fruits, veggies, grains, dairy and proteins? It is common for people to over-do grains or dairy while underdoing vegetables and fruits. If you are vegan or vegetarian, are you eating adequate plant proteins? Is your eating balanced during the day, or are you skipping meals, or hoarding most of your calories at night? Do you throw caution to the wind on the weekends and undo all the good you did during the week? Is your life balanced between work, rest and play?

- *Prana:* Do you feel energized or depleted by the way you eat? Can you sense the varying degrees of life-force in the foods you are eating? Can you sense when your foods are devoid of any life force? Are you overdoing things in your life that are depleting your energy even though you are eating well? Are you making too many withdrawals from your well of energy without replenishing it? Over exercising? Over working? Burning the midnight oil?

- **Mindfulness:** Are you being present when you are eating, or is mealtime filled with distractions? Are you eating in front of the TV, in the car, at the computer or standing at the kitchen counter? Are you eating with all 5 of the senses? Are you present to your life? Do you show up and remain present for whatever is there or do you check out by surfing the web, spending hours on social media, numbing with alcohol or the TV screen.

- **Stretching:** Are you stretching yourself to try new things, new recipes and new foods. Are you open to new and even foreign concepts about eating and food? Are you stretching yourself to try new ways of doing things or are you gripping tightly to your old habits and conditioning about eating and food. Is the way you have been eating in the past working for you? Are you stretching yourself in life? Are you open to learning and trying new things, new adventures and seeing new places or do you settle for the status quo? Do you stay stuck in your comfort zone? Or do you reach for new experiences with an open mind.

- **Releasing:** Yoga releases muscle tension and gripping from the physical body. Can you release habits and patterns that don't serve you when it comes to eating and food? Can you let go of tension surrounding cooking or eating snacks and meals? What learned eating behaviors are not serving you? Where are you still gripping, and holding on to your old ways of eating? Are you clinging to old, comfortable ways of doing things that don't serve you anymore? Can you release these old patterns and conditioned behaviors in order to open to a new way of being?

- **Compassion:** Are you beating yourself up for perceived shortcomings and failures? Are you relentlessly pushing yourself at the gym or on the yoga mat? Do you place perfection above compassion? Are you willing to start over again and again when it comes to eating and food until you find a sense of alignment and balance? Can you return to "beginner's mind" as many times as it takes?

- **Showing-up:** Can you be consistent and persistent? Can you continue to step into the arena and try even if it is challenging, even if some days are better than others? True transformation requires you to show up and do the work. The highest path is not the easy path! Like yoga, eating is a practice. "Practice and all is coming." Pattabhi Jois.

- *Tapas:* In the yoga system *tapas* is not a Spanish appetizer. *Tapas* literally translates as "fire" or to burn, to generate heat and light. Tapas is the practice of taking willful action towards transformation by "burning" away that which stands in the way between you and your highest self, so you can fully light up. Fire purifies gold. Applying heat transforms mud into glass (vitrification). *Tapas* is the practice of self-discipline, self-restraint and self-control which cultivates the building of character and strengthens and grows the mind, body and spirit. By bringing focused determination, commitment, and dedication into your yoga practice and eating practice, self-transformation is not only possible but inevitable! Self-discipline is the foundation of self-confidence. Studies show that children who are given reasonable boundaries, limits and rules are more confidant, secure and content than children who are left to their own devices. It is the same with adults. Without self-imposed discipline and restraint, you lose trust in yourself and you lose yourself in the chaos of life. What does *tapas* look like for you? It may be committing to practicing yoga at a certain time every day, certain days of the week. It may be setting up boundaries with your eating, such as no eating after 7pm, or no eating for 3-4 hours after the previous meal. It may be setting up boundaries about the kinds of foods you purchase and bring into your home. It may be having discernment about the restaurants at which you choose to eat. It is about deliberately choosing foods that nourish and heal the body on a consistent basis. *Tapas* is placing the will and consciousness above the 5 senses. *Tapas* is about presence and perseverance. Self-change is impossible without self-discipline and perseverance. Swami Kripalu observed that, "People who begin practicing yoga, unfortunately stop because the right thing happens. That thing is purification."

Yoga as a tool:

Yoga is a powerful tool that cultivates the art of awareness and presence. The practice of yoga develops new connections, observations and awareness both on and off the mat. Many yoga practitioners notice their eating naturally changing on its own as they cultivate a regular yoga practice. Here are some of the ways the practice of yoga translates into the practice of eating!

1. Yoga installs a keen sense of awareness into the mind-body system. It is almost like installing a software upgrade into a computer. As you practice yoga, you practice awareness, just like working any muscle; the muscle of awareness is thus strengthened. Through this sharpened awareness, yoga practitioners are better able to differentiate whether they are really hungry or just thirsty, bored, tired or stressed.

2. Yoga teaches you to listen to your body, and give it what it truly wants. Yoga connects you to the *annamaya kosha,* or literally "food body." The physical body is considered the "food body" in yoga philosophy because *we are what we eat!* Yoga practice helps you begin to befriend and appreciate the gifts the physical body brings. Practice develops a new sense of connectedness to the physical body as it "unites" the body, mind and soul into their inherent oneness. This sense of oneness helps you begin to discern your cravings. Rather than giving in to sugar cravings, you know what your body really needs is sweet juicy fruit! You are able to listen to what your whole body needs rather than just your tongue. With regular yoga practice the cravings themselves naturally change as the body becomes naturally more sensitized to what brings it a sense of balance and what throws it off balance.

3. Yoga practitioners are also better able to tune into how they feel after they eat certain foods. They begin to make new connections about how good or bad they feel is often directly related the foods they consume. They notice if something they eat is difficult to digest, causing gas, constipation, cramping or indigestion. They notice whether they feel puffy, achy, sluggish or stiff after a big meal. Once these connections are made, it becomes easy to make better choices.

4. Yoga helps you attune to the emotional effects food has on the body. The *manomaya* kosha or "emotional body" layers right over the physical body or "food body." Therefore, the food we eat has a direct effect on the emotions and feelings. Yogis have been aware of the emotional effects of food for millennium. Many sensitive people notice that they feel anxious or fearful after eating meat, or sad and depressed after consuming alcohol. As yoga makes you more attuned to your emotional body, you begin to notice whether you feel cranky, agitated, anxious or depressed after you eat. You naturally begin to move towards foods that bring about a sense of peace and wellbeing. Frequently, regular yoga practitioners notice their cravings for meat become less and less over time as they begin to develop a sense of lightness and ease.

5. Yoga practitioners are able to sense the subtle life-force or *prana* in the food. Because the *pranamaya kosha* or "energy body" also layers right over the physical body, they begin to observe the energetic impact of the foods they eat. They perceive whether they feel enlivened and energized after eating or drained, fatigued, sleepy or depleted.

6. Yoga develops "witness consciousness." In yoga theory, the ability of being able to observe the causes and effects of your own behavior becomes your most powerful teacher. The *vijnanamaya kosha* or "wisdom body" is the part of you who is the passive observer as you go about your life. The more you connect to this observer, the more aware you become of what is and is not working in your favor. Witness consciousness shines the light on your relationship with eating and food! I remember just witnessing myself mindlessly eating a bag of corn chips, and witnessing myself standing at the refrigerator door looking for something to eat, without even being the slightest bit hungry.

7. Yoga helps reconnect our inner wiring to bliss! Yoga helps you do the work to Integrate all aspects of your life into alignment with who you are, how you were created to be and who you will become. This is the path to BLISS! Bliss is who we really are! It is only when we are integrated and whole in every area of existence, that the circuits connect and the "bliss body" or *anandamaya kosha* comes on line. Even when one thing is off, the circuits do not connect for this most subtle essence at the core of who we are. Eating delicious wholesome foods prepared with love is truly a blissful act. Wholeness, alignment, balance and wellness are the path to a blissful life body, mind and soul!

Yoga to detoxify the mind, body and soul!

One of the beauties of yoga practice is that it aids in the detoxification process on every level, body mind and soul. We know the body eliminates toxins through the kidneys, liver, lymph, skin, lungs, and overall blood circulation. Yoga practice can enhance these processes. For example, *pranayama* (yogic breath work) aides in cleansing the lungs. *Asana* practice helps us to sweat out toxins through the pores in the skin. Twists and inversions help to move lymph through the lymphatic system, and redirect the circulation of blood. Specific postures stimulate the kidneys, liver and intestines. Inversions drain lymph and blood and move it in new ways.

It is important to drink a lot of water after yoga practice to help "flush out" the toxins we move, and to get the optimal benefits of the detoxification process we've initiated in yoga practice. We can use saline water in the practice of *neti* to cleanse the nasal cavities, especially with those seasonal allergens in the air. Many yogis use tongue scrapers to cleanse the tongue. Tongue cleaning is likened to teeth brushing, because the tongue is like a little sponge in which bacteria hide and multiply! We can clean up the diet by eliminating processed foods and preservatives, by eating organic, increasing fruits, vegetables and legumes, and by reducing or eliminating meat, sugar, white flour and alcohol.

Detoxifying the mind is no different than detoxifying the body! Clean up what you put into the mind! What are you watching on TV? What are you reading? What music are you listening to? What sites do you go to on the internet? If we clean these things up, then we begin to detoxify the mind! The purer the things which go *into* the mind the more wholesome and clean the mind *is*! Meditation and relaxation also help to reset the mind and spirit!

In the same way, we can detoxify the soul. Are you thinking positive thoughts, or are you drawn to negativity? Are you overly critical of yourself, focused more on your flaws than your attributes? How are your interactions with others? Are you operating from a place of peace and love, or from negativity or selfishness? Negative thoughts and actions are toxic! When we intentionally change our thoughts and our actions, we change our spirits. Setting the intention to think and act in love and light, and to purge negativity, will detoxify the spirit.

> Yoga first removes the dullness of tamas, then the agitation of ragas, finally revealing the intellect in its sattvic purity.
>
> ~Alistair Shearer

Let yoga undo you. Yoga practice helps you undo toxic emotional patterning in the *manomaya kosha*, or mental/emotional sheath, which layers right over the physical body. As yoga practice moves the body in non-habitual ways, we also move out of habitual emotional patterning. Yoga practice helps you to "shed old skin" and old layers of being which are no longer relevant or no longer helpful as we move forward on our soul's path. As we move out of old toxic ways of living, we move into fresh new ways of being. When we move our bodies in new and different ways, it invites us to move our lives in new ways too!

> The Study of asana is not about mastering the posture. It's about using the posture to understand and transform yourself. ~Gary Kraftsow

How Does Yoga Detox the Body, Mind and Spirit?

- *Marmas* and Pressure Points

- Backbends to stimulate the liver and kidneys

- Inversions to drain

- Twists to wring you out like a "dirty rag."

- Moves lymph through the lymphatic system.

- Specific Poses support elimination of waste by stimulating the vagus nerve and toning the intestines.

- Yogic breath-work, or *pranayama*, eliminates toxins through the lungs.

- Undoes patterns of stress and tension in the body-mind system.

- Undoes old stagnant emotional patterns in the *manomaya kosha*.

A balanced yoga practice should be as "yummy" as a delicious healthy meal! You savor and enjoy it as you partake of it, and the feeling of energy and wellbeing continues long after! ~Elise Cantrell

If you only have 12–15 min. a day for yoga, I recommend this sequence of poses.

1. Hero

Kneel with sit-bones on heels, calves tucked under thighs. *Benefits: Stretches the shins, ankles, knees and quads while slackening the hamstrings.*

2. Rabbit

This pose stimulates the thyroid, pineal, pituitary, glands involved in metabolism and regulation of hormones. This pose should not be done by anyone with neck injuries. Seated with sit-bones on heels, one folds forward placing the crown of the head (highest point of the skull) on the floor, and the forehead touching the knees. The hands reach back and hold on to the heels. The sit-bones are then lifted up off of the heels. Most of the body weight remains on the shins. Only about 10% of the weight should be on the crown of the head. The chin should be tucked firmly into the chest, and the navel draws in towards the spine and up towards the heart. *Benefits: This pose stimulates the thyroid, pituitary and pineal glands. Tones the abdominals, opens area between the shoulder blades and the back of the heart, stretches the trapezius muscles, and stimulates the Ayurvedic marma point on the crown of the head called adipati marma.*

3. Cat/Cow

Begin on all fours in a "table top" position. Stack the shoulders over the wrists, and hips over the knees. Arch the back like a "Halloween" cat. Keep the chin tucked into the chest, and open the back of the heart by expanding the area between the shoulder blades as you round the spine. Then keeping elbows straight with just a slight "micro-bend" (to prevent hyperextension of the elbow joint) sink the belly and the heart downward curving the spine in the opposite direction as you move your gaze forward. Sit bones widen apart. Repeat several these cycles of spinal flexion and extension. This promotes spinal flexibility, moves fresh blood in and around the spine, and helps plump up the intervertebral disks, encouraging them to absorb fresh disk fluid. It may also help to realign the spinal disks. *Benefits: Spinal flexibility. Great for lower back pain.*

4. Knee-down Lunge

From all 4's in a "table top" position, step the right foot forward between the hands. The heel should be grounded. Shift the hips forward towards the hands, so the body is in a diagonal line. The heart and crown of the head lift and lengthen upwards away from the big toe in back. The navel draws in towards the spine and up towards the heart. Keep the right knee in towards the armpit. *Benefits: This pose keeps you "regular" as you stimulate the ascending colon and the vagus nerve. You will feel a stretch on the hip flexors at the front of the left hip. Hold for several deep complete breaths, and then switch to the left side. Here you will stimulate the descending colon, and stretch the right hip flexors.*

5. Hindi Squat

(This pose is not for persons with hip or knee issues.) When coming into a squatting position, if your heels do not touch the ground, then place a rolled-up yoga mat, wedge or book under the heels. Place your hands together in prayer position at the heart center. Use the elbows to press the thighs apart, while also contracting the thighs back towards the elbows, creating oppositional energy. Root the tailbone down while lengthening up through the crown of the head. Lift the heart up toward the thumbs. Draw the muscles of the pelvic floor in and up toward the navel. To come out of the pose, place the hands on the floor, and lift the hips, rising into a standing forward bend. *Benefits: strengthens the pelvic floor muscles, opens the hips and groin. Stimulates elimination and increases apana, which is the downward flow of energy.*

6. Ragdoll

A standing forward fold, in which feet are hip width apart, knees are slightly bent, and hands clasping opposite elbows. The head hangs freely between the arms. The legs are strong, supporting the forward bends so that the upper body can lengthen and relax becoming lose like a ragdoll. *Benefits: stretches hamstrings, lengthens spine, increases flow of blood to the heart and brain.*

7. Crescent Moon

Standing with feet hip-with apart, firmly planted, reach arms up over the head, clasp fingers together, with the index fingers pointing up like a church steeple. Hug your ears with the upper arm bones; lift through the heart; contract the abdominals. Bend the spine to the side making the even arc of the crescent moon. Hold. Pressing equally into both feet while simultaneously lengthening out through the crown of the head, heart and the index fingers. Keep the arc an even curve, opening the side of the ribcage. A strong engagement of the abdominals protects the lower back. Using the core muscles return to center on the in-breath. Repeat on the second side. *Benefits: Stretches the intercostal muscles between the ribs and increases lateral flexibility of the spine. Improves core strength particularly through the side body.*

8. Tree

Standing with the hands at heart center in prayer position, shift weight into left foot spreading the toes wide. Find a focal point, a point in front of you to hold a fixed gaze, or *drishti*. This cultivates a steady mind, which in turn supports a steady body. Place the sole of the right foot on the left calf thigh or ankle, finding a "sweet spot" where the foot can stay planted without sliding out of place. Draw the navel towards the spine, lift with the heart and root the tailbone down the standing leg into the earth like the roots of a tree. Hold for several breaths, then repeat on the second side. *Benefits: improves balance, concentration and focus. Strengthens legs and develops proper posture.*

9. Down Dog

Starting on all 4's, hands and feet shoulder width apart, lift the knees, sending the hips towards the sky, forming an upside-down letter "V." Make sure the weight is not on the heel of the hand. Instead it should spread out though the knuckles and fingertips, as you gently "claw" the fingers into the mat. Widen the sit-bones apart. Draw the navel in towards the spine and up towards the heart. Lift the armpits to draw the shoulder blades into their sockets on the back. Lengthen the crown of the head towards the fingertips and let the heels sink towards the floor. *Benefits: develops upper body strength, opens heart, stretches calves and hamstring muscles, lengthens spine, tones abdominals, reverses flow of blood towards head and heart.*

10. Camel

Starting on all 4's, rise into a knee stand. Reach arms over the head first lengthening the spine. Lifting through the heart and contracting the abdominals, bring the hands to the kidney area of the lower back. If possible, turn the fingertips upwards and the wrist down. Contracting the ribcage towards the hip points and the naval towards the pubic bone, lift through the heart and begin to arch back. The entire spine should be in an even curve including the neck. Earlobes press back, ensuring the head does not drop back. Hip points press forward. Stay for several breaths. Squeeze thighs together, lifting through the heart to rise up. Tuck chin towards the chest for a couple of breaths. Release knee stand. *Benefits: Opens front body, improves posture by counteracting hunching, stimulates kidneys and liver.*

11. *Setu Bhanda* or Bridge Pose

Lie on the floor with knees bent. Lift hips off of the floor by pressing into soles of the feet. Weight is on shoulders and feet. Head rests comfortably on the floor. There should be no weight on the neck. Chest lifts towards chin creating a gentle squeeze in the throat area. Lift, hold and lower three times. This stimulates the thyroid. *Benefits: opens the front body, stimulates kidneys, liver and thyroid. Strengthens legs.*

12. Reverse Child's Pose

While reclining on the back, hug both knees into the chest, clasping your hands in the front of the shins or behind the knees. Tuck your chin into your chest and bring your forehead towards your knees. Press navel downward towards the spine. Hold for several deep, complete breaths through the nose. Work up to holding for 1 minute. *Benefits: Stimulates thyroid, digestive "fire" or agni, said to melt away belly fat and strengthen the abdominal muscles.*

13. Reclining Twist

Lying on the back, reach the arms out to the sides at shoulder level. Draw the knees into the chest, and let them fall to the right. Both shoulder blades and arms remain grounded. Roll the head to gaze at the opposite shoulder. Hold for several breaths, and then, shift the knees to the left and hold. *Benefits: Stimulates digestion and elimination. Shifts central nervous system out of fight-or-flight into relaxation response. Twists are very calming to the mind-body system.*

14. *Savasana*

This pose is also called corpse pose. Lie on the back in a comfortable position, with palms open towards the ceiling, hands resting by the sides. Close the eyes, and allow the feet to fall open and gravity to take over. Bring your attention to your breath. The most important pose is "repose," teaching the body-mind system to rest and relax. Even just a few minutes of repose provides lasting benefits. *Benefits: Realigns the spine and resets muscle memory for proper posture. Gives the*

mind-body system the opportunity to "absorb" the benefits of the postures that came before it. Organs and systems are temporary placed in a different, more neutral relationship to gravity, which places less stress on them. The lying position also triggers relaxation response and calming alpha brain wave state.

Because we ARE what we eat, eating itself becomes a catalyst for transforming body, mind and soul. Eating itself is a powerful yoga practice! ~Elise Cantrell

Affirmation: Today I "feed" and move my body in ways that nourish my highest self!

Today's biggest success:

Food for thought: Yoga is Eating and Eating is Yoga! Become aware of the connection between yoga practice and an eating practice! If you haven't done so already, invite yoga into your physical exercise routine and come away with so much more. Yoga is the only way to exercise the body, mind and soul at the same time, and the result is unity and peace! Begin to let yoga feed you!

Journal: What new connections have you made between yoga and eating?

Day 8

Lab Made Foods vs.
Natural Foods

I discovered that the new reality of the world is that chemical companies are feeding us. ~Jeremy Seifert

Food has changed quite drastically since my great-grandmother's generation. My mom still has the churn my great grandmother used to make her own butter after milking her cows! My mom remembers going to her house as a girl and watching her churn butter. That generation knew exactly where their food came from and what was in it. There were no unpronounceable ingredients in my great-grandmother's southern biscuits. There were no GMO's or Roundup® spray in my great-grandmother's creamed corn! My great-grandmother lived to age 92! I remember her as a beautiful woman with a long white braid often coiled up into a bun.

Don't eat anything your great-great-grandmother wouldn't recognize as food. ~Michael Pollan

The body's natural default state is health, energy and wellbeing. When we live and eat in alignment with our body's natural default state, we can't help but feel energized, enlivened, strong and healthy. Modern culture has drastically departed from a lifestyle and diet that is conducive to our natural state of optimal weight, energy and health. If we want to return to the radiance, health and longevity that is our birthright, we simply have to return to "Mother Nature."

Why Organics?

If you think organic food is expensive, have you priced cancer lately? ~Joel Salatin

Conventional produce and meat are found to contain pesticides, chemical preservatives, and additives, which are known carcinogens, neurotoxins, reproductive toxins, geno-toxins, hormone disruptors, and some chemicals referred to as "obeseogens" have even been found to promote weight gain and obesity. There are no studies on the long-term effects of ingesting these toxic chemicals regularly over time. Certified organics must meet a high standard set by the FDA. There is a plethora of studies, which also show that organic produce offers more vitamins, minerals and phytonutrients than conventional produce. In some cases, organics provide more than twice as many of these nutrients. By switching from conventional to organic produce, there is a 19% increase in dietary antioxidants according to the British Journal of Nutrition. One study in which the difference in nutrient content between organics and conventional produce was shown to be negligible was given a great deal of attention by the news media. I thought it was very "interesting" and one sided because there are many other studies whose data shows a wide variation between organic and conventional produce, and these were never mentioned or given any attention! Of course, the news media would not want to offend the food industry who pays big bucks for on-air advertisements for their food commercials during their programming, now would they?

Recently, while giving a talk about healthy eating to a group of women, I was asked what one eating change I have made, which has made the biggest difference for me personally. I reflected on all the changes I have made in my eating practices over the years for a few moments and then told the group, hands down it was going all organic! In addition to dropping several pounds just by dropping the chemicals from my system, what I noticed was I also dropping the aches and pains in my joints, headaches, and mental dullness. In those circumstances when I have had to veer away from organics for a few days such as during vacation while eating out, it doesn't take long for these things to return! One of my students, a cancer survivor, tells me that when she has deviated away from organics, the chemicals in the foods she's eating give her the same symptoms she suffered when she was undergoing chemotherapy!

Here is an observation from another student:

I have to share! I didn't stop at the market yesterday to get organic steel cut oats for my breakfast this morning, but I did find a small container of generic oatmeal. I thought, well okay . . . I've got to tell you that I could immediately taste the chemicals with the first bite. I literally had to run to the sink and spit it out! I couldn't I couldn't even swallow it, my body was screaming in repulsion! ~Dr. Chery Kendrick

The EWG's "Dirty Dozen" most highly sprayed foods:

1. Apples

2. Strawberries

3. Grapes

4. Celery

5. Peaches

6. Spinach

7. Bell peppers

8. Nectarines

9. Cucumbers

10. Potatoes

11. Hot peppers

12. Summer Squash

13. Leafy greens including kale and collards

What Are GMO Foods, and Are They Safe?

GMOs (Genetically Modified Organisms) are crops that have been altered in a laboratory by inserting genes from other plants, animals, viruses or bacteria into the genes of the seeds. These products began to enter the US food supply in 1986. Early on we were all assured by the FDA that GMO foods were perfectly safe and were the answer to feeding a growing world population. As more and more independent research is released, I become less and less comfortable with the idea of GMO or Genetically Modified Organisms in our food supply.

While living in France, I discovered that the French had independently researched the effects of GMOs on animals, and had uncovered disturbing evidence. Based on this evidence and other independent studies, rather than the inside studies done by the biotech industry; **98% of Europe has now banned GMO foods**.

The biotech industry has much to profit from their patents. Their own studies lasted a maximum of 3 months, and from this, they concluded that these crops were safe. There have been no rigorous, long-term, double blind scientific studies done on GMOs by the FDA or the biotech industry. A French study on Roundup® Ready corn, however, lasted 2 years. It found that adverse health effects began to occur **after** the first 90 days! These health effects included mammary tumors, liver and kidney damage and premature death. In fact, 70 per cent of the rats fed GMO corn died prematurely as opposed to 20 percent in the control group!

GMO corn was engineered so that the corn itself becomes the actual pesticide, killing insects as they ingest it. The corn forms what is known as "BT-toxin." This toxin destroys the intestinal tract of the insect, thus killing it. We humans eat corn and BT-toxin in much larger quantities than insects. If it adversely affects the health of smaller living creatures, how could it not affect our own? New evidence links GMO foods to a disturbed gut microbiome. Good intestinal flora, which is responsible for healthy digestion and weight, dies off when exposed to GMO foods.

GMO corn was developed so that the plant can withstand being sprayed by the weed-killer, glyphosate or "Round-up Spray." This allows farmers to conveniently spray their fields with weed-killer without killing the corn. When humans or animals consume this corn, which has been genetically altered to become a pesticide, it has also been doused in weed-killer. Yum, right!? Currently, 89 percent of corn grown in the US is genetically modified. Corn is the main ingredient in the many children's breakfast cereals and eighty percent of the processed food on the grocery store shelves. New generations of GMO corn are emerging, which allow the crops to withstand being sprayed with other toxic agro-chemicals in addition to glyphosate, known on the market as Round-up Spray.

"Roundup® Ready" GMO soy is now being used on a massive scale in Argentina. New human evidence of the dangers of GMO foods is beginning to surface. Infertility, cancer, birth defects, and endocrine malfunction have skyrocketed in Argentina. Children are being born severely malformed at an alarming rate. GMO soy is being widely used in the food supply in the US, and present in things such as baby formula, processed foods, anything containing soybean oil, and any other non-organic forms of soy.

According to one study, when animals are given a choice between GMO feed and conventional feed, they avoid the GMO feed "like the plague". GMO's are also being questioned as a possible culprit in the sudden massive decline in the honeybee population, since it's the bees that pollinate the plants. GMO's are also being questioned as a culprit in the sharp rise in food allergies.

The top selling GMO foods in the US are corn, soy and canola. Tomatoes, zucchini, papayas, salmon, potatoes have also been genetically engineered. Animal feed is now frequently GMO, so if you are eating meat, you are exposed secondhand. If you wish to avoid GMO foods, it is best to either grow your own food from non-GMO seeds, buy products labeled Non-GMO, or buy organic products. Organic foods by law cannot contain GMO's. Produce label numbers beginning with the number 9 are organics. There is currently no required labeling for GMO foods in the United States, yet GMO foods have mandatory labeling in 64 countries around the world and are outright banned in 38 countries at this writing.

Here are the top reasons I choose
not to feed my family GMO foods:

1. Genetic modification does not happen in nature. It takes place in a laboratory. It is not the same thing as hybridization, in which crosspollination is done by a farmer. Crop hybridization is similar to a dog breeder crossbreeding two different breeds of dogs. Genetic modification is like a scientist inserting the genes of a gorilla into the DNA of a dog. Genetic manipulation is not a natural part of the natural evolutionary process.

2. Biotech companies insert viruses and animal genes into plant DNA to alter its genetic make-up.

3. A dramatic rise in inflammatory disorders coincided with the appearance of GMOs in the food system.

4. GMO corn is designed to produce its own insecticide, BT toxin, which damages the stomachs of insects.

5. A spike in digestive disorders including Crohn's Disease, IBS and leaky gut syndrome has coincided with the advent of GMO foods.

6. An upsurge in food allergies has been correlated with GMOs entering the mainstream diet.

7. GMO's adversely affect the delicate balance of the gut microbiome.

8. Autism spectrum disorder, ADD and ADHD suddenly skyrocketed along with the introduction of GMO foods. These disorders are almost non-existent in the Amish culture, where processed and GMO foods are forbidden.

9. Autistic children make significant improvements both cognitively and behaviorally once GMOs are removed from their diet.

10. Children and small animals are more sensitive to the toxic effects of foods at lower levels. Many pet foods contain GMOs.

11. GMO crops have measurably fewer vital nutrients in them than their natural counterparts.

12. Animals fed GMO feed develop sharply increased rates of reproductive disorders, serious birth defects, fetal death, still births, malignant tumors, severe diarrhea, higher rates of disease, and early death. Once removed from this feed these rates return to normal.

13. New unidentified organisms have developed in the guts of animals fed GMO feed.

14. 75% of GMO foods contain glyphosate (Round-up) residue, a broad-spectrum herbicide.

15. Glyphosate has been linked in studies to increased childhood cancers, birth defects, miscarriages, infertility, neurological disorders, Lymphoma: Non-Hodgkin, DNA damage, and Hormonal Disorders. The World Health Organization recently classified glyphosate as a probable carcinogen.

16. Birth defects increase up to 70 times the normal rate in areas surrounding farms growing GMO crops, using round-up spray.

17. Over 30 countries have banned the import of GMO crops. 64 countries require mandatory labeling of GMO foods. The US is not one of these. America is the only industrialized country in the world that does not require labeling of GMO foods.

18. GMO crops can cross-pollinate with and genetically contaminate natural varieties of the same crop.

19. The long-term generational effects of GMOs to humans, plants, animals and farmland soil are unknown.

How to avoid GMO foods:

In the US, it is not easy to avoid GMOs in your home since, unlike the rest of the industrialized world, the FDA does not require mandatory labeling. Right now, consumers have to become "food detectives" if they wish to avoid feeding their families GMOs. All corn, corn syrup, corn oil, corn meal, soy, soybean oil, cottonseed oil, sugar beet and canola oil currently grown in the US is genetically engineered unless it is labeled NON-GMO verified or certified organic. Some of the surprising places GMOs can be found is in baby formula, most breakfast cereals, many processed snack foods such as cookies, crackers and chips, baking mixes, non-organic dairy products, meat from grain-fed animals, vitamin supplements, commercially fried foods, Ketchup, mayonnaise, frozen dinners, canned "heat and serve" meals, frozen pizzas, popcorn, microwave popcorn, prepared sauces and salad dressings. If you do not wish to serve GMOs to your family, opt for "Certified Organic" products or products labeled "Non-GMO verified." Choose grass-fed beef, organically fed chicken, grow your own veggies, or purchase them from farmers and CSA farms committed to GMO-free and organic produce.

Affirmation: I am the architect and builder of my own body. I carefully select foods of the highest quality as building blocks of each and every cell.

Today's biggest success:

Food for thought: Your body-mind system knows the difference between natural foods and engineered foods. The more nutrient dense natural whole foods you consume, the easier it is for your body to default to its natural state of energy, health and wellbeing.

Journal: The purity of what you put in the body has a direct effect on physical and mental health. What changes can you make now to cultivate a cleaner, purer body and mind?

Day 9

The Healing Power of Water

Water represents *soma*, the nourishing, cooling quality associated with lunar energy. It helps with digestion, cools and balances *pitta dosha* supports *kapha*, and counteracts the dryness of *vata*. It nurtures, lubricates and detoxifies as it flows out of the body as urine. ~Maharishi Ayurveda

When I was vacationing on the Caribbean island of St. Kitts, we were able to enjoy fresh pure spring water from the mountain throughout the day for 7 days. I could feel the vitality in the water as I drank it. It was impossible not to sense its charge of vibrant life force! Immediately after drinking the water, my body and mind felt invigorated, refreshed and clear. Over the week, I noticed such a difference in the effect of drinking this fresh spring water in comparison to the chemically treated and ultra-processed water from Lake Michigan that I was astonished! I experienced the healing power of fresh, pure drinking water first hand.

I am not alone in my observation of pure quality drinking water. One of my 40 Days to Enlightened Eating students decided to make an inquiry into the effects that water quality had on her body and mind as she explored her 40-Day journey. She recorded her observations daily. It wasn't long before she noticed the healing power of water for herself. Here is a summary of her observations:

After just one week of drinking distilled water over tap water, I began to feel clear-headed. My mood improved and I felt less bloated. I noticed after drinking tap water that I felt heavy and had a gurgling sensation in my stomach. After drinking distilled water, this feeling was not present. I felt clean and refreshed! ~Caroline Lichucki

There is only one element on Earth that a human being cannot live without for more than 3 to 4 days: *water*. Water is the most plentiful element on Earth, yet the most over looked. We completely take for granted the remarkable powers of water. Water is a powerful transmitter of energy. It is a conductor. If you want to feel more energized, drink more fresh pure water. If you want your thoughts to flow with ease, drink more water. If you want your muscles to work at their peak, drink more water. "If there is magic on the planet, it is contained in water." ~Loren Eiseley

Water is detoxifying!

The human body is 70% water. Water is nature's most powerful detoxifier because it dilutes and flushes toxins out of the cells, organs and tissues of the body. Water promotes the removal of toxins via sweat, urine and waste. Many people who are poorly hydrated might notice scanty urine, saliva and sweat, as well as sluggish bowel movements with hard stools. These symptoms indicate dehydration and that toxins are accumulating in the body. When the body is not properly hydrated, toxins that are not flushed out get stored in the cells. When left unchecked, bodily toxins eventually form a sticky sludge in the body called *ama*, which clogs the channels and causes disease. Toxins cause deteriorating health, accelerated aging, low energy levels and sluggish metabolism. Toxins are accumulated in the body from the environment, foods we eat, health and beauty products we use and household chemical products we are exposed to. Toxins are also a by-product of poor digestion. Drinking ample amounts of water helps prevent toxins from collecting in the body and wreaking havoc on the health, weight, energy and metabolism.

Water is anti-aging!

Water is a primary source of vitality. *Ayurveda* recognizes that the body dries out as we age. Old age is considered the *vata* stage of life. As we age, characteristics of *vata* (wind, air, dryness, irregularity) intensify in the mind-body system. As we lose hydration, the skin becomes dry and wrinkled. The bones become lighter and more brittle. The lubrication in the joints and spine begins to dry out causing arthritis symptoms. Furthermore, as the body gets drier, energy declines, muscles become weak, and tremors can arise. The brain is 80% water. As we age and don't receive adequate hydration, the brain doesn't function at its prime and there is increased fogginess and forgetfulness. Studies show that water alone has a healing effect on Alzheimer's patients. When water intake is increased, improvement can be seen in a matter of weeks! Without proper hydration, brain cells shrink, eventually drying the brain out like a raisin. Proper hydration is also required for the neurons and synapses to fire effectively, since water conducts their electrical activity. The brain cannot function well in a state of even the slightest state of dehydration. Studies show that just a 1% decrease in the water content of the brain has a profound effect on brain function! Most symptoms of aging are simply symptoms of poor hydration! Water plumps the skin, increases production of collagen and elastin, increases the flow of blood and oxygen to the tissues and the brain, and reduces inflammation of every type. Water itself Is the "fountain of youth!" Lao Tzu, one of the greatest sages ever known, put it nicely: "Flowing water never decays."

Ojas, the very "sap of life" in *Ayurveda,* is a vital fluid, dependent upon hydration to remain at adequate levels to nourish the tissues and support the mind. *Ojas* is the vital fuel for the cells that is said to cultivate inner and outer radiance. If *ojas* is optimal, we feel enlivened, energized, have a strong immune system and enjoy a clear, harmonious mind. Ojas puts the sparkle in the eyes, radiance in the skin, and imparts energy and enthusiasm for life. Without sufficient water, this vital essence cannot remain at its ideal level. Youthfulness is really a state of optimum *ojas.* Even the elderly can exude an essence of radiance, vivaciousness and effervescence when their body's alchemy is aligned! Ancient *Ayurvedic* texts emphasize that fresh, pure water is the foundation of "immortality" and that water itself is "life-enhancing" imparting "strength and vigor."

Water is profoundly healing!

Water is the most plentiful and inexpensive medicine on the planet! Water governs **all** bodily functions, and adequate hydration is key to human health. Dr. F. Batmanghelidj, MD has made water his life's work. He has treated thousands of patients ailing from various diseases, successfully with one single medicine: *water*! His extensive research has led him to conclude that most diseases are simply the result of chronic dehydration. He emphasizes that local aches and pains are merely localized dehydration. His work has determined that pain is simply your body's cry for water. Some of the most common ailments which are characteristic of chronic dehydration are: migraines, peptic ulcers, osteoarthritis, rheumatoid arthritis, angina, low back pain, neck pain, high blood pressure, anxiety and depression, high cholesterol, fatigue, weight gain, colitis, asthma and allergies. Dr. Batmanghelidj asserts that most studies on the effectiveness of water as a "cure-all" have been suppressed by the multimillion-dollar pharmaceutical industry, because water is the cheapest and most plentiful substance in the world and stands to upset their profits. His message to the world is that: "You are not sick, you are thirsty. Don't treat thirst with medication." "Chronic and persistently increasing dehydration is the root cause of almost all currently encountered major diseases of the human body." He contends that the only remedy for diseases of dehydration is **water**, and that medications are only masking the symptoms of this chronic problem and leading to the worsening of the condition and the progression of the disease.

Dr. Batmanghelidj's findings correspond to the philosophy and wisdom of the healing science of *Ayurveda*. Water and hydration are age-old treatments for chronic states of disease caused by the aggravation of *vata* and *pitta doshas*, which when out of balance both have a drying out effect on the body. *Ayurvedic* texts explain that water is a "balm" for the human body containing excellent "curative powers." According to *Ayurveda*, water alone "destroys hundreds of diseases." Water's powerful medicine was recognized and revered thousands of years ago. Today the most potent healing agent on the planet is largely ignored!

Water boosts metabolism and aids with weight-loss!

Water is a powerful mechanism in the function of the metabolism. It enables the breakdown of protein and carbohydrates in the body and supports the utilization of stored fat as energy. A German study showed that the metabolism of both males and females rose 30% immediately after drinking a glass of water! Without adequate water, the metabolism cannot function properly. Also, if the body's subtle signals of thirst go unrecognized, hunger symptoms will soon arise. The body knows that it can get some modest hydration from foods. Signs of hunger are often the body's call for water. Sweet cravings are often a signal that the body is craving water. Water has a natural sweet *vipaka* or taste. The body also instinctively knows that fruits are both sweet and juicy containing about 70% water. The body produces sweet cravings in hopes that its need for water will be satiated. When the body gets desperate for hydration, it goes to desperate measures! When we substitute cookies and candy for water, the underlying thirst continues to go unquenched! Many times, we end up eating when all the body really needs is a glass of water.

The most plentiful element on the planet is your closest health allay. Harness the healing power of water beginning today! "Waters are the medicines for everything; may they act as medicine to thee." ~Ancient *Ayurvedic* Text

"Charge" your water!

"Charging" water is an ancient practice of infusing your water with positive energy. Water is a conductor of energy and easily caries any energy infused into it. Holy water has been used in blessings and healings since antiquity. Before drinking water or bathing in it you can bless it, pray for it, say positive words over it or charge it with Reiki energy to elevate the vibration of the water. Dr. Marasu Emoto, a Japanese scientist has spent his career studying the powerful properties of water. He has been a modern-day pioneer in discovering how water is affected by the energy we send it. He has completed countless studies in which water was blessed, prayed over, sent positive thoughts and words, or conversely cursed, sworn at and sent negative thoughts. The energy sent to the water entirely changes the crystalline structure of the water molecules, which is readily apparent with the aid of a microscope. Positive words, thoughts and prayers routinely impart beautiful snowflake like formations of the water molecules, whereas negative energy consistently creates asymmetrical ugly "splats." His studies also prove that at first, the crystalline structure of polluted water appears unsightly under the microscope. Once this polluted water is blessed, prayed over, or sent thoughts of love and peace, the polluted water's structure transforms into very attractive geometrical configurations.

I have begun purifying my own drinking water using the healing power of crystals. Visionary and mystic Kiesha Carruthers, also known as "Little Grandmother" publicly speaks about her own powerful experience of purifying water with crystals. She brought crystals in which she had placed the intention of purification and cleansing to Fukushima, Japan. The crystals were placed into highly radioactive water there. Within just 2 minutes of placing the charged crystals in the radioactive water, the Geiger counter registered zero. Her message is to use crystals to purify not only your own drinking water but to purify lakes, streams, rivers and oceans. Since water is a conductor of energy, whatever intention the crystal is charged with, will be carried from molecule to molecule with the same ripple effects that tossing a stone into the water would have. As Dr. Emoto's body of work with water and intention has shown, our very energy, thoughts, words and intentions change the structure of water molecules of water! I even use crystals to purify the water in my bath! I infuse my bath water with rose quartz or amethyst crystals on a nightly basis to purify the water I am bathing in, and to help to purify my own energy, since human beings are almost entirely composed of water.

"Holy water" has long been known to carry with it sacred energy, and has been used in holy rites for millennia. Holy water is water that has been consecrated and blessed. There are numerous documented accounts of the healing, cleansing and clearing powers of holy water! Water is a conductor of energy, and the energy you give it is the energy it carries in you and around you. In a time when a great deal of our water supply has been contaminated, polluted, or tainted, perhaps it is time to renew the ancient practice of infusing water with the intention of healing, blessings and positivity.

Since water is a conductor of energy, charged water can be spritzed around your home, office or on your person to clear, cleanse and shift the energy in and around you. Adding a few drops of a pleasantly scented high vibrational essential oil (such as frankincense) and or crystals, further charges and imbues the energy of the water. Some people soak specific crystals in drinking water to infuse it with healing energy, while others place it in the sun or moonlight. However you choose to "charge" your water, the key is the power and energy of the intention you put into the charge, that infuses into the water, so make it one of the highest degree of love, joy and healing.

According to the Maharishi Council of *Ayurvedic* Physicians, water has the following healing qualities:

1. Helps lift fatigue

2. Improves brightness and luster of the skin

3. Prevents constipation

4. Increases energy and stamina

5. Promotes healthy mood

6. Heart healthy: Builds blood and promotes circulation

7. Promotes better digestion

8. Cools the body, balances *pitta*, anti-inflammatory

9. Acts as a powerful source of vital life-force energy

10. Has an antioxidant effect

11. Balances *vata*, dryness, and promotes healthy tissue and joints.

Is it okay to drink water with meals?

Many people ask me weather drinking water at meals is a good idea, so I would like to address that here. *Ayurveda* always suggests that the water you drink be warm, and certainly no cooler than room temperature. Many people are disappointed to know that we never recommend ice-cold beverages. The cold effect of iced beverages works counter to the heat of *agni*, the digestive "fire." The stronger the *agni*, the better digestion, and less *ama* is produced. Keeping a strong, hot digestive fire increases the metabolism, and strengthens the immune system. *Ayurveda* maintains that the belly itself is ground-zero of the immune system. If you have a strong *agni*, nothing can get past the belly and infect the body.

It is okay to *sip* warm water with meals to help you wash down the food. How much water you need will vary based on whether your meal is moist and juicy like a soup or stew, or whether it is dry like a sandwich. Of course, with drier food, more water is necessary to help it move through the digestive tract. It is never a good idea to gulp down large amounts of water at meals since this dilutes the digestive enzymes and gastric juices, which are needed in the appropriate strength for optimal digestion. Since the body needs water for the digestive process, the optimal time to begin drinking water is about 45 minutes after a meal when the body naturally begins to experience signs of thirst. Beware that often times between meals, people misinterpret thirst signals from the body as hunger signals. If the body doesn't have sufficient moisture for digestion, it will trigger food cravings, particularly "sweet" cravings. Water has a natural "sweet" *vipaka* or taste as does ripe juicy fruit. The sweet cravings are really just signs your body wants water! Always try satiating your sweet cravings with water first!

Water before a meal is nectar. It replenishes fluids and encourages juicy digestive organs. Small sips during a meal is honey. It helps turn the food into a sauce. Water after a meal is poison because it dilutes stomach acids. ~Dr. Vasant Lad

Affirmation: Today I drink plentiful amounts of fresh pure water. As I drink water I am setting the intention to cleanse, purify and refresh. I consciously and continuously quench the thirst of my body, mind and soul.

Today's biggest success:

Food for thought: Consciously drink plentiful amounts of fresh pure water. In situations when water is not as pure as you'd like it to be, it is often advised that you say a prayer over the water. If you are attuned to Reiki, you can also infuse your water with healing Reiki energy, or use the healing power of crystals. Today be aware if your sweet cravings may really be water cravings in disguise!

Journal: Each day, I fill a large glass pitcher with purified, filtered water. I place crystals at the bottom and have a positive message taped to the pitcher. I make it my goal to finish the pitcher of water by the end of the day. I bathe every evening with rose quartz crystals in the bath as well. What positive changes can you implement to benefit from the healing powers of water?

Day 10

Ayurvedic Dinacharya

Ayurveda teaches that the human body-mind system is best balanced when it is kept in harmony with the cycles of nature. *Dinacharya* is the *Ayurvedic* practice of keeping the bodily rhythms in tune with the natural rhythm of a daily cycle (circadian rhythm). *Dinacharya* literally translates from Sanskrit as "daily routine." An *Ayurvedic* daily routine is the "ideal" way to bring the mind-body system in sync, and keep it balanced, healthy and harmonious. In the modern age, many of us have lost touch with the natural daily rhythms of the body and mind due to spending most of our time indoors in houses, schools and offices with limited exposure to sunlight. Instead we peer for hours on end at a TV or computer screen, even into the wee hours of the evening. By incorporating the following *Ayurvedic* routine into your day, you realign your own rhythms to sync with rhythms of nature.

1. **Wake before sunrise.** (By 6-6:30 am, the body shifts into *kapha* mode. *Kapha* time of day is 6-10am, and waking during that time will leave you feeling sluggish, heavy and slow. 2-6 am is *vata* time of day. *Vata* time of day is ideal for waking, because it is when the body naturally wants to move. The bladder and bowels also begin to awaken naturally at the time and stimulate elimination. By waking later during *kapha* time, you are working against the natural rhythms of the mind-body system. You will awaken feeling groggy, lethargic and sluggish. I notice teenagers tend to sleep right through *kapha* time of day waking up after 10 am, during *pitta* time of day. This is because *pitta* is highly pronounced during the teenage years. The Early morning hours are said to contain the most *sattva* (pure, harmonious energy) of any time of day. *Sattva* can be found in the beauty of the sunrise and the silent stillness of the early dawn.

2. **Tongue scraping:** As soon as you awaken, use a tongue scraper or the edge of a spoon to scrape the toxins or *ama* secreted on the surface of the tongue during the night. This also ignites *agni,* the fire of digestion and metabolism, bringing the digestive system on-line. Tongue scraping also provides helpful feedback about your eating the previous day. If you notice your tongue was coated with a thick whitish sludge, this is an indicator that your body formed *ama* or toxins, which slows the metabolism and clogs the channels, and is the precursor of disease. When consistently eating a clean diet at proper inter-

vals for your digestion, you will find very little if any coating on the tongue. This tells you that your digestion and metabolism are functioning at their optimum. My own morning tongue scraping is a great feed-back system for how well I did with my eating the previous day. Another great benefit of tongue scraping is that it removes the sludge and build-up on the tongue that interferes with the taste buds effectively detecting all 6 tastes. When the brain receives the proper signals from the taste buds, it releases hormones and messages to the body indicating satiation. When these tastes are not well detected, you may continue to hunger for these unacknowledged tastes.

3. **Warm water gargle:** After scraping the tongue, gargle with warm salt water or sesame oil for 1 minute. Both sea salt and Himalayan are ideal.

4. *Neti:* Saline nasal irrigation. Use a *neti* pot with ½ tsp non-iodized sea salt and warm (body temp.) water, not hot or cold. Make sure the salt is well dissolved and mixed in the warm water. Warning: the salt will cause a burning sensation if it is left undissolved at the bottom of the pot. Also, too little salt or too much salt will cause an uncomfortable sensation. When performed properly, *neti* should not feel unpleasant. It may feel strange at first, but is not uncomfortable. Over a sink or large bowl, tilt your head to the side, not too far forward or back, and pour the warm saline water into the top nostril while allowing it to drain out of the bottom nostril until the pot is empty. Repeat on the second side. Benefits: removes, bacteria, allergens and pollutants from sinus passages.

5. *Nasya:* Lubrication of the nasal passages and ear canals with oil. Lying down with the head on a towel, tilt the head back, use a clean dropper to place 5-6 drops of sesame oil, *nasya* oil or ghee *nasya* (not cooking ghee) in each nostril. (Clean cotton swabs, or the tip of the finger can also be used.) Keep head tilted back for several minutes to allow oil to penetrate. Turn head to right and place drops in right ear, hold, allowing the drops to enter the ear canal for about 2 minutes. Turn head and repeat on the second side. This practice helps counter congestion and phlegm. It reduces *kapha* and *vata,* helps relieve stress. It is said to relieve allergies, sinusitis, migraines, cold symptoms and nourish the brain. It improves symptoms of dementia, anxiety, ADD and ADHD. *Nasya* has a host of other health benefits. Herbal *nasya* oils are commercially available for each *dosha.*

6. **Hot lemon water:** This stimulates a bowel movement, and helps to awaken *agni,* the digestive fire. It also awakens the metabolism. I tell my students, if they choose to do only one thing, then choose to start the day with hot lemon water. Among the many benefits, it lifts the mood, having a stimulating yet calming effect at the same time. Squeeze, then drop a small wedge of organic lemon, with the peel, into a cup of hot water. This rehydrates the body after a night of sleep, it helps to cleanse the intestinal walls, and alkalinize the body.

Just as warm water and lemon can remove grease from dirty dishes, it also helps remove *ama* and sticky sludge from the body. Hot lemon water is a blood and liver cleanser, and purifies the skin. I go into great detail about the benefits of hot lemon water in *40 Days to Enlightened Eating*.

7. **Oil pulling:** *The Charaka Samhita*, an ancient *Ayurvedic* text, recommends oil pulling for dental and overall oral health, but also treats over 30 other diseases including migraines, diabetes and asthma with this practice. The oral benefits include:

- Kills bacteria, which cause bad breath and cavities due to its antibacterial properties.

- Prevents and heals mouth sores, cuts, gum inflammation and ulcers.

- Promotes fresh breath, strong, healthy gums, eliminates post nasal drip (clears *kapha* in the form of phlegm and congestion from the nose and throat)

- Is antibacterial, anti-viral and anti-fungal.

- Is said to "heal" cavities over time.

- It whitens teeth without chemicals.

- Removes food debris and plaque, from teeth and gums.

Directions: Simply swish 1 tsp of coconut oil or sesame oil around mouth for 15-20 minutes, then spit out. Coconut oil has a more pleasant taste.

8. *Abhyanga:* Self-massage with oil. *Abhyanga* is a powerful healing and de-toxifying daily practice. It helps remove toxins from the tissues, channels and cells and return them to the digestive channel where they can be eliminat-ed. *Abhyangha* is a form of *snehana,* external application of oil to the body. *Snehana* literally means love and compassion. When practiced regularly, the energy of love, happiness and joy is increased in the mind-body system. According to ancient *Ayurvedic* texts, this practice alone can dissolve away negative thoughts, emotions and energies stored in the body and mind. It is profoundly healing. It is important to use the appropriate oil for your *dosha*. *Vata dosha* should use sesame oil or almond oil. *Pitta dosha* can use coconut oil, sunflower oil or *neem* oil, and *Kapha dosha* can use sesame oil, organic corn oil or mustard oil. Done before yoga practice it can lubricate joints and relax the muscles, allowing the body to safely move deeper into the postures.

9. **Yoga practice:** Yoga is best practiced on an empty stomach. Many of the poses can interfere with the digestive process. For example, forward bends, and inversions on a full stomach can cause reflux. The gravity in an inversion or forward bend works against the natural flow of digestion. In *Ayurveda* digestion uses the energy of *samana vata* and *apana vata*. *Samana vata* is the

clockwise churning energy that moves the food through the intestinal track and *apana vata* is a downward and outward energy that helps the body remove waste through the bladder and bowels. It is best to practice yoga before eating or at least 2 hours after eating. Wait 1 hour after your practice to eat another meal, allowing time for the *subdoshas* to settle back into a regular flow.

10. **Meditation**- Sit in silent stillness for a period of time upon awakening or just following your yoga practice. 30 minutes is said to be ideal, but even 5 to 15 minutes can make a profound difference in your day! A humorous Zen saying is, *"You should meditate for 20 minutes a day. If you don't have time to meditate for 20 min., then you should meditate for an hour."* **(See chapter on meditation for more specific instructions and practice.)**

11. **Breakfast**- Choose an appropriate breakfast for your *dosha*. For detoxing, stewed fruit is ideal for all the *doshas*. (Stewed fruit may not be appropriate for diabetics.)

12. **Lunch**- Lunch should be eaten between the hours of 10am and 2pm. Ideally, this should be your largest meal of the day. During this time of day, the *agni* or digestive fire is at its strongest, and digestion is at its optimum. Frequently westerners eat their largest meal in the evening when the digestive fire has begun to slow. This is a recipe for *ama* and for weight gain. By changing this alone, many folks find this enhances their ability to lose weight, and keeps the metabolism humming!

13. **Afternoon**-this is a good time of day for meditation, yoga *nidra* or an extended *savasana* if your schedule permits.

14. **Exercise**-late afternoon after 4pm is a good time for additional movement, such as a brisk walk, yoga practice, swimming, tai chi, or some other moderate form of movement that you find pleasant and enjoyable, if your schedule allows.

15. **Dinner**-Ideally dinner should be a lighter meal eaten before 7pm. The digestive power is lower later in the day and has less capacity to digest large, heavy meals. Eating a heavy meal in the evening or munching late at night is not recommended because it creates *ama* or toxic sludge. (This sludge will show up the next morning on your tongue when you scrape your tongue. You can't miss it!)

Ayurvedic Daily *Doshic* Cycles

First cycle:

6 A.M. to 10 A.M. – *Kapha* time: Waking before the onset of *kapha* time is suggested to prevent you from feeling groggy, lethargic and sluggish as you begin the day. During *kapha* time of the morning, you may notice more congestion, post nasal drip and throat clearing as *kapha* liquefies. This is a great time of day to exercise in order to clear the sluggish energy of *kapha* and get moving. It is also easier to set an exercise routine in the mind-body system when done during *kapha* time, as *kapha* promotes habit and routine.

10 A.M. to 2 P.M. – *Pitta* time: This is the time of day when focus, concentration and energy are at their height. Take care of any work or activity that demands sharp focus during this time. *Agni* or digestive fire is also at its peak. It is recommended that you eat your largest meal of the day during these hours for optimal digestion.

2 P.M. to 6 P.M. – *Vata* time: Creativity and imagination flow during this time of day, and energy levels should be at their height. Take advantage of this momentum to accomplish your goals. If you are finding yourself crashing during this time of day, you may have fluctuating blood sugar levels. The need to nap during this time of day can also signal weak digestion. It is important to eat an adequate mid-day meal to fuel the mind-body system through productive *vata* time. Be sure not to over-eat at lunch or you may find yourself crashing during *vata* time of day as well. Since *vata* governs elimination, you may experience a bowel movement during this time of day.

Second cycle:

6 P.M. to 10 P.M. – *Kapha* time: Digestion is slower at this time of evening. Ideally one eats the final meal of the day prior to *Kapha* time. If large meals are eaten during this time they tend to be poorly digested, and can cause weight gain. It is best to go to bed before this *kapha* cycle is complete to avoid difficulty sleeping and to ensure restful sleep. This time of the evening is the most conducive to falling to sleep with ease.

10 P.M. to 2 A.M. – *Pitta* time: The mind-body system can become stimulated again during this time of night. It can be much more difficult to fall asleep in *pitta* mode. The mind becomes sharp, clear and focused. It is best to go to bed before *pitta* time begins for a restful nights' sleep.

2 A.M to 6 A.M. – *Vata* time: Waking in the night with anxious, racing thoughts, creating to-do lists, and tossing-and-turning is more likely to happen during these hours. Since *vata* governs the urinary tract, it is more likely that you awaken for a trip to the bathroom during this time. It is best to awaken and arise for the day during *vata* time of morning for increased energy and enthusiasm at the start of the day. Arising during these hours makes it much easier to get going in the morning without the help of caffeine.

Affirmation: I live in harmony with the cycles of nature because I am a part of nature and nature is a part of me.

Today's biggest success:

Food for thought: Beginning today, incorporate some of these daily practices into your routine and by paying attention, note the changes you observe.

Journal: Which practices would you like to begin to incorporate?

Day 11

Ayurveda for the Seasons

Balanced *doshas* (*vata, pitta, kapha*), balanced *agni* (metabolism), properly formed *dhatus* (body tissues), proper elimination of *malas* (waste matter), and blissful state of mind, body and soul define a healthy person. ~Sushruta Samhita

According to the healing science of *Ayurveda*, the seasons of nature are governed by the 5 elements: earth, water, fire, air, and ether. Certain elements tend to be more active during a particular season. Humans are a part of nature, and are composed of these five elements as well and are affected by the forces of them. The elements are classified into 3 categories, the *Ayurvedic doshas*: *vata, pitta* and *kapha*. *Vata* is comprised of the elements of air and ether. *Pitta* contains fire and water, and *kapha* is composed of water and earth. Individuals may have a dominant *dosha* in their constitution such as *vata, pitta* or *kapha,* or they may manifest a combination of these *doshas* such as *vata-pitta, vata-kapha, pitta-kapha* or *vata-pitta-kapha.* (To determine your own unique *dosha,* and understand more about your *Ayurvedic* constitution, refer to the *dosha* quiz and the description and explanation in Chapter 14-16 of *40 Days to Enlightened Eating or* in the appendices of this book.)

The seasons are classified by the characteristics of their own dominant *dosha* just as humans are. The *doshic* characteristics of the seasons increase that same *dosha* in us. "Like" increases "like." As the seasons change, it becomes important to change with them in order to maintain a healthy balance of the *doshas* in our individual constitution. It is particularly critical to incorporate appropriate lifestyle adjustments in a season in which you share the same characteristics of that *dosha.* A *dosha* is more easily aggravated in its corresponding season. Aggravated *dosha* creates imbalance and can ultimately lead to illness and disease if not addressed. *Vata* is twice as likely to come out of balance than *pitta,* and *pitta* is twice as likely to come out of balance than *kapha.* There are twice as many disorders from *vata* imbalance than *pitta* imbalance, and twice as many disorders from *pitta* imbalance than *kapha* imbalance.

Ayurveda teaches that applying opposites is the best way to return and keep the *doshas* in balance. Therefore, we practice the application of opposites to keep the *doshas* in balance during each season. The following are eating and lifestyle practices utilized in *Ayurveda* during each season to promote and maintain balance and wellbeing. These diet and lifestyle suggestions can also be incorporated year-round to keep your primary *dosha* in balance.

Summer: *Pitta* Season

According to the healing science of *Ayurveda*, summer is considered *pitta* season because the elements of fire and water govern the weather. During the summer months, heat and humidity tend to run the show. The heat and moisture of summer often impact our own inner nature or *dosha* as well. Persons with a *pitta*, *vata-pitta* or *kapha-pitta* constitutions tend to be more prone to experience *pitta* related imbalances during this time of year than other constitutions. However, it is possible for anyone to experience the effects of aggravated *pitta,* particularly in a hot-moist climate.

Some common physical and health related *pitta* type imbalances that are more likely to occur during summer are:

Rashes, acne, infections, ulcers or cold sores, fever blisters, sunburn, acid-reflux, hyper acidity, heart burn, peptic ulcer, yellow coating on tongue, hot flashes, heat stroke, fever, heavy menstruation, hair-loss or premature graying, red, stinging eyes, alcoholism, inflammation of any kind, diarrhea and dehydration. If you are experiencing these, your *pitta dosha* is out of balance.

Signs of *pitta* emotional imbalance:

Flares of temper, impatience, irritability, agitation, anger, rage, hyper-competitiveness, bossiness, workaholic, alcoholic, judgmental, fanatical, pushiness, short-temper, becoming easily frustrated, a perfectionist, a strong aversion to the heat or sun and dehydration. If you are experiencing these, your *pitta dosha* is out of balance.

Signs of Balanced *pitta* include:

Even tempered, strong immune system, healthy appetite, strong metabolism, energetic, good digestion, clear soft skin, organized, well focused, a good leader, perceptive, observant, self-disciplined, athletic body type, patient, courageous, successful, a "go getter."

Do You Have a *Pitta* Imbalance?

Pitta qualities correspond with the element of fire and consist of heat, oil, spreading, odor, light, sharpness, and proliferation. People of a *pitta* constitution are more likely to suffer from an imbalance of this *dosha*, but under the right circumstances any constitution can experience a *pitta* imbalance.

Some things which can lead to accumulation of *pitta* might be exposure to extreme heat, a diet of salty, oily, spicy foods, a demanding career, high-stress lifestyle, or a diet high in fried, acidic, spicy foods and alcohol.

According to *Ayurveda*, summer is *pitta* season. When exposed to heat for a duration of time, our own fire-like qualities can become exacerbated and out of balance. If *pitta* imbalance is not corrected, one may experience increased hunger and thirst, rashes and inflammation, irritability, anger, excessive indigestion, ulcers, yellowy skin and eyes and ultimately inflammatory diseases. Take the following quiz to determine whether or not your own inherent *pitta* or fire qualities have been aggravated:

1. Have you felt overheated or experienced hot-flashes?

2. Have you noticed indigestion or stomach hyper-acidity?

3. Has your skin and hair become oilier?

4. Have you been experiencing rashes or acne?

5. Have you observed an increased appetite?

6. Have you observed a slight weight gain?

7. Have you suffered from allergies or inflammation of any kind?

8. Do you feel more aggressive or have more "drive" than usual?

9. Have you had a shorter temper than usual?

10. Do you feel irritated and annoyed by things that wouldn't ordinarily bother you?

11. Have you noticed increased sweating accompanied by a stronger body odor?

12. Do you feel an aversion to heat or direct sun?

13. Have you experienced increased thirst?

14. Have your bowel movements been more loose than usual?

If you find yourself answering "yes" to several of these questions, then your own *pitta* or fire element has come out of balance.

What to Eat?

Ayurveda teaches the practice of eating appropriately for the season to keep the *doshas* in their optimal balance. In order to bring *pitta dosha* back into proper balance, it is helpful make the following changes:

Increase

Sweet, bitter, and astringent tasting foods, add in more raw foods, and eat foods that are lighter in nature.

- **Sweet juicy fruits:** melons, sweet (not sour) berries, grapes, sweet apples, mango, and coconut.

- **Vegetables:** cucumber, okra, squash, zucchini, asparagus, broccoli, celery, artichoke, green beans, cauliflower.

- **Bitter greens:** lettuce, arugula, radicchio, and endive, kale, spinach.

- **Drinks:** cool (not cold) drinks, fruit juices, coconut water, aloe juice, cooling herbal teas, green tea and ample amounts of water.

- **Oils:** sunflower oil, coconut oil, ghee, olive oil.

- **Herbs and spices:** Dill, fennel, cardamom, coriander, saffron, mint, cilantro.

Reduce or Avoid

Sour, salty, and pungent tastes, hot spicy foods, skipping meals, especially lunch, which causes irritability. Specifically reduce or avoid the following foods.

- **Sour fruits:** citrus, sour berries, sour apples, and tomatoes

- **Vegetables:** eggplant, tomato, potato

- **Spices:** chilies, garlic, ginger, black pepper, ginger, cumin, cayenne, fenugreek, clove, celery seed, salt and mustard seed.

- **Meat:** beef, seafood and eggs

- **Other:** roasted, salted nuts, cheeses, sour yogurt, fermented foods, coffee, alcohol, pickles, vinegar, hot sauce. (When imbibing, beer is less *pitta* aggravating than beverages like whiskey, bourbon, rum or red wine.)

Pitta balancing Lifestyle recommendations.

Increase

Entertainment: soft tranquil music, reading, non-competitive forms of recreation.

Practices: Coconut oil self-massage, cool showers, moon bathing, meditation, journaling, affirmations, gratitude.

Exercise: Keep exercise regime light to moderate. Walking or biking outdoors in the cooler morning or evening, swimming, Qi-gong and Tai chi are *pitta*-balancing exercises.

Yoga: Gentle yoga, yoga *nidra*, yin yoga, restorative yoga, SUP (Stand-Up Paddle Board) yoga are yoga practices that calm and cool the body and mind.

Color therapy: Cool colors are best such as soft shades of blue, purple, and green. Wear white, light or pastel colored clothing.

Crystal therapy: Pearl is the best stone to counter *pitta*. Consider wearing pearl jewelry. Consider also purple agate, amethyst.

Aromatherapy: Use the following essential oils to balance *pitta*: clary sage, geranium, rose, jasmine, peppermint, sandalwood, lavender, lime, bergamot, cilantro, fennel essential oils are best for balancing *pitta*. Rosewater mist and rose scented bath soap can work wonders.

Avoid

Avoid direct sun and being outdoors during *pitta* time of day (10am-2pm) Steer clear of heated discussions, arguments.

Practices: Avoid sunbathing, debating.

Exercise: Avoid running, exercising outdoors during the heat of the day and competitive sports.

Yoga: Avoid vigorous forms of yoga such as hot yoga, power yoga and *Ashtanga* yoga.

Entertainment: Avoid competitive and aggressive games and sports (video games included), agitating music, violent movies or TV programs.

Color therapy: Avoid "warm" colors such as yellow, red or orange. Stay away from bright hues and neon colors.

> *****Note:** It is important to be aware that *vata* aggravation begins in the summer, as the heat of summer starts to dry the body out. This is a precursor to *vata* imbalances arising as we transition over to cooler temperatures and autumn winds. In a hot dry climate, symptoms of *vata* imbalance may arise during summer months. It is important to note that fall is the ideal time to treat *pitta* imbalances, as cool dry weather creates the balancing energy ideal for *pitta's* hot, moist nature. In *Ayurveda*, opposites treat each other. Someone working on counterbalancing *pitta* during summer months must be careful not aggravate *vata*, as this imbalance will then worsen in fall.

In summer, the sun's rays become powerful; day after day and appears destructive to all things; *kapha* decreases day by day and *vata* increases consequently. ~Ashtanga Hrydaya Sutrasthana 3:26–27

During the summer, the sun evaporates the moisture of the earth by its rays. In that season, the intake of sweet, cold, liquid, unctuous diets and drinks are prescribed. One should further avoid taking diets that are salty, sour, pungent, or hot. Heavy physical exercise should be given up during this season. ~Charka Samhita Sutrasthan

Auyurvedic **Summer Digestive Drink**

"This drink very good for cooling body and stomach." ~recipe from Sonali Sinha, *Ayurveda* practitioner and friend from India

Ingredients:

2 raw mangoes (green)

1 tsp of ground cumin

1 tsp of ground coriander

2 tbsp of honey

4 mint leaves (crushed)

Pinch black salt or rock salt to taste

Boil or roast the raw mangoes. Peel and puree in blender with 3 cups water, cumin and coriander, mint leaves, honey and salt. Strain then serve cool! It is sweet and tangy in taste and light green in color!

Late Fall/Early Winter: *Vata* Season

According to the healing yogic science of *Ayurveda*, fall is *vata* season. *Vata* is composed of air and ether in the form of wind and space. Autumn hosts dramatic changes. It becomes dry, windy, cold, and is characterized by a lot of harried movement. Animals scurry around collecting their winter stores. Leaves blow in the wind. Birds migrate, insects get into a frenzied mode, and so do we humans! This is the season of autumn harvest, fall sports, raking leaves, and the hustle and bustle of the holiday rush. *Vata* easily brings us out of balance due to its irregular, mobile nature and we begin to feel some ill effects. People tend to feel more forgetful, confused, scattered, worrisome and stressed. As it worsens, they might notice sleep disturbances and other signs of imbalance. Has fall left you feeling off-balance? How do you get back your groove back naturally?

Some common physical and health related *vata* type imbalances that are more likely to occur during autumn are:

Osteoarthritis flare ups, cracking joints, restless legs, tremors, muscle spasms, eye twitching, Parkinson's, headaches, migraine, dizziness, brown coating on tongue, fluctuating blood sugar, asthma, dry coughs, ice cold hands and feet, IBS, chronic pain, back pain, neck and shoulder pain, gassiness, constipation, weak immune system, underweight, excessive weight loss, dry, flakey, itchy skin, dry chapped lips, aches and pains, light restless sleep, waking in the night or insomnia.

> . . . if the level of *vata* increases in the body, there is quivering and breaking pain in the limbs and joints, as if crackling.
>
> ~Charaka Samhita Sutrasthan

Signs of *vata* emotional imbalance include:

Nervousness, anxiety, panic attacks, insomnia, forgetfulness, difficulty paying attention, poor concentration, excessive thinking, racing thoughts, scattered thinking, disorganization, excessive talking, interrupting others when talking, restlessness, overly sensitive to noises and bright lights, easily over-stimulated, can't sit still, spacey, lack of focus, lack of confidence, irrational fear, phobias, ungroundedness.

Signs of Balanced *vata* include:

Creative, intuitive, curious, inquisitive, cheerful, upbeat, exuberant, energetic, animated speech and movement, open minded, good conversationalist, slender but not skinny, loves travel, healthy sleep patterns and eats regular meals.

Do You Have a *Vata* Imbalance?

Vata, which translates literally as "wind", is the force that governs fall and winter months according to Yoga and Ayurveda. It is *vata* that brings on the dryness, cold, wind and stiffness during the winter months. Because of the extreme nature of winter in many parts of the country, many people will find that their own internal *vata* qualities have been thrown off balance during this time of year. Too many raw foods, anxiety, lack of sleep, travel, and exposure to windy conditions can also increase *vata* in the system leading to a *vata* disturbance. When a *vata* imbalance is not corrected, over time one can begin to experience chills, tremors, icy cold extremities, emaciation, constipation, insomnia, rough, dry skin, anxiety, clumsiness, mental confusion, and arthritis. The majority of ailments are rooted in aggravated *vata*.

Take this self-assessment quiz to see if you are experiencing a *vata* imbalance. (*Note these questions came to me via Kristin Bjarnason, RN, RYT 500)

1. Is your skin drier than usual, itching or flakey?

2. Are your lips dry or cracked?

3. Do your throat and nasal passages feel dry?

4. Is your hair dry, frizzy and have more spilt-ends?

5. Have you felt more forgetful, foggy, or absent minded?

6. Has your appetite and digestion been irregular?

7. Do you notice more abdominal gas or constipation?

8. Have you noticed stiffness in the muscles and joints?

9. Have you had increased cracking and popping in your joints?

10. Have you had difficulty focusing and concentrating?

11. Have you felt more fretful, anxious, or worried than usual?

12. Have you had difficulty sleeping, restless sleep or insomnia?

13. Is your mind full of chatter, jumping from one thought to the next?

14. Do you have a dry cough?

15. Do you have a brownish coating on the back of your tongue?

16. Have you been clumsier or more accident prone?

If you answered "yes" to several of these questions, it is a sign that your own *vata* qualities may have accumulated in your body creating a *vata* imbalance.

How to Eat to balance *Vata*?

Eat at regular times every day, meals should be on a predictable routine, do not skip meals, do not over eat, avoid eating when nervous, eat in a calm atmosphere, avoid stimulation when eating such as TV, loud restaurants, arguments. Cooking with ghee (clarified butter) aids in digestion and absorption.

Increase

Moist food such as soups, juicy fruits, cooked or steamed vegetables, stews, curries and stir-fries, stay well hydrated, drink lots of warm fluids, teas, juices, oils, unctuous foods, organic dairy, mildly warming spices to improve digestion.

- **Sweet juicy heavy fruits:** all citrus fruits, banana, avocado, dates, figs, mango, melons, papaya, grapes, cherries, pineapple, papaya, plums.

- **Grains:** Wheat, oats, rice, oatmeal, cream of wheat (Always opt for organic grains.)

- **Vegetables:** Cooked vegetables primarily (as opposed to raw), root vegetables, carrots, potatoes, sweet-potatoes, parsnips, beets, turnips, organic tofu in moderation.

- **Nuts and seeds:** Almonds, cashews, pistachios, walnuts, pecans, sesame seeds, sunflower seeds, nut butters (peanuts are a legume and can be aggravating to *vata*)

- **Drinks:** hot tea, hot lemon water, fruit juice, lassi, kefir, organic milk

- **Oils:** sesame oil, ghee, extra-virgin olive oil, organic butter, Almond, Jojoba, and Safflower.

- **Herbs and spices:** salt, ginger, black pepper, cardamom, cinnamon, ginger, turmeric, clove, basil, oregano, tarragon, thyme, cumin, and fennel.

Reduce or Avoid

- **Reduce or avoid:** Dry light foods, raw vegetables, salads, bitter greens, toast, popcorn, corn chips, crackers, cold cereal, or dry cereal, cold or frozen foods. Avoid raw foods, bitter taste and astringent foods. Avoid the following foods:

- **Fruits:** dried fruit, raw apples, raw pears, cranberries.

- **Vegetables:** Avoid bitter greens, mushrooms, cruciferous vegetables, raw vegetables, legumes, beans, peanuts, peanut butter, eggplant.

- **Beverages:** caffeinated drinks, cold drinks, iced tea, frozen smoothies, milkshakes, frozen cocktails like margaritas, pina coladas and daiquiris.

- **Grains:** Avoid corn, millet, rye, barley

- **Meat:** Avoid red meat, cold cuts

- **Other:** ice cream, popsicles, ices and sorbets, white sugar, white flour, artificial sweeteners.

Vata balancing Lifestyle recommendations?

Increase: warm baths, steam room, massage, whirlpool tub, naps, spending time in nature, grounding: sitting or standing barefoot on the grass, sand or earth. Keep a regular daily routine; waking and going to bed at the same time even on the weekends!

Entertainment: gardening, symphonies, theatre, drum circles, meditation groups, and leisurely dinners with friends.

Practices: Meditation, sacred rest, time in nature (warmly dressed), practice slowing down.

Exercise: walking, hiking, *tai chi, Qi-gong,* swimming,

Yoga: gentle yoga, hatha yoga, yin yoga, and restorative yoga.

Color therapy: earth colors: greens, browns, rust

Crystal therapy: moonstone, opal, pearl, rose quartz, amethyst, onyx, lapis, aquamarine, blue topaz.

Aromatherapy: Incorporate the following essential oils: basil, geranium, rose, citrus, cypress, lavender, patchouli, rosewood, sage, cinnamon, clove, frankincense, pine, thyme, vanilla, vetiver, ylang-ylang essential oils.

Lifestyle Choices to Avoid: overstimulation of any kind, frequent travel, erratic schedule, wind, fans, cold, rough scratchy clothing, erratic schedule, work with irregular shifts, excessive talking, excessive movement, running too many errands, commuting long distances, worry, anxiety fear.

Exercise: Steer clear of long-distance running, swimming in cold water, walking too fast, aerobics classes, kick-boxing, jump rope any exercise with excessive, fast movement, exercising outdoors on a cold, windy day.

Yoga: Aerial yoga is ungrounding. Vinyasa yoga, power yoga, hot yoga are too strenuous, involve too much strain and movement, and the heat is further dehydrating for *vata* imbalance and thus would be aggravating.

Entertainment: Avoid loud music, scary TV programs or movies, bright lights, crowded venues, over-stimulating environments such as fairs, circuses, light shows, loud concerts, chilly, crowded, loud sporting events all derange *vata.*

Color therapy: Avoid cool colors, bright or neon colors which aggravate *vata's* highly sensitive nature.

Ayurvedic **Tea for winter:**
*This tea recipe comes from my friend and Ayurvedic practitioner Sonali Sinha. It is very balancing for a cold climate!

Lemon grass 2-3 leaves
Basil 3 leaves
black pepper 5-6 pods
bay leaves 2
cinnamon 1 stick
cloves 4
ginger small piece crushed

Boil two cups of water and reduce it to 1 cup and strain.

Late Winter/Early Spring: *Kapha* Season

This time of year, nature begins to thaw out and ice and snow begin to melt. The earth is cool, wet and muddy, and animals are just beginning to awaken from a long hibernation. The natural world is slow, damp and sluggish. *Kapha* season is characterized by the wet, heavy, cold, slippery, unctuous characteristics of the elements of earth and water. It is harder for *kapha dosha* to come out of balance that the other *doshas*, but also the hardest to return to balance.

Some common physical and health related *kapha* type imbalances, which are more likely to occur during late winter and early spring, are:

Water retention, weight gain, difficulty losing weight, congestion, post nasal drip, frequent colds, chest congestion, lethargy, low-energy, sluggish bowel movements, pasty white tongue coating, slow to get going in the morning.

Signs of *kapha* emotional imbalance include:

Possessiveness, greed, excess clutter, hoarding, lacking motivation, stubbornness, depression, emotional eating, sloth, excessive sleep, long daytime naps, being overly-sentimental, over-protective, social withdrawal.

Signs of Balanced *kapha* include:

Loving, nurturing, compassionate, protective, well grounded, good stamina, well-lubricated joints, calm relaxed demeanor, forgiving, strong immune system, fertile, loyal, well-nourished body, excellent memory, moist skin with few signs of aging, good physical strength, stable mentally and physically.

Do You Have a *Kapha* Imbalance?

Kapha takes on the qualities of water and earth. It is moist, cool, heavy and solid. When water and earth come together mud is formed. It is the qualities of *kapha*, which give the body form and cohesion. Too much *kapha* can weigh the body down causing it to be sluggish and lethargic. *Kapha* can clog the system with mucus and water retention. Late winter and early spring is the season in which we are most prone to the influence of *kapha* qualities. Left unresolved, a *kapha* imbalance can lead to depression, weight gain, lethargy, sluggishness, fatigue, pale skin, heavy congestion, water retention, and over-sleeping. Take the following quiz to determine whether you have a *kapha* imbalance:

1. Have you felt sluggish and lethargic?

2. Have you had a runny nose or felt congested?

3. Have you experienced weight gain?

4. Do you feel an aversion to cool damp air?

5. Have you noticed water retention?

6. Have you experienced a feeling of melancholy over the last few weeks?

7. Have you been more emotional lately? Cry easily?

8. Have you noticed you are nibbling or grazing more often?

9. Have you been sleepier than normal?

10. Do you feel a bit stuck or stagnated in life?

11. Do you feel you have been lacking in motivation in recent weeks?

12. Are you experiencing a phlegmy cough?

13. Do you feel as if you are moving and talking slower than normal?

If you have answered "yes" to several of these questions, then you are experiencing the symptoms of increased *kapha* qualities.

Balanced *Kapha* is described as expressing strength, for-bearance, patience, and the absence of greed.

~ Charaka Samhita Sutrasthan

What to Eat? Light, dry, warm foods.

Increase

High fiber foods, lightly cooked foods, bitter greens, vegetables.

Fruits: Dried fruit in moderation, light fruits such as apples, pears, pomegranates, cherries, cranberries, other berries.

Vegetables: Most vegetables are suitable for *kapha* with just a few exceptions.

Grains: Buckwheat, corn, quinoa, basmati rice, wild rice, millet, barley, spelt in moderation.

Drinks: Black tea, chai tea in moderation, organic coffee in moderation, pomegranate juice, apple or pear juice in moderation.

Sweeteners: Raw honey is best for *kapha*. Old honey over 1 year old is considered ideal.

Oils: Organic non-GMO corn oil, organic non-GMO canola oil, safflower oil, ghee in moderation.

Legumes: Most legumes are ok.

Nuts and seeds: Pumpkin seeds, sesame seeds.

Herbs and spices: Most spices are great for *kapha*. Especially enjoy black pepper, ginger, garlic, chilies, mustard, clove, cinnamon, peppermint, basil, cayenne, dill, coriander, cardamom.

Other: Caffeine/coffee okay in moderation.

Reduce or Avoid

Excessive intake of fluids, dairy products, salty foods, heavy meals, heavy oils, nuts, sweets, grazing, munching between meals, over-eating, over-cooked foods, overly sweetened foods, left-over foods, cold foods.

Fruits: Avocado, banana, mango, papaya, sweet juicy melons, dates, figs, citrus.

Vegetables: Cucumber, olives, sweet potato, sweet winter squash.

Grains: Bread, oatmeal, rice, wheat, pasta.

Legumes: Kidney beans, tofu.

Drinks: Sweet fruit juices, smoothies, juicing, cold drinks, soft drinks, diet drinks, sweet thick sticky beverages, milkshakes, protein drinks, nutritional shakes.

Sweeteners: It is best to avoid using sweeteners other than honey, which is the only sweetener that has *kapha* balancing properties when used in moderation. Sweet taste in and of itself increases *kapha*.

Spices: salt.

Meat: luncheon meats, red meat, fatty meat.

Kapha balancing Lifestyle recommendations?

Increase

Movement, warmth, stimulation and travel.

Entertainment: Stimulating music, action films, dancing, active sports, puzzles, classes, books, games, and taking classes that interest and inspire you

Practices: vary daily routine, clear clutter, regular vigorous exercise, travel, dry sauna, *garshana* (dry brushing)

Exercise: *Kapha* benefits from breaking a sweat and varying their exercise regime in both type and time of day: Fast walking, jogging, biking, hiking, aerobic exercise, dance.

Yoga: *Vinyasa* yoga, power yoga, hot yoga, vigorous yoga, aerial yoga

Color therapy: Warm, vibrant, bright colors

Crystal therapy: Ruby, garnet, coral, diamond, clear quartz, rose quartz, carnelian, red jasper, orange calcite, fire agate, pyrite

Aromatherapy: Stimulating warming scents such as anise, bergamot, cinnamon, clary sage, clove, eucalyptus, frankincense, geranium, grapefruit, ginger, juniper, lemon, lemongrass, neroli, myrrh, peppermint, orange, oregano, tea tree, and wintergreen essential oils.

Avoid

Naps, excess sleep, lack of physical activity, weight gain, damp cool climates, being overly materialistic.

Practices: getting stuck in a rut, hoarding, strict routines

Exercise: Heavy weight lifting, body building, being inconsistent with exercise.

Yoga: Yoga nidra or restorative yoga (Avoid in excess)

Entertainment: Too much television.

Color therapy: dark, cool or "heavy" colors.

Kapha Tea

Recipe from Sonali Sinha, Ayurveda practitioner in India.

3-4 Tulsi or basil leaves
Ginger, 2-inch piece
5 Black pepper corns
Turmeric, just a pinch
4 Cloves
1 tsp Honey- (optional)
2 cups Water

Method 1: After crushing them little bit, put all the ingredients together in two cups of water and soak them overnight. In the morning, strain and add honey. This method is best for *kapha* during spring/summer.

Method 2: Keep the ingredients on the strainer add 1 1/2 half cup water. Boil for 5 minutes, then strain and drink with honey! This method is best for winter *kapha*.

Affirmation: Today I practice seeking and maintaining balance and wellbeing in my eating and in my approach to life.

Today's biggest success:

Food for thought: Beginning today, incorporate seasonally appropriate eating and lifestyle practices into your routine. Over the coming weeks, note the difference in your emotional and physical sense of balance and wellbeing.

Journal: Note any seasonal imbalances you recognize in yourself now or in the past. These are areas where you are constitutionally vulnerable during the corresponding season.

Day 12

Agni, Key to Weight and Health

The food is consciousness.

The plasma in the body is the Protector.

The fire which digests the food is the destroyer of the impurities in the food.

If you know this,

The food becomes pure consciousness.

~Yatha Pinde Tatha Brahmade

According to *Ayurveda*, a well-functioning digestive system is fundamental to optimal weight, energy, youthfulness, and immunity. A healthy digestive fire or *agni* is the single most important element necessary for optimal weight and health. The impact of digestion on the mind-body system is profound. If you have any health issue, you can be assured that digestion is involved in some way. The *agni* is the first line of treatment at the sign of disease. In *Ayurveda*, if digestion is optimal, the result is wellness. If digestion isn't optimal, the result is *ama* (toxin accumulation) which is the precursor to disease.

If digestion is ideal, and diet is correct, the result is optimal weight. If it is not ideal, the result is unhealthy weight. *Ayurveda* emphasizes digestion over dieting in order to lose weight. Strictly limiting calories overtime slows digestion, dampens the digestive fire and lowers the metabolism. Often people are perplexed as to why they begin to gain weight yet haven't altered their eating or exercise routine. They begin to ramp up their exercise routine and cut calories more sharply, with little or no results. The culprit is most likely sluggish *agni* and the resulting buildup of *ama*, slowing the metabolism.

If digestion is optimal, the result is sustained energy and vitality. If digestion isn't optimal, the result is fatigue and lethargy. It doesn't matter how well you eat, if *agni* is not functioning properly. The nutrients in the foods you eat cannot be properly digested and absorbed. Is your *agni* functioning as well as it should be? If not, what can you do to get it back into balance?

Symptoms of an under-functioning *Agni*:

- Poor appetite
- Sleepy after meals
- Weak immune system
- Food allergies
- Sluggish energy, fatigue
- Bodily aches and pains
- Brain fog, cloudy thinking
- Aching joints
- Bloating, burping up the taste of food, gassiness with odor
- Constipation
- Weight gain, overweight, ongoing weight accumulation despite healthy diet and exercise
- Heavy coating on tongue
- Bad breath, bad taste in the mouth
- Fluid retention, edema, water weight, puffiness
- Phlegm, drainage, frequent clearing of the throat
- Lack-luster skin, eyes and hair
- Excess sleep
- Difficulty waking or getting moving in the morning

Symptoms of over-functioning *Agni*:

- Powerful appetite
- Acid indigestion/ heartburn
- Feeling weak or lightheaded if hungry
- Mouth ulcers
- Loose stools/diarrhea
- Skin rashes/acne
- Aversion to heat/sun
- Agitation, irritability, easy to anger
- Weight-loss
- Sweating and feeling over-heated
- Fever

- Burning sensation in stomach
- Burning sensation/aches in the joints and tissues

Symptoms of Irregular *Agni*:

- Alternating appetite from strong to weak
- Abdominal cramping
- Constipation, or alternating constipation and diarrhea
- Gurgling sounds in the abdomen, burping with odor
- Muscle pain, cramping or twitching
- Dry cracking joints
- Anxiety/sleeplessness
- Anemia
- Lackluster skin, nails and hair

Signs of a properly functioning, balanced *Agni*:

- Bright, clear eyes
- Healthy, lustrous nails, skin and hair
- Sweating without odor
- Pleasant breath
- No coating on the tongue
- Clear urine as opposed to cloudy
- Vibrant energy
- Mind is clear and alert
- Regular bowel movement without strong smell
- No bloating, cramping or discomfort after eating
- No belching or foul smelling intestinal gas
- Normal appetite
- Enthusiasm for life
- Cheerful disposition
- Strong immune system
- Healthy appetite
- Fresh breath
- Stable and healthy weight

Causes of *agni* Imbalance:

- Grazing, eating frequently throughout the day
- Overeating (even healthy foods)
- Fruit fasts, water fasts
- Too many cold foods or iced drinks
- Eating a large meal late at night
- Anxiety, depression, anger
- Cigarettes, alcohol, drugs
- Certain medications including acid inhibitors
- Drinking excess fluids or iced beverages at meals which dilutes gastric digestive juices
- Under-eating, not eating an adequate amount of food
- Exercise on a full stomach
- Yoga just after eating
- Chewing food insufficiently
- Eating while having a heated discussion or arguing
- Eating while watching violent or disturbing television programs/ music
- Spending too much time in a cold, dry or windy environment
- Spending time in an overly hot environment
- Spending time in an excessively damp environment

How to optimize digestion and support a balanced *agni*:

1. **Eat at regular, predictable times every day.** The digestive system can be trained like a dog when it comes to eating and food. Set meal times help regulate the secretion of digestive juices optimally, and influence the regulation of circadian rhythms.

2. **Do not graze.** Give your digestive fire at least 3-4 hours to digest the previous meal. Otherwise you are putting undigested food on top of partially digested food. Your gut does not know the difference and both pass through the system simultaneously, dampening *agni* and forming toxins.

3. **Do not eat late at night.** Give your *agni* time to digest the food before you lie down. Gravity aids the digestive system in keeping its proper flow. When you are in a lying position, it is more likely for undigested food to back up into

your esophagus, and not stay where it can be properly digested. Secondly, when we sleep, the nervous system slows down. Agni is reduced, and your digestive system cannot properly digest your food when it is in "rest mode."

4. **Do not overeat.** Overeating smothers *agni*. Fire needs air and space to burn sufficiently. Overeating overloads your *agni* causing it to dull and diminish. I've heard this compared to shoveling dirt over a camp fire so that it only smolders rather than burns brightly. Regularly overeating fosters a chronically low *agni*. Eat until you are only 70-80% full. Aim for the feeling of satiation, not a food coma!

5. **Use a small amount of *ghee* (clarified butter) in your cooking.** It is known to improve digestion.

6. **Spice things up:** If your *agni* is sluggish, try adding digestive spices such as black pepper, cinnamon, anise seed, cardamom, ginger, cumin, fennel, turmeric, cayenne, pippali, cloves, mustard, oregano, basil, rosemary, cilantro, licorice. These spices/herbs stimulate the secretion of digestive enzymes, and support the digestive fire. The *Ayurvedic* herb *hingavastak* or *asafetida* is formulated to awaken *agni* and promote proper absorption and assimilation of nutrients. It is especially recommended for *vata* disturbed digestion or imbalanced *agni*. Try drinking **Agni Tea** which contains digestion enhancing spices. The recipe is at the end of the chapter.

7. **Be sure and thoroughly chew your food.** Digestion begins in the mouth. Chewing is a part of the digestion process breaking down the food into digestible sized particles. Digestive enzymes are also secreted in the saliva during the chewing process. If your food is swallowed without first being properly chewed, *agni* is taxed, and *ama* forms. Poorly chewed food happens when people eat in the car, standing, watching TV, or working at the computer. When people are not mindful about eating, they tend to swallow food without chewing well.

8. **Avoid heavy or overcooked foods.** For example: deep-fried foods, meat, heavy cream sauces, gravy. Opt for lighter foods like fresh fruits and lightly cooked vegetables.

9. A *kitchari* **cleanse** (see day 1) *Ayurvedic* detoxification is a great way to balance *agni* and flush out *ama* as well as excess *dosha*.

10. **Drink hot lemon water.** This helps increase *agni* if it is diminished. This practice alone can have a positive effect on weight-loss.

11. **Probiotics.** Eat yogurt with live active cultures, or drink *lassi,* an *Ayurvedic* drink for balancing intestinal flora. Lassi is best taken after lunch or in the late afternoon rather than in the evening or after supper as it can increase *kapha*. See *lassi* recipe at end of chapter.

12. **Agni** *mudra*- a powerful yoga pose for the hands: place tip of ring finger at base of thumb. Press thumb down on 2nd knuckle of ring finger to hold it in place at the base of the thumb.

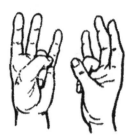

13. **Tongue scraping:** The *Ayurvedic* daily practice of scraping the tongue with a tongue scraper or an inverted spoon first thing in the morning is said to awaken and stimulate *agni*. This should only be done before eating the first meal of the day.

Ayurvedic Food Combining

*for optimal digestion and robust *agni*

(From Dr. Vasant Lad, Director *Ayurveda* Institute)

Incompatible food combinations:

Milk Is Incompatible With:

• Bananas	•	Sour Fruits
• Fish	•	Kitchari
• Meat	•	Bread containing yeast
• Melons	•	Cherries
• Curd		

Melons Are Incompatible With:

• Grains	•	Fried foods
• Starch	•	Cheese

Starches Are Incompatible With:

• Eggs	•	Bananas
• Chai	•	Dates
• Milk	•	Persimmons

Honey Is Incompatible With:

Ghee (in equal proportions)	Heating or cooking with.

Radishes Are Incompatible With:

• Milk	•	Raisins
• Bananas		

Nightshades, (Potato, Tomato, Eggplant, Chilies) Are Incompatible With:

• Yogurt	• Melon
• Milk	• Cucumber

Yogurt Is Incompatible With:

• Milk	• Fish
• Sour Fruits	• Mangos
• Melons	• Starch
• Hot drinks	• Cheese
• Meat	

Eggs Are Incompatible With:

• Milk	• Cheese
• Meat	• Fish
• Yogurt	• Bananas
• Melons	

Mangos Are Incompatible With:

- Yogurt
- Cheese
- Cucumbers

Corn Is Incompatible With:

- Dates
- Raisins
- Bananas

Lemon Is Incompatible With:

• Yogurt	• Cucumbers
• Milk	• Tomatoes

The above guidelines are by no means an exhaustive list. It must also be remembered that a proper *Ayurvedic* diet should consider nutritional value, constitution, seasons, age and any disease condition.

Incompatible Food Combining

Don't eat:	With:
Beans	fruit, cheese, eggs, fish, milk, meat, yogurt
Eggs	fruit, especially melons; beans, cheese, frish, kitchari, MILK, meat, yogurt
Fruit	As a rule, with any other food (there are exceptions, such as certain cooked com-binations, as well as dates and milk, which have the same taste, post-digestive effect, and the energy)
Grains	fruit: tapioca
Honey	when mixed with an equal among of Ghee by weight (i.e., 1 tsp. honey with 3 tsp. Ghee); boiled or cooked honey.
Hot drinks	mangoes, cheese, fish, meat, starch, yogurt
Lemon	cucumbers, milk, tomatoes, yogurt
Melons	EVERYTHING – especially dairy, eggs, fried food, grains, starches. Melons more than most fruit – should be eaten alone or left alone.
Milk	BANANAS, cherries, melons, sour fruits; bread containing yeast, fish, kitchari, meat, yogurt
Nightshades (Potato, Tomato, Eggplant)	melon, cucumber, dairy products
Radishes	bananas, raisins, milk
Tapioca	fruit, especially banana and mango; beans, raisins, jaggary
Yogurt	fruit, cheese, eggs, fish, hot drinks, meat, MILK, nightshades

1. These guidelines are by no means an exhaustive list. It must be remembered that a proper *Ayurvedic* diet should consider nutritional value, constitution, seasons, age and any disease condition.

2. Foods in CAPITALS case are the most difficult combinations.

3. According to ancient *Ayurvedic* literature, honey should never be cooked. If cooked, the molecules become a non-homogenized glue that adheres to mucous membranes and clogs subtle channels, producing toxins. Uncooked honey is nectar. Cooked honey is considered poison.

– Source *Ayurvedic Cooking for Self-healing* by Mrs. Usha Lad and Dr. Vasant Lad

In *Ayurveda*, the digestive fire or '*agni*' is considered your inner alter to God. Are you offering up foods that are whole and pure or are you offering up junk? ~Elise Cantrell

Affirmation: As I enhance my own internal "digestive fire" or agni, I become radiant from the inside out! My healthy digestion, give me a healthy glow.

Today's biggest success:

Food for Thought: An optimal *agni* or digestive fire is synonymous with optimal health, energy, youthfulness and weight. By focusing your efforts on *agni* alone, you cannot help but see positive results in all areas. The glow of that internal fire will show in the gleam in your eyes, the radiance of your skin, and the fire of your spirit!

Journal: What habits or patterns do you have that work against a well-functioning *agni*? What are some simple changes you can make personally to optimize your *agni*?

Day 13

Space in Your Belly, Space in your Life

In general, mankind, since the improvement of cookery, eats twice as much as nature requires. ~Benjamin Franklin

Your outer life mirrors your inner world. Those of us, and I am guilty of this myself, who over fill our calendars are often the same ones who over-fill our plates and over-stuff our bellies. Overdoing, overfilling and overeating is a chronic and interconnected pattern. Chinese philosopher and sage, Lao Tzu states, "When your cup is full, stop pouring." When your calendar is full stop committing to more. Present day cultures need to get comfortable with the concept of space; space in our belly and space in our lives. We get anxious when there is empty space or unfilled time in our day. Downtime during the day, week or weekend causes many of us restlessness and unease! We have lost our sense of spaciousness both inside and out! We get uncomfortable if we aren't "full" after a meal. North Americans often end a meal by saying, "I am full", as if this is a way of measuring satiation. We are conditioned to believe that "full" is better than enough.

If one bite fills you, you don't need two. ~Marty Rubin

When you are full, that means no space is left. "Enough" means that you are satisfied. As a culture, we need some reprogramming around the concept of being *satisfied* rather than *stuffed*. Satisfied means we are fulfilled, contented and gratified. Once we experience these things on an external level we can become comfortable with a sense of "enough" within as well. Many of us continue to purchase more "stuff" for our homes, continue to "stuff" one more thing into our day and generally overcommit to stuffing as much into our lives as possible. An overstuffed belly feels no better than an overstuffed life. I have noticed it is when I stopped putting "too much on my plate" in life; I naturally began to put less on my dinner plate. If you find yourself overeating, it could indicate that you need to slow down and make space in your life!

If you envision your stomach as a furnace or cauldron, you'll realize that if you pack it too tightly, things will not burn efficiently. If you leave space for air, the fire of your digestive process will work its magic, giving you energy and vitality, rather than slowing you down. ~Baron Baptiste

A key *Ayurvedic* eating principle is that your portion size for a meal should be no larger than what you can cup in two hands. This measurement is called 2 *anjali*. The space in the belly is 3 *anjali*. By leaving 1/3 of the belly empty there is space left for the digestive fire to breathe and burn stronger. It is recommended in *Ayurveda* to fill the stomach with 1/3 food. 1/3 water, and leave 1/3 empty with air to help oxygenate and fuel the flames of the digestive fire or *agni*. This space is the key to optimal digestion of foods and absorption of nutrients into the body. Leaving this space is critical in preventing the accumulation of *ama* in the body, which is the root of all disease according to *Ayurveda*. *Ama* adheres to the *doshas*, causing toxic build-up of *doshas* in the channels and tissues.

Another thing I hear over and over, "I don't have time to cook. I don't have time to eat lunch. I need to eat in a hurry. Eating healthy takes too much time," . . . etc. Ironically, not eating the way we were designed to eat, robs us of time. It robs us of years of our lives and the life in our years. We sell out our own energy and health for the illusion of more time. The very time we steal from our health and life, ends up getting hijacked by obligations and more "to dos." When you give yourself the gift of health, you are giving yourself the gift of time. Eating well is the gift of time. It is all in how you look at it!

There also has to be space in your life for "slip-ups." You must hold space for imperfection not only in your eating, but in everything you do! Occasionally having a dessert or special treat is good for the soul. When I go on vacation, although I truly try to do my best, I may indulge or splurge a little. I do this knowing that I will get right back on track when I get home. I also know that if necessary I can reboot and recalibrate with the 3-day cleanse. As long as it doesn't become a regular thing, there has to be space to fall off the wagon once in a while. One of my 40 Days students had decided to experiment and go meat and sugar-free for the 40 days. Her birthday happened to be right in the middle of the journey, and her son invited her over for a birthday dinner. He made her a birthday cake and lasagna with meat. Instead of being inflexible, she gave herself the space to indulge in these things her son so lovingly prepared for her birthday, knowing she would go right back to her resolve the very next day! It is healthier to create space for whatever arises, than to be rigid and obsessive when it comes to eating and food. She would have stolen the joy from her birthday celebration had she made a big fuss about the meat and the sugar!

Space for Grace

Looking for a necklace to wear, I pulled a tangled mess of chains from my jewelry box. At first, I attempted to undo the knots by pulling on the chains, only to find the knots got tighter, more rigid and fixed and the chains more deeply ensnared. The "aha" moment happened when I began to loosen the chains from each other, creating space to disentangle, the knots. The necklaces almost freed themselves as I simply loosened their grip on each other!

How often do we get ourselves caught in the same kind of trap, pulling ourselves tighter and tighter, creating more and more tension, rigidity and constriction? We pack our calendars, we tighten our schedules, we stuff our bellies, and we crowd our minds. We cram our drawers, cupboards, refrigerators, closets, basements and garages. We squeeze our budgets and overextend ourselves until we are as tied up as the entangled necklaces in my jewelry box!

We never allow ourselves breathing space, space to move, space for change, space for mistakes, space to be human, space for growth, space for transformation, space for the unexpected, unforeseen and unanticipated! We crowd out the lessons, the blessings and the peace that life so desperately wishes to bring us! We stay stuck in our own tightly embedded knots! We pull ourselves every which way. Our busy, hectic, overfilled, overflowing lives have crowded out grace. The constant hunger for news reports, for the latest trends, the newest gadgets, and the next big hit has overcrowded our minds leaving no space for us to digest and absorb what comes in. Our overstuffed mouths and bellies lead us to a tangled mess of illness and disease. We crowd ourselves to death, suffocating in our own entangled snares. We unwittingly form our own noose, leaving no space to breathe, no room to move.

We talk, but do not leave space to listen; we "DO" without giving ourselves space to "BE." We acquire without leaving space to enjoy or appreciate. We give without space to receive. We live without space for life! Thread by thread, chain by chain, knot by knot we too can disentangle ourselves from the knotted-up mess we have become. Where can you loosen yourself? What can you untie, undo, slacken and release? Where do you need to come undone in order to create space for grace?

> Those who think they do not have time for healthy eating, sooner or later will have to find the time for illness.
>
> ~Unknown

Meditation on space: Begin by lying down. Take a moment to notice the space between the fingers and toes. Become aware of the space between the body and the floor. Sense the space between the torso and arms. Notice the space between your legs. Become aware of the space in your nostrils. The space inside your ears. The space inside the mouth. The space between the lips. The space inside the sockets of the eyes. The space between the upper and lower eyelids. The space between the upper and lower lashes. As you breathe in, feel the space in the windpipe. The space in the lungs. Notice the space between the ribs. Sense the hollow space of the esophagus. Follow the esophagus downward into the empty space of the stomach. Explore the empty space in the belly. Travel the hollow space of the intestines. Sense the pores in the skin. Ponder the space between each vertebra of the spine. Become aware of the space in your joints. Imagine the hollow space inside of your bones. Sense the space in the pores of the bones. Sense the space inside of each cell. Each cell in your body is 95% space. Who and what would you be without the space that is always there within you? How could you live, function and thrive without space? We are creatures of space. How then can we function in life if we do not have breathing room? Space is an open invitation for grace to flow in. Sense the space inside your head. Envision the empty screen of your mind. Allow your consciousness to enter into that spaciousness. For the remaining moments of this meditation, settle into that space within yourself for silent stillness. Be open to this space. Own this sense of spaciousness and allow yourself to just BE in this sense of space. Now just BE space.

You must have a room, or a certain hour or so a day, where you don't know what was in the newspapers that morning, you don't know what you owe anybody, you don't know what anybody owes to you. This is a place where you can simply experience and bring forth what you are and what you might be. This is the place of creative incubation. At first you may find that nothing happens there. But if you have a sacred space and use it, something eventually will happen.

~Joseph Campbell

Affirmation: Today and every day I have time and space in my schedule to cook, savor and eat the foods I was created to eat. I give myself room to digest my food and my life experiences. I give myself room to breathe and space just to be and to enjoy the life I have created.

Today's biggest success:

Food for Thought: Beginning today, notice where in your life you need more space. Pay attention: Do you pack your calendar, your desk, your closets, your drawers in the same way you stuff your belly? By clearing space in the physical world, you create space in life. By giving yourself permission to have empty space in your home, office and life, you begin to realize a little space in the belly is not such a bad thing! You become more comfortable with inner space and outer space simultaneously. Give yourself space to be less than perfect. Make an intention to create pockets of space in your life to reflect the inner spaciousness that we explored in the meditation. Let pockets of life fill your space; let pockets of space fill your life!

Journal: Where in your life can you create more space, more breathing room? Where do you need more open pockets to allow for the magic and mystery of grace to flow in? What do you need to release now to create new space in your life?

Day 14

Samskaras: Are You Stuck in an Eating Rut?

All things are difficult before they are easy. ~Thomas Fuller

Are you stuck in a rut and don't even know it? "*Samskara,*" is the Sanskrit word for "rut." It literally translates as "deep impression" or "groove" which is set in the unconscious mind through our thoughts, habits and patterns. *Samskaras* cause us to keep falling back into the same way of doing things over and over again like a CD or vinyl record replaying the same sound-bite over and over. *Samskaras* typically are habits, which have become so ingrained, we're often not even aware of them.

Oftentimes, even well intended people are unconsciously stuck in patterns or *samskaras*, which sabotage their ability to lose weight and look and feel their best. By becoming aware of our habits, patterns and ruts, we can consciously create new, healthier *samskaras* to replace the old ones. Replacing old, unproductive patterns is the doorway to transformation. Perhaps you recognize yourself in some of these patterns, which often start with good intentions, but sabotage your weight, energy and health.

12 Habits Sabotaging Your Weight, Energy and Health

1. A vegetarian or vegan "junk-a-holic" – People mistakenly think that just by cutting out meat they are instantly healthy. Unless the whole diet changes, eliminating meat alone does not amount to perfect health and weight. I have known many a vegetarian who believes that as long as meals don't contain any meat (or dairy in some cases) it is healthy! I did this myself in my early 20s! I simply cut meat from my junk-food diet and replaced it with more junk. Within a month, I felt exhausted and lethargic and didn't lose an ounce of weight! I've known vegans who eat Oreos, chips and soy ice cream because they contain no meat or dairy. However, these also contain nothing of nutritional value with the addition of toxic additives! They are loaded with chemicals, sugar, artificial flavors, coloring and preservatives.

There are numerous vegetarians who adore processed meat substitutes. I am horrified to read the lengthy list of chemical ingredients in these "meatless" imitation meats! These substitutes are much worse than eating meat, especially if the meat is grass-fed or free-range!

There are people who believe they are "vegetarians," who don't even eat vegetables! There are also those who think they are eating vegetables because they eat potato chips, French fries, corn flakes, and "fruit snax." I have to emphasize that the word "vegetarian" comes from the word the word "vegetables." Vegetarians eat foods grown on plants, bushes, trees and vines. Processed foods are no substitute for veggies. I am a much more balanced vegetarian now in my 40s, eating vegetables, fruit, whole-grains, organic dairy, beans, nuts and seeds rather than junk!

2. Evening or Weekend Bingers – These are people who eat well all day long but blow-it at night, or people who eat well all week long only to blow it on the weekends. They are also the "teetotalers" who don't drink all week only to have 6 cocktails on Friday night! This is a pattern of imbalance and we know that imbalance never leads to health and harmony. This all or nothing philosophy puts the mind-body system on a roller-coaster ride, never knowing what to expect and never finding stable ground. Steadiness, stability and consistency create balance and harmony and progress towards transformation. Instead of undoing all the healthy affects you gain from eating well, begin to build upon them. Huge beautiful cathedrals were built one stone at a time. In order to make progress, you have to keep heading in the right direction, not taking 2 steps forward and 2 steps back. Binging at night or on the weekend is self-sabotaging. This habit causes cravings to continue to arise, preventing you from breaking unhealthy patterns permanently!

3. Exercise fanatics – These are folks who exercise excessively, too vigorously or overly-strenuously. I had a friend who exercised 4 hours a day thinking she was being "healthy." She ended up with countless health problems including digestive issues, thyroid issues, hemorrhoids, arthritis, sleep problems, not to mention a myriad of injuries. In *Ayurveda*, over-strenuous, excessive exercise burns up our vital "life-sap" or *ojas*, which is the essential substance underlying the immune system, and is the critical basis of energy, vitality and youthfulness. Depleting *ojas* causes a break-down of the immune system, premature aging and drains away life-force energy like a sieve. Studies show that the body-mind system interprets extreme exercise as stress! Vigorous exercise triggers the release of cortisol, a stress hormone. Over time, increased cortisol levels eventually lead to insulin resistance and weight GAIN! Cortisol is a fat storage hormone. In addition, it creates a multitude of free-radicals in the body which trigger premature aging and can lead to cancer. Overly-strenuous exercise includes "boot-camps," marathons, and Iron mans.

I have cringed while watching the commercials for "Biggest Loser" as the trainers pile on excessive exercise as if they are *punishing* people for being over-weight. Participants even pass out and throw up! Pushing yourself to unhealthy extremes is never the way to achieve your optimal, healthy weight, energy and vitality. You can never beat yourself up at the gym, "whip" yourself into shape or punish yourself to the best version of YOU.

We tend to think that if a little exercise is good, then more must be better. Too much of a good thing is a bad thing! You can only love and nurture yourself into health and vitality. Regular moderate exercise is key.

4. Obsessive counters (calories, fat, carbs, or points)-I have had only **one** student over my years of teaching *40 Days to Enlightened Eating* classes who wanted to lose weight but failed to. This student insisted on counting carbs during her 40 day journey. Carbohydrates from natural whole food sources like whole grains are NOT the problem. Weight gain comes from processed carbs found in bagels, muffins, breads, breakfast cereals, snack crackers, pretzels and chips. Problem carbs are also in processed sweets such as cookies, cakes, pies and candy. If you are eating real whole carbohydrates in moderate portions counting and weighing is completely unnecessary! Counting is not only unnecessary; it is an obstacle. Trust that eating the foods we were designed to eat is the only counting you need! Counting leads to needless focus on "lack" and deprivation. This scarcity mentality causes us to pay attention to what we can't eat, rather than what we can eat. Because of this negative focus, we energetically "hold on" to the weight we are trying to release. Eating well should be a lifestyle, not a math exercise!

5. Living on bars or shakes – There are those who are living on meal substitutes such as packaged "health" bars, shakes or even "healthy" prepackaged meals. I've had a couple of readers tell me they had previously relied on Protein bars for ALL meals. People who think protein bars are healthy should take a moment to read the ingredients! Most commercial protein bars contain highly processed ingredients, are loaded with fillers and are fortified with synthetic vitamins. They are no substitute for real food! It is important to understand that bars and shakes are processed food! Our bodies are made to live on natural whole LIVING foods, not laboratory created substitutes. Would you rather have a synthetic diamond made in a lab or one made by nature itself? One is way more valuable than the other! Your body is no different! It craves the real McCoy when it comes to eating and food. I have spoken to people who have tried to lose weight eating "healthy" prepackaged frozen meals. They were baffled that these meals contained fewer calories than their previous meals, yet they still weren't losing weight. The truth is these meals contain very few nutrients, very little real food and very little life-force! In addition, freezing and microwaving in a plastic tray, compromise even further, the already sub-standard qualities of factory-made foods. A calorie is not a calorie! Cooking and preparing fresh whole foods is the only ticket to healthy weight! We cannot "trick" the body mind-system. If we do not eat the natural whole foods we were made to eat, it is impossible to feel the way we were created to feel, think the way we were created to think or look the way we were created to look. *Ayurvedic* eating philosophy is designed to bring us into our highest state of health and wellbeing. Our mind, body and spirit will always reflect back exactly what we put in.

6. Juice junkies – Juicing has been all the rage over the past few years. Juicing in moderation is great, but people who are living off of juices are doing themselves more harm than good! Juicing is definitely an improvement from a lifestyle of cheeseburgers, fries and pizza, but juicing can raise blood sugar as there is no fiber, fats and very little protein. This makes most juices high glycolic. Juices can also be too acidic for the system. *Ayurveda* teaches that we need all 6 tastes to stay in balance, however, juicing primarily contains sweet and sour tastes. One must consciously make a point to incorporate bitter, astringent, pungent and salty tastes. *Kapha dosha* is the most negatively impacted by a lifestyle of exclusively juicing. *Kapha* is increased by cold, wet, sweet and sour foods. Increased *kapha dosha* is the basis for weight gain (See chapter 14 in *40 Days to Enlightened Eating* which explains the *Ayurvedic doshas*) Humans were not designed to live on juices. They are designed to eat whole foods as they come from nature.

7. Health and exercise "yo-yos" – These people get on a bandwagon or health-kick, only to fall off again and again! Their weight and health "yo-yo" back and forth, and their body-mind system stays confused. It takes these people longer to shed pounds because the body recognizes the pattern and becomes habituated to it. I find when people start to look and feel their best, they seem to begin to unconsciously sabotage themselves. In part, this may be a feeling that they can now afford to "relax their efforts." I also find it is because they are subconsciously holding on to the old parts of themselves that they are afraid to let go of. They may hold on to old patterns of poor eating and exercising because somewhere they feel that they don't deserve to look and feel their best. They are afraid of the changes that will take place if they do look and feel their best. Some people fear their own transformation, and as it comes closer and closer into being, they bolt like a rabbit, resuming old comfortable patterns instead of embracing real change, and letting the butterfly emerge from the cocoon.

8. Falling for "healthy" processed pre-packaged food. Many people are fooled by marketing labels such as low-sodium, low-fat, organic, whole-grain, high-fiber, "baked, not fried," no sugar added, all-natural, preservative-free. This is only marketing! These labels in no way make a food healthy! These foods are still processed and contain very little *prana* or life-force energy. Since food is a major source of our own life-force energy, it is important that we are eating as many fresh, living foods as possible! In addition, it is not uncommon for these same packaged foods to contain Genetically Modified Ingredients, chemical pesticides, herbicides, artificial flavors, colors, and preservatives. Many foods labeled "whole-grain" contain very little fiber. Don't be tricked by food industry's crafty marketing strategies to get you to buy their processed foods under the pretense that it is healthy! Trust in Mother Nature, as she is not in it for profit!

9. The Extreme Cleanser – This is someone who is always on a detox or a cleanse, or that uses extreme measures to detoxify. *Ayurveda* recommends a cleanse two or three times a year, particularly in fall and spring. If you are eating clean, there is no need to go on a detox every other week! If eating well isn't your lifestyle, then you are just retoxifying after detoxifying and the cleansing is pointless! There are some people who go on severe fasts only drinking water, fruit juices, or eating just fruit for days. These extreme cleanses bring the body out of balance rather than into health and harmony. They do more harm than good. They deplete vital energy, cause the immune system to flag, and cause the blood sugar and digestive acids to come out of balance. Extreme cleanses cause weakness, dizziness and fatigue. They sabotage the metabolism putting it into fat storage mode. They deplete *ojas*, the vital "life-sap" of health, energy and immunity. An *Ayurvedic* detox is a balanced approach designed to help bring all systems back into health and balance, and help your body improve and optimize its own natural detoxification organs and systems. *Ayurveda* knows that harsh extremes never serve the body, mind or spirit.

10. Exercisers who think they get a free-pass when it comes to eating. Some people think the treadmill entitles them to cookies, brownies, candy bars, potato chips, ice cream and all sorts of unhealthy junk. Some people think that time at the gym is an excuse to overeat, and then use the overeating as a reason to abuse themselves at the gym. It is a cycle of being at war with food, and quite frankly at war with yourself. Healthy weight is 20% exercise and 80% eating! No amount of exercise ever undoes overindulging or eating junk. I have heard it said that "You can't outrun your fork!" I have also observed people who purchase a gym membership thinking that belonging alone entitles them to overeat. They belong, and they think about going, but never follow through. Others go to the gym for an hour and stand near the equipment chit-chatting and gossiping, but never lift a finger! They think that just "going" to the gym is the ticket to health and that just being in the presence of exercise equipment works wonders. (I am not exaggerating; I have seen it!) The only way to become and stay at your optimal weight and health is to commit to regular moderate exercise and a lifestyle of healthy eating. There is no cutting corners, no shortchanging yourself, no tricking yourself and no beating yourself up on the way to the best version of you! There is no way you can outrun an unhealthy diet! It will eventually catch up with you!

11. Food Ruts-People get stuck in a rut with meals or snacks. They eat the same tired dish every day, every week. I often hear people eat the same thing for breakfast every day, whether it be yogurt, oatmeal, granola, cereal, etc. They may eat the same health bar daily for snack, or bring the same lunch to work. *This is a food rut.* The problem with food ruts is that even with a "healthy" food, eating it daily increases the properties contained in the food in your body creating an imbalance. *Vata* type foods are dry, light and cold and they increase these mental and physical properties in the body, which can lead to nervousness, insomnia, and irregular digestion. *Pitta* type foods are hot, spicy, sour, acidic and oily. Eating these type foods on a regular basis leads to inflammation, hyperacidity, ulcers, acid indigestion, anger, agitation, and irritation. *Kapha* type foods are heavy, cool, sweet, sticky, wet and dense. These foods increase these properties in the mind-body system. They increase phlegm, mucous and congestion. They cause weight-gain, create heavy, sluggish energy and a sense of dullness and lethargy. They cause the mind to become slow and sluggish as well. (For more details about the *doshas* and foods see chapter 14 and 15 in *40 Days to Enlightened Eating*.) It is very important to vary your diet day-to-day to stay energetic, youthful, in balance and at a healthy weight. Also, a varied diet exposes you to a host of various nutrients, and supplies the body with all the vitamins, minerals, and micro-nutrients it needs.

12. Under-eaters – These are people who are not eating enough intentionally or unintentionally. Some eaters are severely restricting calories to maintain a low weight. In other cases, eaters forget to eat or are not eating foods that contain sufficient nutrients. This causes several problems. The first problem is it inhibits the ability to replenish *ojas*, the vital fluid from which the mind-body system is nourished and rejuvenated. When this fluid becomes low, immunity becomes low, and there is susceptibility to all forms of disease. This fluid is also critical for youthfulness. The first outward sign of low *ojas* is apparent in the skin. The skin loses its outer glow and vibrancy and becomes dull and lack-luster. Low-ojas also shows up as low-energy or chronic fatigue.

Secondly, adequate nutrients are necessary to build and rebuild the tissues in the body. There are layers of tissues according to *Ayurveda*. One layer builds upon the next in hierarchy of each tissue's necessity for survival. Each tissue draws upon the nutrients left over from the one that precedes it. When eating is not sufficient or nourishing, the rebuilding only goes so far and stops. For example, the body will build bone before it will build hair or nails which are less critical. Hair-loss and dry, brittle nails are a sign of in adequate diet or poor digestion. Infertility also shows up this way. The body builds vital plasma before it builds reproductive fluids and tissues.

When eaters are eating too much food that contains little or no nutrition, tissue building can get "stuck" at the fat layer. Fat keeps building, but there are no satisfactory nutrients left to build the next tissue layer which is bone-hair-nails, marrow-nerve and reproductive tissue. Thus, the fatty tissue is overdeveloped yet the tissues that develop next on the hierarchy are unable to be built or maintained because of the poor quality of raw materials. This is why you will notice some overweight people who appear to be getting enough calories, suffer low-quality hair, bones, skin, infertility, etc. Calories do not equal nourishment. Under-eaters who over-exercise will amplify the ill effects of undernourishment, low-*ojas* and poor quality tissue, having poor immune systems, fatigue, premature aging and poorly developed tissues.

Bringing unconscious patterns into conscious awareness is the first step forward on any journey to transformation. What goes undetected has much greater power to affect us adversely. What becomes seen, becomes known, and knowledge plus action equals transformation. If you recognize yourself stuck in one of these patterns, it is time to leap out of your rut and move forward on the journey to the best version of YOU!

Affirmation: Today I empower myself to break free of old patterns that do not serve me.

Today's biggest success:

Food for Thought: By becoming aware of your own patterns that are unhelpful, you empower yourself with the opportunity to make conscious change.

Journal: What *samskaras* have you wrapped around their finger? Create your own action plan of change.

Day 15

Eat the Rainbow:
Food and the *Chakras*

The rainbow is pervasive in nature. We live in a world of light and color. As "light beings" who are part of nature, human beings reflect the energy and light of the rainbow in our energy body! Each *chakra* represents a different wavelength of light vibration emanating within us and shining through us! We are human rainbows!

The *chakras* are energy centers found in the physical body and in the energy field around our body. These energy "vortexes" or gateways help to regulate energy flow through the energy channels or *nadis* similar to the way that the heart pumps blood through the blood vessels. Each *chakra* has a specific function and duty. The *chakra* system is part of the "energy anatomy," just as organs, tissues and bones are a part of the physical anatomy. Without this energy flow, we could not move, function or live. With improper energy flow, we are susceptible to imbalances of the mind and body.

The *chakra* system is ancient. It cropped up millenniums ago all over the world on various continents and in cultures that had no communication or contact with each other. In addition to ancient India, the ancient Egyptians, Chinese, Tibetans, Aborigines, Mayas, Aztecs, Incas and Native Americans are all civilizations, which had discovered the *chakras* and the energy body independently. Ironically, these are not yet recognized in western medicine because they cannot be seen or measured with our current technology. Although there are numerous minor *chakras* and sub-*chakras*, our focus in this chapter is on the 8 main *chakras*, which form a harmonious "full octave" of vibrational energy in and around the human body.

Like the other rainbow aspects of nature, foods too come in a rainbow array of colors! It is no surprise then that what we eat affects our energy anatomy by targeting specific *chakras* through their specific color vibration! Eating colorful whole foods and using affirmations are powerful ways to heal and balance the *chakras*. I invite you to discover the *chakras* and experiment with food and using affirmations to bring your *chakras* into harmony and balance.

The *Chakras*: Nourishing Our Own Inner Rainbow

1st *Chakra*: *Muladhara* – "The root" *chakra*. It is located at the coccyx and perineum and extends energy out to the souls of the feet. This energy center is responsible for a sense of groundedness, stability and security. This is the most primitive *chakra* whose purpose is "survival" and the will to live. Its color is red. This *chakra* is governed by the earth element.

When unbalanced, a person my feel insecure, unstable mentally, emotionally or physically, or ungrounded. On the other end of the spectrum, the unbalanced root *chakra* may present a sense of heaviness, lethargy and greed.

Balancing foods: Root vegetables such as carrots, parsnips, beets, turnips, rutabagas, potatoes and sweet potatoes balance *muladhara*. Root vegetables are inherently grounding because they grow in the earth. Roots nourish our root. They have an earthy taste and they are moist, dense and heavy. Salt and other earth minerals are also very balancing and grounding. Garlic, grown in the earth is also very grounding. Since the root *chakra* vibrates with the frequency of red light, produce which is red in color such as strawberries, raspberries, cherries, beets, radishes and tomatoes are said to balance the first *chakra*. Red meat, which is considered *tamasic*, can be used in certain situations to ground a patient.

Affirmation: I am stable and secure. I feel grounded and peaceful. I am firmly rooted in who I am. I am safe.

2nd *Chakra*: *Svadisthana* – "The sacral *chakra*." Its association with the sacrum, alludes the "sacredness" of this *chakra*. Located in the pelvis, this is the area of the body where human life is created and sustained. If this *chakra* is not functioning properly it is difficult to become pregnant or to maintain pregnancy. The second *chakra* is also the location of the *"hara center"* a vast "ocean of energy and strength. Yogis and martial artists learn how to tap into this "well" of energy to do the seemingly impossible. This *chakra* oversees the reproductive organs, the movement of reproductive fluids, the flow of the kidney channel and the bladder. The function of the *chakra* is creativity, pleasure, abundance, procreation, enthusiasm and vitality. It is said to be the seat of *"Shakti,"* the force of sacred creative feminine energy. Its color is orange. This *chakra* is governed by the water element.

Foods that balance *Svadisthana*: It is important to ingest adequate fluid for this *chakra* to stay balanced as it governs the bladder, and movement of menstrual flow and sexual fluids including semen. Fluids and fresh juicy fruits keep the body moist and hydrated, also helping to flush out toxins. The juicy, sticky sweetness of fresh fruits nourishes the reproductive fluids. Seeds, nuts and avocado are nourishing to the reproductive organs and 2nd *chakra*. Orange colored produce such as tangerines and oranges, apricots, carrots, peaches, papaya, pumpkin, mango, salmon, sweet potatoes and yams, are said to help balance and energize the second *chakra*.

Affirmation: It is safe to take pleasure in life and to embrace the joy of living.

3rd *Chakra*: *Manipura* – "The city of jewels" *chakra*. Located in the solar plexus region of the abdomen, where our "inner jewels," or our vital organs are found. This *chakra* is responsible for self-confidence, courage, willpower, assertiveness and self-esteem. It is also responsible for regulating he energy of digestion. Its color is yellow and it is ruled by the fire element. I like to call it our "inner sunshine!"

When out of balance, a person lacks confidence, will-power and self-esteem. Conversely, they may be overpowering, bossy, forceful and pushy.

Foods to balance *Manipura*: High fiber foods, spices that promote digestion such as ginger, cumin, coriander and fennel, as well as probiotic foods to balance digestion. It is equally important not to over or under eat to keep this *chakra* in balance. Yellow colored produce such as grapefruit, corn and yellow squash and whole grains, are also said to balance the third *chakra*.

Affirmation: It is safe to be powerful. I own my power and shine my light.

4th *Chakra*: *Anahata* – "The heart *chakra*." Located at the heart center and extending out through the palms and soles of the feet, this *chakra's* function is love, joy, compassion, inner peace, gratitude, self-love and appreciation. The heart *chakra* governs the heart, lungs and circulatory system. It is ruled by the air element. This centrally located *chakra* is responsible for transformation of lower energies into the energy of love. Its color is green.

Foods which balance *anahata*: comfort foods, sweet juicy foods, *sattvic* (pure, harmonious) foods, food that increase *ojas,* the vital sap of life, such as raw honey, *Chavanprash*, an *Ayurvedic* jelly compound, raw milk, ripe, juicy fruits, figs, dates, almonds, sesame seeds, sesame oil, ghee or clarified butter. *(Ojas* is stored in the heart center. See upcoming chapter about increasing *ojas.*) Foods that improve circulation and heart health are beets, dark chocolate, sweet berries, cherries, organic red grapes and good fats. Green produce such as artichokes, broccoli, bok choy, green beans, honey dew, kiwi, peas, zucchini are said to balance the heart *chakra*. Too many bitter greens however, can promote a sense of bitterness according to *Ayurveda*. Pink is also harmonizing to the heart *chakra*, so guava, pink grapefruit, and watermelon are helpful.

Affirmation: It is safe to love and be loved. I freely give and receive love.

5th *Chakra*: *Vishuddha* – "The throat *chakra*." It is located in the throat and extends into the shoulders and ears. It governs the thyroid, parathyroid glands and the ability to hear and speak. It is responsible for communication, sound, self-expression, speaking your truth, speaking from the heart, and hearing the truth. Its color is blue. It is ruled by the element of ether or space, because the throat is an open cavity or channel in the body.

Balancing foods: Moist foods that lubricate the throat without creating phlegm or postnasal drip. Licorice tea soothes the throat as does gargling with salt water, coconut oil or sesame oil. Avoid: excessive dairy and overly sweet food that can congest and block the throat *chakra*. Blue produce such as blueberries, blue potatoes, blue cauliflower, blue corn and juniper berries balance the throat *chakra*.

Affirmation: It is safe to speak and be heard. I speak from the heart. I voice the truth to make the world a better place. I am able to clearly, kindly and safely express what I think and feel.

6th *Chakra*: *Ajna* – "The 3rd eye." Located in the center of the forehead between the eyebrows, it is responsible for inspiration, insight, creative ideas, introspection, intuition, imagination, vision, dreaming, and clairvoyance. It governs the pineal gland, which is considered our "inner eye." This gland is shaped and pigmented like the "Egyptian eye" depicted in that culture's hieroglyphics. Kissing someone's 3rd eye helps to calm and balance this energy center. This *chakra* is the place from which prayers are sent out. Its color is indigo. The third eye is ruled by the element of ether or space in a more light and subtle sense than the throat *chakra*.

Balancing foods: Vegetarian or vegan diet. Eat foods that increase *sattva,* or mental clarity and harmony, especial fresh sweet juicy organic fruits and vegetables, ghee and honey. Drink adequate fluids. Avoid the following foods/ beverages which imbalance the 6th *chakra* and block the 3rd eye: Fluoride in drinking water and toothpaste, aluminum cookware, neurotoxins, heavy metals, meat, alcohol, caffeine, left-overs, overcooked foods, artificial colors, flavors or preservatives, and chemical ingredients or chemically sprayed foods. Indigo colored foods such as black beans, black cherries, black currants, black raspberries, blackberries, boysenberries, dark olives, plums, prunes and raisins nourish the third eye.

Affirmation: I trust the vision, intuition and guidance within me. I am full of creative ideas and trustworthy insight. It is safe to use my inner vision and look within.

7ᵗʰ *Chakra:* *Sahasrara* – The "thousand petal lotus" or the "crown *chakra*" is located at the highest point of the crown of the head. It is centered around the fontanel, as this is said to be the spot where the soul enters the body in the womb and leaves the body at the time of death. This is the area where we receive the answers to our prayers and communications from God, angels, spirit guides, etc. Here we receive insight, knowledge and Truth from beyond ourselves. This *chakra's* function is Truth, higher consciousness, and bliss. It governs the pituitary gland, cerebral cortex and the Central Nervous System. Its color is violet. The 7ᵗʰ *chakra* is ruled by a lighter and subtler essence of the ether element.

Balancing food: Sunlight, the breath, *pranayama* (yogic breathing techniques) prayer and meditation feed the 7ᵗʰ *chakra*. Violet colored foods such as eggplant, figs, purple grapes and plumbs are said to balance this *chakra*.

Affirmation: The essence of my being is light and peace. I am open to the infinite power of God. I have a unique spiritual destiny. I am divinely guided on the path that is right for me.

8ᵗʰ *Chakra:* *Padaka* – "The halo" and the auric field that surrounds all beings. This *chakra* is located an arm's length above the head and has been depicted across cultures and time as a halo, because it becomes increasingly radiant in those with a deep and pure spiritual connection. Here is where spiritual awareness, ultimate truth and awakening reside. The 8ᵗʰ *chakra* is an energy portal where we can access divine healing energy for the highest good. It is the doorway to spiritual abilities such as healing gifts, prophecy, and doing works on behalf of humankind for the greater good. Here we disconnect from ego and become selfless. From this higher place of awareness, we are able to watch the drama of life unfold without attachment. Here we access the infinite, which surrounds and envelops the window of time-space. Beyond all constructs of time, space, mind, ego, and illusion, it is our doorway to *eternity*. Its color is white. The 8ᵗʰ *chakra* is ruled by the subtlest and lightest form of ether element.

Balancing food: Meditation, silent stillness, time in nature, prayer. White foods such as cauliflower, coconut, garlic, jicama, white mushrooms, quinoa, organic tofu, turnips, white beans are said to balance the eighth *chakra*.

Affirmation: I am infinite, eternal and whole. I am beyond time, space and illusion. I am the healer and the healed. I accept and honor my spiritual gifts. I live my divine purpose.

Today's biggest success:

Food for Thought: Beginning today, notice which *chakras* need balancing. Use the affirmation and eating suggestions listed for that *chakra* to promote wellbeing and balance.

Journal: Note any *chakra* imbalances you have become aware of. Create your own action plan using the information above to return them to their natural state of balance.

Day 16

Eating and Exercising the "Middle Way"

If we could give every individual the right amount of nourishment and exercise, not too little and not too much, we would have found the safest way to health. ~Hippocrates

Ironically, our culture places more emphasis on what the body looks like on the outside, than what it feels like on the inside! Our culture's ideal of a "perfect body" is at odds with optimal health. As we restrict calories, fats, carbs or food itself, we are inhibiting our own vibrancy and vitality. We deplete our vital energy and age our bodies with punishing exercise regimes, eliminating entire food groups, and fad diets. Feeding ourselves with kindness and exercising ourselves with compassion is the path to transformation. Eating and exercising "the middle way" is the only path to wholeness, harmony and balance.

"The middle way," according to the Buddha, is the path to enlightenment. He came to this revelation after meditating and fasting for 40 Days under a Bodhi tree by a river. As he observed a lute player in a passing boat, he suddenly realized that if the string of the lute was tuned too tightly, it would break. He also noticed that if the string was too flaccid, it would not emit sound. The ideal, he realized, was in the middle, when the string was tightened just enough, perfect harmony resulted. This realization led to a key life principle called "the middle way". The middle path is a life lived without extremes. Neither self-deprivation and harsh regimes, nor overindulgence and laziness lead to a life of harmony and balance. The answer lies in the middle.

If there is no pleasure in eating, then there is no balance. We have been conditioned to bounce back and forth between extremes: overindulging followed by harsh dieting, from junk food to rice cakes! What if I told you the answer is the "middle way?" With the right recipes and ingredients, healthy eating is delicious, joyful and balanced! There is no need to go hungry or eat boring, tasteless foods again! When the healthy food you are eating is delicious, you don't feel the need to splurge, binge or "pig-out" on the wrong foods! You begin to trust that the opportunity to savor and enjoy your food is available at every meal. Don't eat foods you dislike just because they are deemed healthy. This does not benefit the body-mind system. Find healthy foods you love, and enjoy your way to looking and feeling your best, rather than punishing yourself into it. Health and wholeness are rooted in happiness. Your food should make you feel both happy and healthy! There is no need to give up one for the other as we have been made to believe!

The Art of Savoring:

Savoring means to perceive by taste or smell, especially with relish, to give oneself to the enjoyment of. Savoring is an essential part of the eating process, which other cultures such as the French and Italians have turned into an art form by serving dishes in courses. While not eating more, they have mastered the art of allowing the pleasure of a wonderful meal to linger for hours. Savoring is really a form of mindfulness. It is about being present and aware in the eating process from beginning to end. Eating is truly the most sensual act there is, as it involves all the 5 senses. You can hear the food simmering on the stove, you can smell its delightful fragrance, you first devour it with your eyes, and then you feel its texture on your mouth while tasting it on your tongue. When you allow yourself to savor and appreciate your food more, you eat less, because savoring allows less to become more. Let less be more, by really savoring what is there before you. I had a student tell me she had a hard-boiled egg and 15 almonds for lunch every day. Where is the Joy in that? Where is the savoring?

When you truly savor what is before you; there is no need to overeat or over do.

Ways to savor your food:

1. Plan your meal and look forward to it. Savor your meal as you shop for the choicest ingredients.

2. Choose ingredients you truly love, and be open to experimenting and experiencing new flavors, recipes and ingredients!

3. Enjoy every step of preparing the meal. Don't rush!

4. Tune into to the scents, smells, sounds textures and colors of the meal you are cooking.

5. Be fully present while preparing the food.

6. Cook with LOVE.

7. Sit down to eat. Let the meal be your full focus.

8. Never "wolf down" a meal. Eat with your eyes, nose and mouth, seeing, feeling and relishing the full sensory experience.

9. Don't eat standing at the kitchen sink, sitting in front of the computer or TV or while driving in your car.

10. Don't try to satisfy yourself, with flavorless commercial shakes or bars in order to save calories. Instead enjoy a flavorful soup or salad. Meal substitutes always backfire, as your body-mind system craves the missing flavor and texture! Flavorless foods lack life-force or *prana*. Only real food carries *prana*, not commercially prepackaged foods.

Are you savoring your life or hungering for more? Your eating mirrors your life! The inner is always a reflection of the outer.

Imbalanced Exercise Patterns:

Excessive or extreme exercise is a sign of imbalance. This imbalance usually signals there is another imbalance going on such as over-eating or distorted body image. *Ayurveda* teaches that excessive exercise creates further imbalance in the mind-body system. It causes the body to hold on to weight, creates toxins, causes inflammation, and premature aging. Excessive exercise is at odds with health and wellness. Moderate regular exercise is key to a balanced, healthy body and mind. Extremes are never a balanced solution; the answer lies in the "middle way!"

I recently saw several posts on Facebook from a group of runner friends who had just spent the day on a 40-mile run. This is quite a feat, and they appeared to be smiling and having fun. What I found disturbing though was that they were posting photos of the gruesome blisters on their feet and the photos of the very "unenlightened" meal of deep fried foods they shared afterwards, as if this was a badge of honor for their huge undertaking. Everything about what they were doing, the excessive running, the greasy fast food meal and the nasty blisters on their feet were all signs of imbalance, rather than wellness. One imbalance inevitably leads to another and another according to the science of *Ayurveda*. Imbalance has a domino effect! Some people have made these imbalances the pattern of their life. This is not what mind, body and soul wellness is about. Ultimately, imbalances left unchecked lead to injury, premature aging, illness, and chronic disease. Your exercise regime has to be good for the body, mind and soul, or it is not working for your highest good.

Without rest, a man cannot work; without work, the rest does not give you any benefit. ~Abkhasian Proverb

I tell my students often that too much of a good thing becomes a bad thing! Extremes of any kind lead to a rebound effect as the body attempts to compensate for the imbalance. Your body is always working towards balance and wholeness. When things are out of balance, your system will attempt to counterbalance the issue with its opposite. This can create a vicious cycle! Too much caffeine promotes too much alcohol consumption, which in turn promotes too much caffeine. Too much sugar stimulates salt cravings, which encourages too much salt intake. This in turn stimulates stronger sweet cravings. Punishing workouts cause strong sweet and salt cravings. When blood sugar drops due to excess exercise, sugar is a quick fix for the body. Also, electrolytes get depleted from the body, which triggers salt cravings to restore things to balance. Sweet and salt cravings often result in people consuming foods that undo any benefits of the exercise itself. I remember a friend telling me that after a long run, she couldn't help but devour a king-sized bag of M&Ms! Instead of creating energy, this creates fatigue and inflammation along with guilt! Out of guilt, my friend went and did the same long run the next day continuing the same pattern of imbalance!

Exercise: The faster we move the faster we age.
~Dr. Mark Halpern, founder of the California College of *Ayurveda*

The human body is evolved to equate struggle and strain with survival. If you have to struggle, strain and starve to maintain a certain weight, it is not your healthy weight! If maintaining a certain weight steals your joy, it is not in alignment with your wellbeing. Stop fighting your weight and start befriending the optimal you! The field of love is where the magic happens!

If you love running, then run. If you love swimming, then swim. If you love walking or biking, then by all means do those. Don't force yourself into doing an exercise that you hate thinking that it will in any way benefit the mind-body or spirit. Instead, trust what you love. Trust in your body's inner wisdom to guide you towards the exercise that serves you best.

"Enlighten" Your Exercise to Lose Weight

We Americans have much to learn about the "middle way". We are under the **illusion** that if a little is good, then more must be better. We go over the top! The most startling way Americans sabotage their weight-loss efforts is **over-exercising**! **Ayurveda**, yoga's healing sister-science, teaches that we should exercise at only 50% of our capacity: the **middle way**! With trepidation, I gave this concept a try, and after 5 years of trying to lose baby weight after my second child, the weight finally began to come off. This ancient science was right!

At first, I too fell for the "more is better" approach to exercise! I kick-boxed, ran, lifted weights, did spinning, step aerobics, boot camp, power yoga. My workouts could last 2 hours or more. But I wasn't losing weight! Moreover, I felt depleted and had little energy left to enjoy my life. I remember continuously kicking up my workouts striving to lose weight. The more strenuous they got, and the more time I spent exercising the more weight I gained! I realized 4 things from this:

1. I was caught in a cycle that was not working. "Insanity is to keep doing the same thing and expecting a different result." I had to do something different! I was exhausted and I was not losing weight!

2. I found that the more I harshly I treated my body; the more it came into a state of resistance with me, and I with it. My mind and body were in opposition, not in harmony. We were in a battle of wills.

3. I found that the more I exercised and pushed myself, the hungrier I became for 2 reasons. First, my body was building up reserves bracing itself against the next exercise assault. Second my soul was craving for comfort, compassion, sweetness and contentment, which it was not getting from me and the lifestyle I was caught up in, so it settled for the next best thing: food! This kept me locked into a cycle of excess. Excessive exercise led to excessive eating which led to excessive weight.

4. I discovered that harmony was the secret weapon I had been missing to lose unwanted pounds. Once I consciously shifted away from hardcore workouts into moderate exercise, my body began to shift. It became happier, felt better, and as I released the struggle and the strain, the weight released along with the cravings!

I am now at my healthy weight! What's more, I have newfound time and energy for family, hobbies, and cooking healthier meals . . . and the enthusiasm to enjoy it all. My exercise regime consists of **moderate yoga practice**, and, when the weather is nice, walking the dog. No more hard-core workouts for me!

I teach this "middle way" of exercise in my *40 Days to Enlightened Eating* classes. I have seen this moderate approach profoundly impact my students. One of my students worked out during lunch, and then returned to the gym after work for a second session. When she gave up the evening workout, she did not gain weight, but gained more time to enjoy life with her husband! Another was taking several intense boot-camp classes a week, and found herself exhausted and depleted afterwards. When she tried a moderate exercise approach, she lost 13 pounds and found her energy.

People often use harsh exercise regimes as a form of "self-punishment" for over-eating or making poor food choices. Not one study correlates increased exercise to increased weight-loss! However, studies do show that the more strenuously one exercises, the more hunger increases, creating a vicious cycle of exercising to undo overeating!

Overly strenuous exercise is not maintainable. Overdoing it results in injury or just giving up. Exercising the "middle way" is safer and doable. The body no longer holds onto weight, preparing for the next exercise assault. It *liberates time and energy* for *enjoying life*, and is more likely to become habitual. The "middle way" *lightens your body* on the scales, while *enlightening your mind and spirit too*! When it comes to exercise, most of us don't need more, we just need a little **enlightenment!**

Side effects of excessive or overly-strenuous exercise:

1. Increased cortisol: Overly intense exercise triggers the release of cortisol, a stress hormone, which triggers fat storage especially in the abdominal area. Excessive exercise makes the body think it is in a "flight-or-flight" situation day after day. It stresses and strains the mind-body system, creating a pattern of tension, tightness and anxiety. It keeps cortisol continuously circulating in the blood.

2. Fatigue: One of the most common symptoms I observe in over-exercisers is a chronic sense of exhaustion and fatigue. After exercising, they have little energy for anything else. This is because their *prana, chi,* or life-force becomes depleted. From an *Ayurvedic* perspective, they are also depleting *ojas* or vital life-sap, the "well-spring" of energy, immunity and vitality.

3. Pre-mature Aging: Excessive or overly-strenuous exercise causes free-radicals to circulate in the body and attack the integrity of the cells. Free-radicals are atoms or molecules containing unpaired electrons.

Damage occurs when the free radical encounters another molecule and seeks to find another electron to pair its unpaired electron. This sets off a chain reaction of cells seeking electrons from other cells, ultimately damaging the cellular structure. Free-radicals have been shown to cause cancer, heart disease and pre-mature aging. Free-radicals break down collagen fibers in the skin which ultimately causes skin sagging. Strenuous workouts cause a look of strain on the face. Examine the face of someone you know who is addicted to high-intensity exercise regimes. You will notice a number 11 between the eyebrows, or frown lines. This is a facial characteristic of a *pitta* imbalance, showing the signs of pushing too hard, overstraining and driving too hard.

4. Increased hunger: Excessive exercise is shown to trigger excessive hunger. Research shows that people who over-exercise, end up over-eating! In fact, studies show they end up consuming more calories than they burned off! This reaction is simply the body's own protective mechanism. It knows it needs to refuel itself in preparation for the next exercise attack!

5. Joint damage: Pounding on the joints over time causes wear and tear, and can deteriorate the cushioning in the joint causing pain and discomfort and even the need for joint replacement.

Exercise is food for those people whose muscle mass it helps increase; it is medicine for the obese, and poison for those who become addicted to it . . . Excessive exercise may cause physical injury and may actually shorten your lifespan. It can create severe and lasting *vata* imbalances. In fact, over exercising can be positively dangerous for *vata* types.

~Dr. Robert E. Svoboda

Affirmation: Today I exercise my body in a way I truly enjoy at a duration and intensity that leaves me feeling energized, uplifted and invigorated.

Today's biggest success:

Food for Thought: Beginning today, adjust your eating and exercise routine as if tuning a fine instrument to emit the most melodious sound. Your body is that instrument, and when it is tuned *not too tight* and *not too lose*, you will naturally find it in perfect harmony!

Journal: Note any eating or exercise imbalances you have become aware of. Create your own action plan to tweak your eating and exercise plan to a more moderate approach.

Day 17

Ahimsa: Are You Doing Your Body More Harm than Good?

True yoga is not about the shape of your body, but the shape of your life. ~Aadil Palkhivala

Ahimsa is a Sanskrit word, which translates as "non-violence." *Ahimsa* is the first *yama* or ethical observance from the yoga tradition recorded in Patanjali's *Yoga Sutras*. According to renowned yoga sage, Patanjali, when the *yamas*, or tenets for harmonious living, are not put into practice, the consequence is suffering. *Ahimsa* or "refraining from harm" is practiced by refusing to cause injury, hurt, pain or suffering to the planet and any creature, including you. It includes avoiding violent or forceful actions, unkind thoughts, and hurtful words. I have observed that the average human being strives not to harm other beings, but the biggest struggle seems to be practicing *Ahimsa* with the **self**, especially when it comes to our perceived faults and flaws and our dissatisfaction with the physical body!

We verbally berate ourselves for what we've eaten. We use unkind thoughts against ourselves, like "I'm not skinny enough." "I'm fat." "I hate my thighs." We beat ourselves up at the gym by over-exercising. We abuse ourselves in yoga class by forcing our bodies into postures or positions against our own inner wisdom. Somehow, we've been brainwashed to believe that to look good, we must treat ourselves bad!

I have watched episodes of *The Biggest Loser* in horror while participants are pushed so hard at the gym that they literally collapse, pass out or throw-up! They are humiliated in front of their peers for their weight, lack of stamina, and food choices. Torture is not the path to wellbeing or the optimal YOU! No one becomes the enlightened version of himself or herself by inflicting pain and abuse. Never beat yourself up for not measuring up to the almost superhuman physical ideals that are worshiped in our culture.

As already discussed, *Ayurveda* teaches that overly vigorous exercise does more harm than good to the body-mind system. In the body it causes premature wear and tear on the joints, leads to arthritis and inflammation, creates imbalances in *vata* and *pitta doshas,* causes sciatica, tremors, constipation and depletes *ojas,* the vital "sap" of health, strength, stamina and immunity. In the mind, it creates a pattern of tension, stress and strain. *Ayurveda* recommends moderate exercise at about fifty percent of your maximum capacity . . . the "middle way." Copious sweating, being out of breath and not being able to talk while exercising are signs that you are exercising beyond your current healthy capacity. The goal of *Ayurveda* is not 6-pack abs, a beach body, or being a "skinny bitch." *Ayurveda's* goal is optimal health, balance and longevity. We have allowed airbrushed magazine covers, emaciated models and Hollywood housewives to erroneously define the modern-day ideals of what a "perfect" body looks like. This has dictated a way of living, being and exercising that is in opposition to health and wellbeing!

Prajnaparadha is the *Ayurvedic* term for insisting on taking an action that goes against your health and inner wisdom. *Prajnaparadha* literally translates as, "an offense against wisdom." "This happens whenever one part of you insists on an action that is detrimental to the rest of you. It happens when you know deep inside that something is not right for your body-mind-spirit, but you obstinately go ahead and do it anyway, ignoring Nature's warnings." ~Dr. Robert Svoboda

As already discussed, *Prajnaparadha* is at work when we engage in punishing exercise regimes, crash diets, or forcing our bodies into yoga positions that are not yet appropriate or available to us. Stop rejecting yourself, your body, your weight, the lines on your face, the shape of your tummy or size of your thighs! Self-abuse is never the path to transformation. The path to wellbeing is one of self-love, not of self-abuse! Use the following guidelines to find out whether you are doing your body more harm than good.

How to tell whether or not you are Practicing *Ahimsa* in your exercise regime:

- Does it hurt?

- Are you miserable? Do you hate every moment?

- Is your exercise regime causing injuries?

- Are you exercising with an injury, just ignoring the pain?

- Do you feel like you have been "beat-up" or "hit by a bus" afterwards or the next day?

- Do you feel depleted and fatigued the rest of the day with no energy left to do the things you enjoy?

- Do you enjoy your exercise routine?

How to tell whether or not you are Practicing *Ahimsa* in eating:

- Are you going hungry, letting your stomach burn, growl or cramp?

- Are you forcing yourself to eat foods you don't even like just to lose weight?

- Are you leaving no room for error, no room for fun?

- Have you eliminated entire food groups?

- Are there more things you can't eat than you can? Some dieters find reasons to eliminate almost everything!

- Are you berating yourself and mentally beating yourself up after eating the "wrong" foods or eating too much?

How to practice *Ahimsa* in your exercise regime:

- Exercise moderately-not too much, not too little.

- Exercise between 30 min. to 1 hour daily. 2 or 3 hour workouts are excessive.

- Find an exercise regime that you enjoy. Exercise in a way that brings you joy not misery.

- Exercise should not hurt, injure you, or make you feel bad afterwards; it should energize and enliven you.

- Do not power through your workout, ignoring injuries, fatigue or your *body's* messages to stop.

- Are you allowing yourself time to rest? Make sure you are balancing physical exercise with appropriate rest.

How to practice *Ahimsa* with your eating:

- Never "diet," severely restrict calories or "starve yourself. Instead, nourish yourself with vibrant, wholesome, living foods.

- Eat enough, not too much and not too little. Don't leave yourself feeling stuffed or feeling hungry.

- Find and prepare healthy recipes that taste delicious.

- Never deprive yourself when you feel hungry.

- If you make a poor food choice or over-eat, let it go, move on, and start over. Never berate or insult yourself!

- Choose foods grown in sustainable ways that do no harm to the environment.

- If you eat meat, choose clean meats that are humanely raised and minimally processed.

- Avoid GMO foods which are proven to cause environmental harm as well as harm to animals' and humans' health.

If you perceive yourself as "battling" with your weight, what you are really doing is "battling" against yourself! In a battle against yourself, you are always destined to lose. When the mind and body are at war with each other, the soul is always wounded! End the battle, the violence against yourself, and you have already won! Put down your weapons and create a self-care plan that nourishes you into the best version of yourself body, mind and soul.

Yoga is not about attaining any form of external perfection. It is not about developing the perfect body, doing perfect yoga postures, or living the perfect yoga lifestyle. Kripalu Yoga is a way to be fully present to the reality of life unfolding in the moment—however it is showing up. Rather than teaching you how to get somewhere else, it helps you be fully where you are. ~Richard Faulds

Affirmation: Today I am kind to myself. I accept my body just as it is, and thank it for safely carrying my beautiful soul!

Today's biggest success:

Food for Thought: Become aware of any ways you may be consciously or unconsciously harming yourself rather than healing and nourishing yourself.

Journal: Create your own action plan to tweak your eating and exercise plan to a more kind, compassionate approach.

Day 18

What Are You Feeding Your Skin?

I often get complements on my skin. Many people ask which skin care products I use, expecting that I use expensive, exotic or rare products. However, that is not the case. I spend my "skincare allowance" at the grocery store and farmer's market! After all, *Ayurveda*, teaches that beautiful skin shines from the inside out! No creams, potions or scrubs will mask a bad diet. The foods you feed your body, build the health and luster of the skin from the inside out! The radiance of your skin is a direct reflection of how you eat! Many people who spend a small fortune on the latest "breakthrough" skin products may be throwing their money away by eating a poor diet. *Ayurveda* practitioners can tell much about the state of the diet, the state of digestion and the state of health, just by observing the appearance of your skin. What is exciting to know is that the skin cells completely renew themselves every 2-4 weeks. By improving the diet, you can quickly and dramatically improve the skin in a matter of weeks! In each 40 Days class I have taught, there comes a point when I look around the room, and notice the renewed radiance and glow on everyone's face!

Answer the following questions to see if you are properly feeding your skin from the inside out:

1. My complexion is dull, washed-out, sallow, or ruddy.
    Y or N

2. I often experience breakouts of pimples, acne, rosacea, rashes, eczema or psoriasis.
    Y or N

3. I experience skin inflammation, blisters or sores.
    Y or N

4. My skin is dry, flaky, scaly or itchy.
    Y or N

5. I have rough, bumpy "chicken-skin" on the back of my upper arms.
   Y or N

6. My skin has lost its suppleness, elasticity and radiance.
   Y or N

7. My skin appears to be prematurely aging.
   Y or N

8. I have dark circles underneath my eyes.
   Y or N

9. My skin lacks luminosity, radiance and luster.
   Y or N

10. My skin is sallow, ruddy, or has a lot of redness.
    Y or N

If you have answered "YES" to any of the above questions, your skin is not getting the nourishment it needs from the inside out.

Ayurveda teaches that you should not feed the skin anything you would not ingest with your mouth! In fact, we use the skin as a transdermal delivery system of medicinal herbs and oils into the tissues and cells much like conventional medicine uses the Nicotine or estrogen patch. Whatever you apply to the skin is absorbed and delivered to the blood, tissues and cells. The skin "drinks" in whatever we put on it though the pores. If we are slathering toxins all over the body, we are literally "feeding" ourselves toxins. If your grooming, skin-care or make-up products contain chemical ingredients, you are *contaminating* your skin and body rather than nourishing it.

It is estimated that the average woman comes in contact with 515 chemicals daily through her beauty routine alone. Forty years ago, one in twenty women was diagnosed with breast cancer in the U.S., and today it is one in eight. Alone, in small doses, the FDA deems these cosmetic toxins safe, but what about the "toxic load" of "day in and day out" contact with this "chemistry set" on the body? In addition, what about other chemical contaminants we come into contact with unintentionally, through the air, in our drinking water, in household cleaning products, insecticides, and in the foods we eat. What is the cumulative effect of all this daily toxic exposure?

Be sure to check your skin and beauty care products' ingredient list just as carefully as you would read the ingredients before ingesting a food product. What you feed your skin; you are feeding the entire body-mind system!

What we feed the skin goes directly into the bloodstream, bypassing the digestive tract and gets delivered to the tissues and cells of the body where they are stored! As we walk the 40 Day Journey to Enlightened Eating it is critical that we rethink the ways we feed our skin! After decades of chemically laden skin care products and miracle creams, there is now a growing trend back towards plant based natural beauty products. Ironically, recent progress in the cosmetic industry is essentially a return to the ancient wisdom of *Ayurvedic* medicine, using natural oils, herbs and plants, to rejuvenate the skin and to bring about a more healthy, luminous and youthful appearance in a safe and effective way. We have literally traveled "back in time" to discover a modern health and beauty breakthrough!

Ayurveda teaches that there are several ways to keep the skin healthy and bright.

1. Diet One of the first things my students observe as they take the 40 Days to Enlightened Eating journey is how much softer, clearer and more radiant their skin becomes as they make food choices that nourish the tissues, blood and cells and reinvigorate the digestive fire.

2. Detox The blood feeds the skin. When we begin to remove toxins from the cells and blood, the skin naturally and dramatically improves. The daily hot lemon water has a host of benefits for the skin! (See "Day 1" for information on *Ayurvedic* detoxification.)

3. Balance your *dosha*. *Doshic* imbalance is easily observable in the skin. In order to maintain beautiful skin, it is necessary to eat to keep your *Ayurvedic* constitution in balance. (For more information about eating for your *dosha* and how to determine your *Ayurvedic dosha* please refer to chapters 14 and 15 in *40 Days to Enlightened Eating*)

- *Vata* type skin is prone to dryness and premature aging. It is typically cool and dry to the touch and *vata* types sweat very little. *Vata* type skin imbalance appears as dry scaly patches, cracking, chapping, premature wrinkling, appearing weathered looking, lacking radiance and luster.

- *Pitta* type skin is fair in complexion, often with freckles, and these individuals blush easily. It tends to have soft red or yellow undertones. *Pitta* types tend to sweat liberally and have oily skin especially in the T-zone. *Pitta* type skin imbalance shows up as rashes, acne, pimples, rosacea, inflammation, and excessive oiliness. They may experience hot flashes, and pronounced red or yellow tones (ruddy or sallow) to the skin.

- *Kapha* skin tends to maintain its youthful appearance longest due to its natural moisture. It tends to be pale, have larger pores, good skin tone, and few lines or wrinkles. When out of balance, *Kapha* skin can take on enlarged pores, become cold, damp and clammy, and become particularly pale and dull. Edema can also result from out of balance *kapha*.

4. Regular exercise: Exercise circulates the blood, which feeds the skin. Exercise encourages the circulation of blood to the skin and extremities by increasing *vyana vayu*, the outward movement of blood, oxygen and the circulation of *prana* or life-force energy from the internal to the periphery. This increases skin radiance. Regular yoga practice is said to especially help increase the luster and radiance of the skin. Because it enhances digestion, elimination, detoxification, sweating and circulation, the skin cannot help but benefit from regular yoga practice.

5. *Abhyangha* and *snehana*: Both *Ayurvedic* massage practices involve oiling the body, and both Sanskrit words mean "to oil" and "to *love*." Oiling the body promotes a sense of self-love and self-care. Use oils according to *dosha*. For *vata skin,* sesame oil is recommended. For *pitta* skin, coconut oil is recommended. *For kapha skin,* mustard oil is recommended. Simply massaging the oil onto the skin nourishes, supports and moisturizes the skin, builds *ojas,* and nurtures the body-mind system.

6. *Svedhana* – Intentionally provoking a sweat. This practice helps move blood to the skin and helps to detoxify the pores of the skin, by moving toxins and debris out of the skin pores through the sweat.

7. Water – Drinking ample water keeps the complexion clean bright and clear. Water helps hydrate the skin, while also helping to keep it cleansed, purified and detoxified, by supporting it to continually move out toxins through sweat, blood and urine.

8. *Garshana*/Dry Brushing – *Garshana* is an *Ayurvedic* dry massage using a body brush or exfoliating gloves with strokes moving toward the heart. Before showering, begin by massaging from your feet up the legs, circle clockwise at joints buttocks and the belly several times, continuing up your torso. From here, brush up from the hands to the shoulders circling at the joints. Practice this daily for at least five minutes. *Garshana* improves circulation of blood and lymph. It is detoxifying and helps to exfoliate the outer layer of the skin. It is excellent for *kapha* because it is stimulating and invigorating and simultaneously has a calming effect on the nervous system. This practice is less helpful for *vata dosha*. Rough sensations on already dry, rough *vata* skin, aggravates *vata dosha*.

Affirmation: My physical body is a divine gift. I choose natural, wholesome products to care for my body, and give it the best that nature has to offer. My body is pure, clean and safe.

Today's biggest success:

Food for thought: Become aware of how well you are feeding your skin both on the inside and on the outside. Read the ingredient lists for skin care products as avidly as you do your food products. Avoid any words you cannot pronounce or chemical ingredients. Do not feed your skin anything you would not eat with your mouth!

Journal: List any changes you need to make in your diet and in your skin care routine, to better nourish your skin outside and in!

Part 2
Food for the Mind

Day 19

The 5 Hindrances:

Obstacles on the Path to Transformation

The obstacle is the path. ~Zen proverb

According to ancient Buddhist tradition, there are 5 destructive mental states that can hinder our spiritual progress and even lead us to harmful actions and unpleasant outcomes as we walk the path to transformation. These obstacles are known to block the path of transformation and enlightenment. By becoming aware of these often-unconscious mental barriers, we are empowered to consciously overcome them. The following are the 5 Hindrances as I have observed them arise on the journey to Enlightened Eating!

1. Restlessness: This hindrance comes in the form of ambivalence, apprehension, worry, confusion, second-guessing. Not being focused and clear of the path. It can be seen as not staying on course or weaving your way down the path rather than making your way clearly forward. Confusion is the most prevalent form of restlessness. We are constantly being bombarded with conflicting dietary information. One day kale is in, the next day it is out! Food bloggers put fear in us about any and every food, making so many foods off-limits, many folks just give up and give into their bad habits, figuring it really doesn't make a difference anyway. Confusion is a way we stay stuck in our old habits without a clear way forward. In my philosophy, if it is grown on a vine, a tree, a plant, or bush, and not chemically sprayed or genetically modified, it is what we humans were made to eat. The real question to ask yourself is, "Is this REAL food?" Check the ingredient list. Is there a 16-letter-long mystery ingredient? Is the ingredient list a mile long? Is this food highly processed? Can you recognize it from its original form?

Focus is the second way I observe this obstacle arise. People start out with the right intentions, and clear focus, but they are quickly side-tracked and distracted by temptation, and their focus dissolves. When you find yourself losing focus, or falling off track, go back to Day 1 and Reboot! Detox instead of "retox!" I have rebooted over and over again to keep my own efforts moving forward!

2. Aversion: Aversion is a strong dislike or resistance. A yoga instructor friend of mine who was teaching "Enlightened Eating" classes emailed me about a student who LIVED on packaged "bars." The student was an older single adult, who would cook for her children when they came to visit, but didn't want to take the time to make nourishing meals for herself. She was taking the class, but very resistant to cooking, and to giving up the convenience of her bars. She was experiencing resistance or *aversion* to cooking. I suggested she return to a state of "beginner's mind" or Day 1 of *40 Days to Enlightened Eating*. I told her, you can't keep doing what you have done and expect different results. Transformation requires openness and willingness to change. Without making changes, it is impossible to change! I also believe this was a deeper issue of self-love, as she was willing to cook for her children whom she loved, but not willing to make those same efforts for herself.

I have had students who have thanked me over and over for getting them to try cooking, and they ended up discovering they LOVED it! One was a bright, beautiful, single young lady who skipped meals, ate out, or ate packaged bars. She worked long hours and traveled a lot in her job, which made it challenging to eat regular meals. At first, she wasn't into cooking. Early on, she set the intention to cook for herself, and she came to the class meetings every week proud of this achievement. She noticed food tasted better when she put time, thought and love into it. I ran into her again about 6 months later and she was radiant and vibrant, noticeably more so than she had been in class. She reported that enlightened eating had changed her life! She took pleasure in cooking even if just for herself and said it was a true act of self-love to choose to set aside time to nourish herself. She was now considering a career change. She was in a much more stable place just by learning the act of nourishing herself which now flowed through all aspects of her life, not just eating!

I also had a working mom of 4 young children who had never really cooked. She had relied on packaged foods, pre-made food, frozen meals and take-out. She kept an open mind and was thrilled about cooking for the first time as she made her first batch of kitchari! She was really proud and felt successful about cooking her first "real" meal! She was delighted that her husband and oldest kids loved the kitchari she had made. She returned a second and a third time to "Enlightened Eating "classes to improve her skills! She felt she was modeling healthy eating and self-care to her four children, and felt even better about herself as a mom by feeding her children healthy, nourishing foods.

I have had students who were resistant to the kitchari cleanse, and there has been resistance to spending extra on organics. Each time they ran into resistances and moved through them anyway, transformation happened! I remember one mom who was resistant to paying extra for organic dairy, but acquiesced to giving it a try for the 40 days. She was astonished to find that her two teenage children's acne visibly cleared up, which she attributed to this simple change!

When you notice yourself running up against the obstacle of aversion or resistance, try embracing what you don't like. Remember the Zen philosophy that the obstacle is the path. Be with what you don't like. Practice openness, beginner's mind, and non-judgment. The very thing you are resisting is most likely the single most important obstacle between you and your own transformation. "What you resist persists."

3. Doubt: This obstacle or hindrance comes in the form of self-criticism, self-doubt, finding holes, mistakes, problems, and questioning the direction. This can take the form of falling into insecurity, self-doubt or negative self-talk "I have no will-power, so I'll never be able to do this." "I hate my body." "I am fat." "I have a slow metabolism and nothing works for me." "I hate to cook." "I never stick with any program." "I have no willpower." *Thoughts are powerful.* When you entertain negative thoughts, they quickly get a foothold in your life, setting the intention for where you are going next. To change your life, you first must change your thoughts! Choose positive thoughts to replace the thoughts of self-doubt. In order for anything to work, you first must believe in yourself, and secondly you must believe in what it is you are doing!

Another way this hindrance can show up on the journey to self-transformation is starting to doubt the path. Thoughts like "This isn't working for me." "It's too hard to eat healthy." "It takes too much time to cook my own food." "I am too busy for this." "Healthy eating is boring." Doubt can show up as these negative thoughts that keep you standing still and not moving forward. When doubts arise, let that be the signal that you need to push through them with determination and commitment, instead of letting them rule you. Instead of doubting yourself or doubting the path, celebrate each and every step in the right direction, no matter how small! As long as you keep moving forward, no matter how slowly, you are moving through doubt.

4. Clinging: This comes in the form craving, desire and attachment. Often, we cling to our old habits, comfortable ideas and familiar ways of doing things. Over the course of teaching the *40 Days to Enlightened Eating* classes, I have noticed students each come with something to which they are attempting to cling. For example, I've had several students who were terrified to give up artificial "calorie-free" sweeteners, for fear of weight-gain. Thankfully they trusted the process for 40 days, and were astonished to see that they lost weight when they switched to natural sweeteners like raw honey or maple syrup. Interestingly, the one student I had who claimed she didn't lose weight during the 40 Days, was a student who insisted that she needed to count carbs. As she clung to her obsession with carbs, she lost the essence of what the 40 Days was about. Often, I've had students who were reluctant to give up their evening cocktails or glass of wine during the 3-day cleanse, but they did! After the cleanse, they felt "freed" from "needing" a drink every night and realized they certainly could do without it. Often students think they can never do without meat every day, even for the 3 days of the cleanse.

Some of these same students went through the entire 40 days and beyond without returning to meat. Others, were surprised to find that eating meat only a few times a week worked amazingly well and were thrilled to save money in their grocery budget, and feel increased energy too! I have had students who were "addicted" to diet soda, but have let it go for good without looking back.

Clinging can be attachment to a certain outcome. Perhaps it's the strong desire to be a size 4 or be a certain number on the scales. Perhaps the weight or the size you are clinging to is not reasonable or healthy for you! When you observe yourself *clinging* to a particular habit, food, or outcome, this is your obstacle. The antidote to clinging is letting go. Let go of preconceptions, fixed ideas, old habits, and patterns to step forward into transformation. Is there a food or habit you can let go of which is standing in between you and your optimal self? What are you still clinging to?

5. Sloth and torpor: These obstacles take the form of complacency, laziness, half-heartedness, and inconsistency-(a lack of *tapas* or fire) Just reading the book or joining the gym will not help you reach your optimal weight and health. You have to walk the path. Teachers open the door, but you must enter on your own. I've known people who sign up for a gym membership, but never actually go, thinking the membership alone will help them lose weight. People buy a new yoga mat, but never attend classes! People buy a cart full of healthy produce, and let it spoil in the fridge! Is this you? You have to meet your intention halfway by taking action! Have you become lazy about making healthy meals? Have you been inconsistent about your yoga practice or exercise? Are you half-heartedly engaged in the 40 day journey? Your results will reflect your efforts. Perhaps it is time to recommit, to redouble your efforts, to rekindle the fire of *tapas* or self-discipline. The struggle with temptation to eat unhealthy foods is your soul giving you the opportunity to learn discipline and self-control. It is discipline that ultimately leads to freedom... Freedom from disease, excess weight, low-energy and premature aging. Those who become lazy and complacent on the journey never arrive at the destination; they stay stuck right where they are behind the obstacle. Only you can take action to move forward, no one else can do it for you and nothing happens all by itself!

Food for Thought: What are your obstacles? Once you become aware of them, meet them head on and move through them. Trust that overcoming the obstacle is the path to transformation. The obstacle is the path. Meet it head on!

Today's biggest success:

Affirmation: The places where I struggle are simply opportunities for great breakthroughs to happen. I move through my obstacles with awareness, determination and self-compassion.

Journal: Which obstacles do you need to move through on your path to transformation? What is your action plan to step through your obstacles?

Day 20

What are you Really Hungering For?

Time is the missing ingredient in our recipes—and in our lives. ~Michael Pollan

On a vacation to the picturesque island of Aruba, I curiously began to observe that I had little appetite. At regular meal times, I just wasn't hungry. I'd nibble on a few berries at breakfast, thinking that by lunch I'd surely have an appetite, only to find that still I wasn't hungry. I'd nibble on something light just because skipping meals is a migraine trigger for me, but I was not feeling hungry. As the afternoons wore on to evening and we went out to dinner, I left much food on my plate, still I just wasn't hungry.

As I practiced yoga and meditated on the balcony of our room overlooking the ocean, feasting my eyes on the tropical foliage, birds, white sand and the turquoise sea, I realized that I was already being fed, and I was in the process of digesting a delicious experience in my life.

I thought about the numerous times back at home when I sense sensations of hunger, and wind up standing at the cabinet or fridge searching for something to fill that void. It dawned on me that in Aruba, I was feasting fully on what I was really hungering for: rest, quiet, warmth, sunshine, fresh air, nature, the calm of the sea, the splendor of the natural world, and the care-free ease of island life. Now that I had it, I wasn't hungering anymore.

A dear friend of mine struggled with her weight for years. For many of these years she believed her weight struggle to be about poor will power or a slow metabolism. As her yoga and meditation practices deepened, she began to realize the weight wasn't really about those things at all. She lived in and "unfulfilling" marriage and worked in an "unfulfilling" job. She began to realize that her addiction to food, eating and shopping were her unmet need to fill her empty life rather than an empty belly. She was using food and material things to fill a much deeper hunger. All at once, she found the courage to leave her empty marriage and job and change careers. Once she acknowledged to herself that it was really these things, which made her "hunger" for something more and made the appropriate changes, the weight began to almost dissolve! Once she found herself in her "dream job" and with her "soul mate," she was no longer constantly thinking about eating and food to fill a void!

Is there something deep within that you are really hungering for? Hunger has many qualities and multiple appetites, desires and cravings that don't necessarily involve eating or food. Hunger is emptiness, longing, craving and yearning for what is most needed to nourish not only the body, but the mind and spirit too. Our culture tends to over-feed the body, yet starve the mind and soul.

What are you hungering for in life? We use food to mask feelings of a deeper hunger, the inner hunger for our inmost desires. Perhaps we are hungering for love, companionship, human touch, connection, space, time, rest, self-care, or to feast the eyes on a relaxing and scenic panorama! Perhaps we are hungering to follow our dreams, to live out our life's purpose. Perhaps we are hungering for a career change or a happier more connected relationship. What I do know is that hunger is not always about food. Hunger is about feeding the whole self. Hunger is about feeding deeper needs. Once we receive the nourishment that we are really seeking, refilling our soul, hunger simply evaporates. It is only when the body, mind *and* spirit are fed, that we are at last truly satiated.

If you are satisfied in your life, you won't be tempted to stuff yourself with food to feel contented. Using food to satiate these deeper needs, only anesthetizes the deeper hungering, putting off further the fulfillment of what your soul is craving. If you are prone to overeating, examine your life for areas that lack fulfillment. Consciously work to bring about renewed contentment in these areas rather than using food to fill this void. When you don't feed yourself what it is you truly want and need, you continue to hunger.

Affirmation: When I feed my deeper needs, I cease to hunger for that which isn't truly nourishing me. I nourish myself body, mind and soul.

Today's biggest success:

Food for Thought: Sense what it is you are really hungering for in your life beyond physical food. Begin to focus on feeding your deeper needs, and notice if your appetite for less than optimal foods begins to diminish.

Journal: What are you really hungering for in your life? What needs are unfulfilled right now that leave you wanting and craving? What changes can you make to ensure that those deeper needs are fulfilled?

Day 21

The Real Messages
Behind Your Cravings

If you are feeling stressed or depressed, don't look in the fridge or the cupboards to heal, look inside yourself.

~Elise Cantrell

As I write this chapter about food cravings today, I write from visceral raw experience. I experienced the passing of my beloved 93-year-old grandmother yesterday morning. At first, of course I had no appetite whatsoever. As the day wore into evening, I experienced a deep sense of emptiness inside, and I experienced the need to fill this deep emptiness with food . . . comfort food. Grains and cheese are heavy, grounding, and most of all, filling. As I ate bread and cheese trying to fill the void, I recognized that no amount of food seemed to fill that hole inside of me. I also craved wine that evening. I wanted to feel numb. I wanted to dull the ache in my heart. The next day I noticed myself craving chocolate, milk and sweets. I was missing that nurturing, love and sweetness that only a grandmother can give. I consciously observed my cravings shift and swing as I endured this emotional rollercoaster.

What I realized from this experience, is that overall I live a pretty balanced life and normally have natural, steady and balanced food cravings, but this was different. Through no fault of my own, I had been thrown for a loop. My own mind-body system was thrown way off balance. It made me aware that many folks who are regularly living lives out of balance, experiencing daily wild swings of cravings as the mind and the body, desperately try to bring themselves back to the center.

I think about my students who are caring for elderly parents and their children at the same time. I think of students who struggle with cravings for sweets because their jobs are so demanding, hectic and stressful. Many folks have regular stressors, which send the body into food craving mode in order to bring them back into some sense of harmony. I am fortunate to have a job that I absolutely love and a peaceful home life, so through this experience, I could clearly witness the effects our emotions have on cravings. I believe that when you're in the trenches 24-7, it is hard to step back and see what "normal" feels like. I had the unique occasion to step out of my "normal" and feel what it felt like to be caught up in stress-induced foods cravings.

Food cravings are messengers sent from your mind-body system. They arrive to tell us something is out of balance, and to compel us to take action to regain equilibrium. Depending upon the severity of the imbalance, cravings can become quite powerful.

Here are what your food cravings are really trying to tell you:

Junk food: The message here is that your body is so out of balance that it no longer intuitively knows what you need. Its messenger system becomes "deranged" causing cravings for things which only further imbalance the mind-body system. In *Ayurveda*, like attracts and increases like. When your body-mind system is toxic, it craves more toxins. This should be a strong warning signal that toxins have accumulated in your body and it is now hospitable to disease. In *Ayurveda*, these deranged cravings occur in the 3rd stage of the progression of disease called *prasara*. Symptoms have not yet begun to manifest, but the disease process is already underway. Mild symptoms begin to manifest in stage 4 when disease moves into the body's weakest areas. These worsen in stage 5 and become fixed and very difficult to cure or treat by stage 6. If you are craving junk food, this should be a wakeup call! It is time to cleanse, detoxify and reboot, making immediate positive lifestyle changes. At this stage disease can be reversed. As disease moves into its later stages it becomes increasingly difficult to reverse, treat or cure.

Salty food: Salt balances *vata*. If you are craving salt, you are likely experiencing *vata* imbalance, which is often associated with anxiety, nervousness, sleep disruption, dehydration, cold extremities and feeling chilled. Salt treats the anxiety and sleep difficulties because it is a mild sedative. It counters dehydration by causing the body to hold on to fluids (increasing *kapha* which is heavy and stable). Salt also has a warming or heating effect on the body. Salt is an earth mineral and creates a sense of groundedness to balance the light, airy and disconnected sense *vata* can bring about.

Spicy Food: Spicy flavors balance *kapha*. Spicy cravings are the mind-body's way of helping to balance a sense of fatigue, dullness and lethargy. Spicy cravings may indicate the need for more play and to "spice" things up. Spicy foods are known to activate feelings of excitement, energy and enthusiasm. This taste promotes a sense of putting more "spice" into your life. Spicy foods are also warming. These cravings indicate that perhaps you need more emotional warmth in your life. Spicy foods include garlic, black pepper, hot peppers, cayenne, hot sauce, ginger, cinnamon, cardamom and cumin. It is not a bad thing to eat spicy food to break up feelings of sluggishness caused by *kapha dosha*. I recommend chai tea, as a perfect spicy remedy to afternoon *kapha*. However, spicy foods can aggravate *pitta dosha*. Cravings for spicy foods can also indicate stage 3 of *pitta* imbalance.

When *pitta dosha* has reached this stage of imbalance, cravings become perverted, and you begin to crave the very things that aggravates the *dosha* further. If you have a *pitta* constitution, and you begin to crave heating spices, let this be a sign to you that you are possibly in a state of imbalance. Rebalance by cleansing and rebooting in chapter 1.

Sugary treats: Sweet taste balances *pitta dosha*. If you are craving sweets, you are likely experiencing emotions like frustration, irritability, agitation or anger. Energetically you probably have been pushing yourself too much, concentrating too hard, being overly competitive, experiencing depleted energy, feeling burnt-out and in need of a pick-me-up. Physically or emotionally, you may feel overheated. Sweet taste is cooling to the emotions and to the physical body. Sweet taste mimics sweet emotions like love compassion, kindness, and self-care in the mind-body system. Have you been "sugar-coating" your lifestyle, moods and emotions with candy, cookies and sweets? Bringing about pleasant, sweet emotions like love, joy, playfulness, uplifted moods, and a kinder, gentler lifestyle counterbalances the heated emotions of *pitta* banishing *pitta* related sweet cravings. Sweets are known to provide a quick energy boost, livening up the body and mind during energy and mood dips. The best way to solve sweet cravings is with sweet, juicy fruits such as melons, berries, apples, pears, and sweet, juicy citrus (as opposed to sour). **On a side note:** Our family lived in France for a couple of years. The French eat their meals in *courses*. I remember my daughter came home from French school one day quite dismayed. She had gotten in trouble at lunch for eating her orange first! In France, the fruit course comes *after* the main meal. Counter intuitive to our culture, *Ayurveda* teaches that sweet taste should come first. Little did she know it at the time, but Hannah was eating things in exactly the right order for optimal digestion, and to create the least amount of *ama*.

Fats/Oils: Fats and oils balance *vata*. They bring on a sense of heaviness which helps stabilize the light airy, unstable qualities of *vata*. Oils also help to smooth and lubricate the rough qualities of *vata*. Emotionally, fat brings about a sense of satiety, protection, ease, comfort and love. Fat is very steadying to the *manomaya kosha*, or our "mental body" which includes the mind, emotions and thoughts. Fat is instantly grounding and improves the ability to concentrate as well as supports emotional balance. Healthy fats are proven to help improve focus and concentration in kids and adults with ADD and ADHD, which are *vata* disorders. The brain is 60% fat. Fats protect the brain and nervous system from anxiety and depression. In addition, body fat is protective of the fragile internal organs, nerves, vessels and systems, so craving fat is in a sense a craving for protection, safety and security. Healthy fats to solve this craving in a balanced way are: ghee, olive oil, sesame oil, coconut oil, grapeseed oil, pumpkinseed oil, walnut oil, fish oil, nuts, seeds and whole dairy.

Dairy: Dairy balances *vata* and *pitta*. Dairy also has a calming effect on the *manomaya kosha,* our mental-emotional self. Dairy brings about a sense of unconditional love and acceptance according to *Ayurveda*. Dairy is the first food we receive in life from our mother. This rich, sweet, fatty substance brings about a sense of being loved, nourished, cared for and nurtured. *Ayurveda* considers whole organic dairy the best way to balance this craving. The fat in the whole dairy is nourishing to the brain, and prevents a surge in blood sugar, due to the lactase content in milk, a natural sugar. It has been found that skim and "light" dairy cause the blood sugar to rise rapidly triggering insulin release. Insulin is a fat storage hormone. Organic whole dairy from well-treated cows is the best way to satisfy a dairy craving because it will satisfy the craving in the form that is the purest and closest to nature. The more dairy is modified and processed, the more it will take to satisfy the craving. This is what causes weight gain. Craving cheese, milk or other dairy products is a call from the mind-body system for self-nurturing and love.

Alcohol: Alcohol is numbing to the mind-body system. In times past, it was given to patients to anesthetize pain from injury or even surgery. Many people use alcohol to anesthetize or self-medicate mental-emotional pain as well as physical pain. Alcohol dulls the mind-body system and creates the illusion of comfort without solving what is causing the discomfort. It slows thoughts and reactions, dampens inhibition, clouds the thinking, and blunts instincts and intuition. Alcohol initially relaxes the nervousness and awkwardness often experienced by the *vata dosha*. *Vatas* are the most likely to act goofy, giggly, clumsy and talk too much when drinking, and are more prone to vomiting. After first dulling *vata,* alcohol has a strong *vata* disturbing rebound effect, causing agitation, worry, and interrupted sleep. Alcohol dulls the sharpness and focus of *pitta*. *Pittas* tend to crave alcohol the most because of its sweetness and sensory dulling effect, but they are the constitution most easily aggravated by alcohol. They are most likely to experience impatience, irritability, anger, rage, skin flushing or become overheated from alcohol. Drinking alcohol will also cause diarrhea in *pitta* types. *Kaphas,* tend to retain fluids, and become melancholy or depressed after imbibing. In other words, if you are looking to numb-out, alcohol is not the answer, because it further imbalances the *doshas*! Opt for calming teas such as tulsi, chamomile, kava, lavender, or other teas containing calming herbal compounds. A healthy and powerful nervine formula (nerve calming) in *Ayurveda* is warm milk with nutmeg and saffron. It will work wonders without the side-effects of alcohol.

Crunchy foods: This craving is not covered in *Ayurveda* texts, but crunching is a craving that seemed to arise frequently among my Enlightened Eating students as they gave up processed crackers, chips, and junk foods. They noticed that they missed the "crunch" more than the foods! It was the "crunch" itself that they were craving! This may be one of the reasons that junk foods can be so addicting. I began to note that this seemed to be a common craving among *pitta* types. I have come to believe the crunching relieves or pacifies feelings of aggression. One student put it like this: *"Crunching makes me feel like I am destroying the things in my life that are causing me irritation and aggravation."*

Soul Cravings: Your soul has CRAVINGS too! It is important to satisfy your SOUL'S cravings, or they may surface in the physical body as unsatisfied FOOD cravings! The soul craves the following: joy, purpose, creativity, fulfilling work, pleasure/playfulness, sweetness/beauty, loving relationships/connection to other souls, connection to God, and to serve. If you are not feeding your soul any one of these things, you may misinterpret your soul's cravings for food cravings. Read more on this subject in the upcoming chapter *Are You Feeding Your Body but Starving Your Soul?*

One of the reasons people consume anything too much is because they don't consume other things enough. You tend to take in too much material substance when you are starving yourself of spiritual substance. ~Marianne Williamson

Affirmation: I crave foods that are both healthy and delicious! I recognize emotional cravings for what they are, and I quickly and easily note and address signs of imbalance.

Today's biggest success:

Food for Thought: Sense where your food cravings are really arising from. When you address the actual source of the craving rather than just the craving itself, you can quickly and easily return to a state of balance and equilibrium.

Journal: What food cravings frequently arise for you? Describe any new insights you have into why these cravings arise for you.

Day 22

Food for Thought . . .

We are shaped by our thoughts. We become what we think.

~The Buddha

Many people are aware of the dramatic impact food has on the physical body. Certain foods can enhance health, energy, youthfulness and wellbeing, while other foods promote fatigue, dullness, disease and decay. What most people aren't aware of is that foods can have the same effects on the mind. There are numerous studies noting the effects of certain foods on children and adults with neurological disorders such as autism, Alzheimer's, ADD, Dyslexia, and others. These studies show that foods containing artificial preservatives, colors, chemical pesticides, insecticides, herbicides and other chemical ingredients have adverse effects on these disorders, worsening the symptoms. With these disorders, when diet is clean, pure and nourishing, sufferers notice marked improvement.

For the average person, side effects of foods are subtler, but they are still present. The science of *Ayurveda* has recognized the connection between food and the mind for millennia. *Ayurveda*, yoga's healing sister science, teaches that foods either elevate the thoughts and the mood, or aggravate the mind by increasing agitation, confusion, fogginess, distractibility, anxiety, nervousness, moodiness, dimness, depression and negativity. After all, the mind operates through the brain, and the brain is a very sensitive part of the physical body. The brain is the mind's "OS" or *operating system*!

Foods which compromise the mind and cause negative mental effects are foods that are stale, canned, processed, artificially flavored or preserved, foods which have been sprayed with chemical pesticides and herbicides, as well as alcohol and meat, especially the meat of poorly treated animals, which carries the stress hormones and fear energy from the animals and thereby impacts our own mind-body system. Sages throughout history have stated, *"Everything is mind."* However, I beg to differ. "Everything is food" because what you eat has a powerful impact on your thoughts and your mind, yet the state of the mind has a direct impact on the foods you choose to eat. Food is mind and mind is composed of the things you feed it. When you change your eating, you literally recreate the brain (rewiring the operating system) and therefore the mind. The very thoughts you have are a direct reflection of the "energy" and vibration of the foods you put into the body. What you feed the body is what you feed the mind. What you feed the mind brings about the quality of thoughts projected on the mental screen.

I am often asked why it is so important to eat organics since they can be more expensive than their conventional counterparts. My reply is that most non-organic produce is contaminated with insecticide, pesticide and/or herbicide sprays. The suffix "icide" comes from the Latin word *cidere,* which means "to kill." Pesticide, insecticide and herbicide, homicide, suicide and genocide are different means of causing death. In *Ayurveda,* the foods we eat either build momentum towards health and longevity or conversely towards decay and death. The foods we eat carry intentionality and energy. They either carry the energy of life and vitality or disease, decline and demise. Any food containing an "icide" in it is like eating small doses of death. Each dose builds upon the last, affecting the body and mind on a cellular level. Energetically speaking, intent is very powerful in our own energy body, the *pranamaya Kosha.* Chemical sprays containing the purpose of "icide" or death, energetically communicate this subtle message to every cell.

Recently, my next-door neighbors had their yard sprayed with a pesticide spray to kill dandelions. I broke out in hives and had an excruciating migraine headache for days straight. My daughter also had a prolonged migraine. I spoke to the neighbor on the other side of them, and she and her 2 young children had also experienced a migraine for days on end triggered by the spraying. Anything causing such a reaction cannot be good for the body or the earth.

Foods containing artificial colors and flavors are meant to "trick" the mind-body system. These foods may fool the tongue, but they don't fool the mind-body system! Fake foods impart the energy of deception, deceit and inauthenticity into those who eat them. I propose that this intention imparted in our food can affect our own mind-body system in our personal ability to be authentic and true to ourselves, and live impeccably and with integrity. Everything is energy!

Energy and intention are so important in the *Ayurvedic* system that it encourages us to cook with love, noting that the energy of the chef is imparted into the meal. We are reminded not to argue or get into heated discussions during our meals because we digest this energy along with our food. We should avoid watching the evening news, violent television shows or listening to harsh music while eating. It is also critical that we do not tell ourselves, "This food is bad for me." Because this intention works its way into your body, which believes everything you tell it!

Foods that contain vitality, health and vibrancy, impart these same characteristics to the mind: well-being, ease, positivity, harmony, joy, intuition, insight, clarity, clairvoyance and creativity. Such foods are fresh, chemical-free vegetables and fruits, nuts, seeds, whole grains and dairy products from well-treated animals. When people begin to eat a clean, pure diet, they often report that colors appear more vibrant and vivid, and vision becomes more clean and crisp. There are even reports of eye color changing from brown to green or blue!

The idea of eating fresh organic foods sounds extreme to some people because our current food system has been corrupted. However, eating foods that contain artificial ingredients and chemical pesticides would have seemed quite extreme only 100 years ago! The food industry has done a great job of marketing and making acceptable, foods that have scientifically amped up flavor along with an endless shelf-life, and high profit margin. They have successfully packaged these aberrations as the "norm," and natural foods now seem alien to many folks.

I remember experiencing the effects food has on the mind while on vacation. As someone who eats fresh, pure, natural foods as a life-style choice and only seldom drinks alcohol, I began to notice the effects of eating restaurant foods and having a glass of wine each night with dinner by the 4th night of vacation. I noticed a change in not only my energy levels, but I began to notice aching in my wrists, ankles and lower back. The striking part was how much of a change I noticed in my mind and thoughts. Normally my thoughts are upbeat, positive and happy. I rarely have difficulty sleeping or experience worry, anxiety, doubt or negativity. By the 4th night these all began to creep in like insidious beasts. I recognized and knew these were not my own thoughts, but had been triggered by the less than optimal foods I had been eating, although I can attest that I was doing my best eating the healthiest foods available at the time. I am not used to preservatives, additives, and chemical contaminants. What this experience showed me was that many people are experiencing thoughts of doubt, self-judgment, fear, worry, and negativity on a regular basis, and they think that's normal. They think those thoughts belong to them when they are simple a biochemical effect on the mind. It is *their* norm only because of their diet, but it doesn't have to be.

Here is an experience shared by a yoga instructor friend of mine about the effects of food on the thoughts: "We had a birthday in the training group last night, I managed to stay away from the cake until just before bed. Within minutes of eating it, my mood plummeted, feelings of self-doubt arising, hatred for every aspect of myself, the desire to get in bed and not get up again . . . when will I learn that sugar is not my friend!" ~Sara B.

Personally, I am often frustrated and baffled by how difficult it can be to find REAL foods! I recently went to 3 grocery stores looking for non-GMO corn, because I don't want to feed Roundup sprayed, genetically altered foods to my family. At most restaurants, more often than not, there are no ideal or even adequate options. Our culture has embraced substandard fare as the norm, and we are paying the price with our health and wellbeing not only physically, but *mentally*. I hope I have given you some "food for thought."

Affirmation: My thoughts are as pure as my foods. Today I choose foods that elevate and empower my body, mind and moods.

Today's biggest success:

Food for Thought: You choose your thoughts by choosing your foods. Empower your self today to have clear, positive uplifted thoughts by choosing pure, clean foods.

Journal: Have you had your own experience when you became aware of a food affecting the quality of your thoughts positive or negative? Describe this experience and what insight it brought you.

Day 23

Eating Your Way to Enlightenment

To keep the body in good health is a duty . . . otherwise we shall not be able to keep our mind strong and clear. ~Buddha

Growing up in the 1970s, I recall my daily breakfast consisted of Pop-Tarts, Fruit Loops, Cap'n Crunch or Lucky Charms. Snacks were usually junk-food and soda. I have not always been an "enlightened eater"! As a teen, I suffered from mood swings and irritability, and I was plagued by fear and self-doubt, not to mention a bad case of acne! Although I was an honor student, I still made some pretty "unenlightened" recreational choices during my teen years that I regret to this day. Before studying *Ayurveda*, it never occurred to me that my moods, fears, insecurities and acne might have had something to do with the foods I ate!

As a new mom 18 years ago, I suffered from a paralyzing case of Irritable Bowel Syndrome (IBS). What seemed then like a horrible curse became one of the greatest gifts life has ever given me! I was forced to change my eating! **When I changed my eating, my whole life changed!** I suddenly had more clarity, insight, perception, and understanding, not to mention boundless energy, steady moods and ideal weight. I healed myself completely with food, and a whole new way of seeing things flooded open for me! I felt awakened for the first time in my life! I was suddenly able to tap into my own inner wisdom, which was already there, but just shrouded by the toxins I had been dumping into my body for years!

As they say, "Once you are awakened, you can't go back to sleep." It has become my passion and my mission to show others that **by changing your eating, you change your life** . . . for the better! Food has a direct effect, not only on the body, but on the mind and spirit too!

Today, I understand much more deeply the connection between food and states of consciousness. *Ayurveda* has understood this relationship for thousands of years. The food we eat corresponds directly to our **mental states** and to the **levels of consciousness** at which we operate.

According to *Ayurveda*, there are three *gunas*, or intrinsic qualities, that are present in all matter in the universe, including our foods, our bodies and state of mind! **The three *gunas* or inherent qualities are: *rajas*, *tamas*, or *sattva*.** These three states exist in the foods we eat, and the foods we eat are directly reflected in our own mental, emotional and spiritual states.

Rajas is a quality of agitation, restlessness, and change.

A *rajasic* diet includes:

- caffeine
- tobacco
- fried foods
- white flour
- white sugar
- meat or fish of any kind
- hot, spicy foods
- overly salty or overly sweet foods

A diet consisting primarily of these foods *over-excites* the system, creating **disharmony** and **discord**. These kinds of foods, promote **irritability, moodiness, anxiety, worry, restlessness, poor concentration, distractibility, anger, aggression** and **hostility**. With this diet, the ego can become unstable and inflated, causing one to make choices to further the self at the expense of others, lacking compassion and sensitivity. Indian militaries were fed a primarily *rajasic* diet in order to stimulate the aggressive, combative temperament needed for battle. A *rajasic* person lacks the stability and integrity necessary to reach higher levels of consciousness.

*Tamas i*s a quality of dullness, density and inertia.

A diet of *tamasic* foods consists of:

- junk foods
- fast foods
- processed foods
- artificial flavors, colors, and preservatives
- canned foods
- left-overs
- frozen TV dinners
- red meat
- alcohol
- stale, over-ripe or over-cooked foods

Tamas carries the energy of **ignorance, disease** and **decay**. A *tamasic* eater may suffer from **depression, delusion**, or **darkness** in thinking. Someone who eats a primarily *tamasic* diet, invites upon themselves a *tamasic* state of consciousness. A *tamasic* person makes choices from a place of **unawareness, dimness**, and **lack of perception**. This person is **disconnected** from spirit, higher consciousness, and their divine nature. Their diet prevents them from being the best version of themselves.

Sattva is a quality of **harmony, purity**, and **balance**. This is the optimal way to eat and to live. *Sattva* is the highest level of **cleanliness** and **wholesomeness**. A *sattvic* diet includes fresh, juicy, nourishing foods. These are real foods, grown on vines, trees, stalks or plants, and consumed at the peak of ripeness and freshness. These foods are not sprayed with herbicides, pesticides, or genetically modified, but grown in harmony with nature. These foods are filled with nutrients and micronutrients, and abounding with *prana* or life-force.

A *Sattvic* diet includes:

- fresh whole grains
- freshly prepared foods, lightly seasoned and lightly cooked
- organic fruits
- organic vegetables
- nuts and seeds
- legumes
- natural herbs, spices and sweeteners
- fresh organic dairy from well-treated cows

These foods are grown, prepared and cooked with the energy of love. **The most *sattvic* foods in *Ayurveda* are considered to be:**

- fresh juicy fruits
- raw honey
- almonds
- rice
- sesame oil
- ginger
- *ghee* (clarified butter)
- herbal teas and infusions

A *sattvic* diet promotes **joy, lightness** and **positivity**. It fuels **clarity, insight**, and **creativity**. It supports the **highest states of consciousness**, is said to bring about a state of **self-realization**, and to fertilize the seeds of **enlightenment**.

Since discovering and incorporating a more *sattvic way* of eating, my own life has transformed. My moods, thinking and concentration are calm, crisp and clear. Doubt and insecurity have all but evaporated! I no longer get moody or cranky. My children have said, "You're not like the other moms; you never get mad and yell at us!"

The other pleasant side effects of this way of eating have been excellent health, ideal weight, boundless energy and spiritual growth. I notice a considerable sense of ease, positivity and a brighter, lighthearted approach to life. I am aware of subtle energies, thoughts, and insights in myself and in others. My intuition is at an all-time high! My creativity has awakened! I feel enlivened on every level. Life moves along harmoniously as things seem to just fall into place. Answers come when I seek them, and miracles unfold on a regular basis. Moments of synchronicity are frequent. I feel mysteriously guided to make "enlightened"" choices. My life path is clear. I live with a sense of peace, contentment and gratitude. Prayer, yoga and meditation are a daily ritual, and I am connected deeply to spiritual practice, and to the Creator.

Food clearly has the power to open or close our channels of perception, awareness and clarity. Food can either be poison or nectar to the spirit. You can choose to eat your way into darkness, or **you can eat your way to enlightenment**.

Take the following "3-*Guna*" self-quiz. See which of the three *gunas* is predominant in your eating. This will give you a good idea whether or not you are eating your way to enlightenment.

Is my eating *Rajas, Tamas,* or *Sattva?*

(Check the one that applies in each row.)

1. I most often eat: ___ homemade food ___ in restaurants ___ reheated, prepared, convenience, or fast food.

2. I often eat my fruit and vegetables: ___ fresh ___ dried or canned ___ I don't like fruit or vegetables.

3. I often buy my food at: ___ the local farmers' market ___ the supermarket ___ the convenience store.

4. My diet is: ___ vegetarian ___ some meat ___ heavy meat.

5. I tend to: ___ chew each bite 20 times ___ eat rapidly ___ overeat.

6. I stop eating at: ___ 70-80% full ___ 100% full ___ 120% or more full.

7. I eat: ___ at regular times each day ___ sporadically or skip meals ___ by "grazing" all day.

8. I order pizza delivery or pick up take-out: ___ rarely ___ once or twice a month ___ weekly.

9. I drink alcohol: ___ rarely or never ___ 1 or 3 drinks a week ___ daily.

10. I use tobacco: ___ never ___ only when I drink alcohol ___ daily.

11. I use caffeine or stimulants: ___ never ___ a few times a week ___ several times daily.

12. My favorite foods are: ___ natural foods ___ fried foods ___ fast foods.

13. I sweeten with: ___ natural sweeteners ___ white sugar ___ artificial sweeteners.

14. I prefer: ___ whole grains ___ white bread, flour, rice ___ Cheetos, Doritos, and doughnuts.

15. I enjoy drinking: ___ herbal teas or fruit juices ___ sports drinks ___ diet sodas.

16. I crave: ___ fresh whole foods ___ salty or spicy foods ___ junk food.

17. Usually my food is: ___ organic when possible ___ convenience ___ leftovers.

The first choice in each row is *sattva,* the second is *rajas,* and the third is *tamas.* Total your check marks for each.

Total: _____ sattva _____ rajas _____ tamas

Affirmation: I am eating my way to enlightenment!

Today's biggest success:

Food for Thought: *Ayurveda* teaches that you can eat your way to higher states of living and being! Food directly affects our levels of consciousness.

Journal: Have you noticed changes in your own state of consciousness and being since you have changed your eating? If so, please describe the changes you have noted. When you are not eating your best, do you notice any mental and spiritual changes connected to it?

Day 24

Choosing Foods to Nourish Your Moods

So, to begin healing, stop kidding yourself that a little feel-good of the wrong sort will take care of a broken leg. Tell the truth about your wound, and then you will get a truthful picture of the remedy to apply to it. Don't pack whatever is easiest or most available into the emptiness. Hold out for the right medicine. You will recognize it because it makes your life stronger rather than weaker. ~Clarissa Pinkola Estes, *Women Who Run with the Wolves*

Do you experience any of the following: mood swings, irritability, anxiety, poor sleep, dullness, clouded thinking, lethargy, sadness or depression? Have you ever considered that the foods you eat are influencing your moods? For millenniums, *Ayurveda* has known that diet directly affects the mental-emotional body or *manomaya kosha*. It teaches that certain ways of eating can result in agitation, aggression, mood swings, quick temper, irritability, sleep disturbance, darkness, dullness and even depression. Most people don't associate their eating habits with their emotions and moods; however, the food we eat creates who we are physically, mentally, emotionally and even spiritually. If we are experiencing unwanted moods, often we can look to our diet for answers. Let me explain how – through the ancient wisdom of *Ayurveda* – you can eat your way to a better mood!

Ayurveda teaches that all matter in the universe, including the foods we eat, are composed of varying proportions of 3 "qualities" or *gunas*: *rajas*, *tamas*, and *sattva*. *Rajas* is the quality of motion, agitation, and change. *Tamas* is a state of darkness, heaviness and inertia. *Sattva* is the state of harmony balance or purity.

Foods that contain more *rajas*, exacerbate over-stimulation, restlessness, agitation and irritability. A diet heavy in *rajasic* foods such as caffeine, tobacco, red meat, deep fried foods, white flour, white sugar, highly sweetened, overly salted or hot, spicy foods is known to agitate the mind-body system and can create over-excitability, difficulty concentrating, impatience, aggravation, even anger and aggression. In fact, the Indian army was intentionally fed a *rajasic* diet to promote aggression and agitation to give them an edge in battle. Is this the "edge" we want to encourage in ourselves?

A diet heavy in *tamasic* foods is known in *Ayurveda* to cultivate, dullness, darkness, depression and a lower "animal-like" nature. A *tamasic* diet is composed of foods that contain few if any vital nutrients or energy. *Tamasic* include processed foods, fast foods, junk food, alcohol, left-overs, cured meats, fermented foods, stale food and foods containing artificial ingredients. Not only are these foods devoid of life-force, they contain toxins. These foods slowly poison and deplete the mind-body system. *Tamasic* foods are energy and mood "robbers" which impart a sense of feeling weighted down physically, emotionally and spiritually. Over-eating in general is also known to increase these same *tamasic* effects. If you are looking to lift, lighten and elevate the mind, body and spirit, then it is essential to eliminate these foods and avoid over-eating.

Foods that contain more *sattva* on the other hand, are foods that are clean, pure and full of vital nutrients. These foods promote harmony, balance, lightness, joy and positivity. They cultivate optimal health and promote functioning at the highest potential in mind, body and spirit. These are "God-made" foods such as fresh, juicy, seasonal fruits, vegetables, grains, legumes and nuts. Organic dairy products from well-treated livestock are also considered *sattvic* in nature. It is through eating in harmony with nature and the way we were created, that balance, peace and calm are restored. If you are looking for improved mood, then these are the foods you should seek out!

Yes, diet alone has the potential to recreate, not only the ideal healthy body, but mind and spirit too. So much so, that studies have shown that when vending machines for soda and junk foods are removed from school cafeterias, violent outbursts and aggressive behavior in students decrease dramatically! In another study, juvenile delinquents who were incarcerated had their diet switched from junk food, meat and sugar, to one mainly consisting of vegetables, fruits, grains and nuts. Within days there was a 48% decrease in all types of violent behavior.

As someone who has traveled extensively and even lived outside of the country, I have become aware that the American diet is primarily *rajas* and *tamas*. Not unlike the Indian army, Americans are eating a diet that encourages aggression, agitation, darkness, depression and even violence. If obesity, cancer, diabetes, and heart disease are not reason enough to change what and how we eat, perhaps we will be motivated by food's potential and power to change the way we think and act. Our moods are in our control, and they no longer have to control us! By consciously choosing the foods we eat, we are choosing our state of consciousness.

I clearly recall one of my students in Enlightened Eating class tearfully sharing that since she has cleaned up her eating, she has noticed her moods have evened out. Through tears she recounted that she no longer found herself exploding at her children or husband. She observed that she was so much more patient during moments of frustration at work, running errands, with the store clerk, in the car and with herself, and her family. Her mood had completely evened out! She was astonished that all along it was foods that were affecting her moods!

I have personally noticed the way I eat affects my moods and even my THOUGHTS! As someone who eats clean the majority of the time, it becomes crystal clear when I notice my moods and thoughts have suddenly shifted after eating certain foods. One of my biggest "aha" moments was after a New Year's Eve celebration. I had had several glasses of wine which in turn lowered my resistance to impulses to eat foods which I know don't serve me well. I woke several times in the night filled with anxiety for no reason. I noticed my thoughts had shifted too. My mind was suddenly telling me I was a failure, I wasn't worthy, I'd never succeed at anything I did, etc. I immediately recognized that these thoughts were not my normal disposition, or my regular way of looking at myself or at life. Thankfully, I did not believe these thoughts, and called them out for what they were . . . the toxic effects of the evening's toxic dietary choices! Toxic thoughts are the result of putting toxins in your body. The brain is part of the physical body or *annamaya kosha,* which directly translates as "food body". In other words, what we do to our body, we do to our mind, and when what we do to our body and mind does not serve it, we impair our spirit, which inhabits that space.

I can't help but consider how deeply affected the minds of people who drink heavily and eat toxic foods all the time must be. It occurs to me how people who seemingly have no optimism, no inspiration, no enthusiasm, no hope or faith in themselves, and no peace, have given all those gifts away for the sake of food and drink! Foods have not only temped us into ill physical health, but into a lower state of consciousness, with troubled thoughts and disturbed moods.

The more harmoniously people eat, the more harmonious their thoughts. The more harmonious the thoughts; the more harmonious the actions. The more harmonious the actions; the more harmonious the life. The more harmonious the life; the more harmonious the world. What goes in, although it may be transmuted into a different energy form, is what comes out. The inner creates the outer. We truly are what we eat.

*Tip: Omega-3 fatty acids have a profoundly positive effect on the part of the brain that supports joy, positivity and bliss. It also is known to help improve focus and concentration. Make a conscious effort to add ample amounts of omega-3 containing foods to your diet for elevated moods!

Dietary sources of omega-3 fatty acids include:

- Flax seeds/oil
- Walnut seeds/oil
- Chia seeds
- Seafood, especially salmon, anchovy, and sardine
- Beans/legumes
- Olive oil
- Winter squash

B-vitamins have a stress relieving, calming effect on the mind-body system. The following are great food sources of B-vitamins:

- Leafy greens
- Whole grains
- Nuts and seeds
- Legumes including peanuts and green peas
- Fish, seafood and shellfish
- Eggs
- Organic soy
- Organic dairy, especially cheese and yogurt
- Avocado, sweet potatoes, potatoes, mushrooms and broccoli

Affirmation: Healthy foods create harmonious, balanced and uplifted moods. What I eat forms who I am. I empower myself by eating foods that nurture and nourish a positive mind.

Today's biggest success:

Food for Thought: You choose your moods by choosing your foods! You no longer have to be held hostage by your moods! A life filled with positivity and good moods starts in your refrigerator and cupboards!

Journal: Have you noticed changes in your emotions and moods since you have changed your eating? Please specify the changes you have seen.

Day 25

What Weights Are You Carrying?
The Weight of Our Emotions

Everything held on to, everything suppressed, everything not allowed to go is a burden. ~OM C. Parkin

Are you carrying too much "weight" on your shoulders? Are you straining with the weight of too many responsibilities? Emotional weights, obligations, duties and responsibilities weigh heavily on us. Stress depletes our body of essential nutrients, triggering food cravings to arise as an attempt to bring the mind-body system into balance. Stress depletes *prana* (life force) and *ojas* (the juice of vitality), *which* triggers our bodies to crave quick, cheap energy from the wrong foods or overeating the right foods. Tension releases brain chemicals, which stimulate overeating. It is important to understand how the weights of the emotions you are carrying translate to physical weight in the body-mind system.

In *Ayurveda* emotions and thoughts are known to carry weight. Feelings are the emotions we *feel* in the body! The *gunas* (3 humors, *rajas, tamas and sattva*) constantly interact with the *doshas* informing and impacting the quality, influence and nature of the emotions we are carrying. *Sattvic* emotions are light, pure and harmonious. *Rajasic* emotions are in flux and ever changing moving between heavy and light, including mood swings.

Tamasic emotions are heavy and dark. These carry the most energetic weight and baggage. When *kapha dosha* is overrun with weighty *tamasic* emotions, the natural density of *kapha* is compounded by dense emotional weight. In other words, heavy *tamasic* emotions imprint themselves on the mind-body system and materialize as excessive weight. After all, the *manomaya kosha* or the "emotional body" layers right over the physical body.

Tamasic kapha emotions are the heaviest emotions and negatively impact physical weight the most. These include dullness, lethargy, boredom, apathy, melancholy, depression, grief, holding grudges, shame and lack of motivation. *Sattvic kapha* emotions include: loyalty, love, affection, kindness and compassion. *Rajasic kapha* is a state of vacillating between the two extremes and would include stubbornness, greed, possessiveness and attachment.

Tamasic pitta emotions include anger, rage, jealousy, envy, control, lust and hatred. Energetically and vibrationally, these emotions carry more weight than *rajasic pitta* emotions such as disgust, judgment, irritation, frustration or desire. *Sattvic pitta* emotions include attraction, passion, curiosity and longing. These are the lightest *pitta* type emotions.

Vata is the lightest *dosha*, therefore *vata* type emotions are the lightest emotions to carry, but they too still vary in weight. Heavy or *tamasic vata* emotions include confusion, uncertainty and fear. Lighter, *Rajasic vata* emotions include forgetfulness, worry, nervousness and excitement. In particular, *sattvic vata* emotions are the lightest and highest vibrating emotions of all. These emotions include unconditional love, joy, inspiration, playfulness, enthusiasm and wonder.

It is important to witness your emotional energy and your thoughts and bring conscious awareness to them. Your thoughts create your emotions. As you learn to witness and to carefully pick and choose your thoughts and emotions as wisely as you pick and choose the foods you eat, you become a conscious participant in how you look, feel and vibrate in the material plane as a physical being. As you become aware of how emotions affect your physical weight, you may choose to release unwanted emotions to release unwanted weight!

Kapha **Emotions** (From heaviest to light)

Tamas: dullness, lethargy, boredom, apathy, melancholy, grief, depression, shame, no motivation.

Rajas: attachment, stubbornness, greed and possessiveness.

Sattva: loyalty, love, affection, kindness and compassion.

Pitta **Emotions** (From heaviest to light)

Tamas: anger, rage, jealousy, envy, control, lust, and hatred.

Rajas: disgust, judgment, irritation, frustration, desire, nosiness and aggression.

Sattva: attraction, assertive, passion, inquisitiveness, longing.

Vata **Emotions** (From heaviest to lightest)

Tamas: confusion, uncertainly, fear, anxiety.

Rajas: excitement, forgetfulness, worry, nervousness.

Sattva: unconditional love, joy, inspiration, playfulness, enthusiasm, and wonder.

Emotion is energy in motion. ~Panache Desai

Heavy emotions are energy that is stagnant or sluggish with little motion due to their mass and weight. Excess weight is not always about what you are eating. Einstein mathematically established the theory of mass-energy equivalence. His equation $E=mc2$ directly connects the mass of an object or person with its energy. This theory states that mass can be converted to energy and energy can be converted to mass. In other words, the weight of the energy you are carrying, is directly proportional to your physical weight.

Are you holding on to heavy emotions such as angst, anger, frustration, resentment, unforgiveness, grief, guilt or shame? Perhaps you are carrying more than your share of the chores at home or at work. Perhaps you have put "too much on your plate." Do you pick up on and carry around other people's heavy emotional burdens for them? Do you take on everyone else's problems as well as your own? When we always take on other's weights and worries, that allows these people to continue to make the same poor choices that landed them there in the first place, instead of gaining an awareness that they need to change.

We energetically stuff heavy emotions down like food right into the center of our being – the belly. Because we cannot digest them, we unconsciously carry them. These undigested emotions show up physically as excess weight and girth right around the tummy and waist. As you process, digest and release the heavy emotional weights you are carrying, your pounds begin to shed away. The longer we carry them around and allow more to accumulate, the heavier we look and feel!

The next layer of emotional energy is where stagnant heavy emotions are being moved, shifted or broken-up. These emotions carry the lighter energy of change, motion and transition as heavy emotions are dislodged from the body-mind. As the emotions are released, our own energy body feels lighter and freer, with the ability to move and flow with ease. This lightness begins to manifest in the physical form. Are you clinging to anything? Regrets, past resentments, guilt, shame anger or even other people's emotional baggage? What do you continue to carry with you that it is time to put down and let go?

There is a Zen story about a group of monks making a long journey. They carried along a boat with them on the journey because they had a great river to cross. Once they crossed the river, they set the boat down and left it behind. Because of their wisdom to leave behind that which was no longer necessary, they continued on their journey with greater ease, lightness and freedom. Are you still carrying the boat even though you crossed a river long ago? What weights can you set down to experience lightness, ease and freedom as you continue the journey of life?

Defeat is not bitter unless you swallow it. ~Joe Clark, former Prime Minister of Canada

By releasing heavy emotions and consciously replacing them with light, high vibrational emotions such as love, peace, joy, compassion, kindness, forgiveness, we begin to let go of excess weight physically and energetically. I like to ask myself, "How would my soul feel without this, lighter or heavier?" How could I choose differently in order to feel "lighter?" Lightness in feeling and emotion becomes lightness in body! Heavy physical weight is a reflection of the heavy emotional weight you have been stuffing down deep inside.

Affirmation: I consciously choose to embrace light emotions that elevate, enliven and liberate me.

Today's biggest success:

Food for Thought: Emotions carry weight. There are heavy and light emotions. We have a choice as to which emotions we nurture and cultivate, and which emotions we release. What can you choose to do differently today that will begin to make you feel lighter?

Journal: Are you aware of any heavy emotions that you may be carrying around. List them here. Awareness is the first step! What light emotions would you like to begin to cultivate more?

Day 26

Emotional Cravings

Do you experience sugar cravings? Crave salty foods? Alcohol? Comfort foods? What are these very different kinds of cravings trying to tell you about your lifestyle? How do you tell if your cravings are coming from true hunger and your body's need for a certain nutrient, or if they are coming from your emotional body's attempt to deal with uncomfortable emotions?

We often crave the answers and solutions for difficult emotions, but take the quick and easy way out and "band-aid" the wound with food! Emotions are intelligent messages from the mind-body system attempting to get your attention for a reason! When we bypass our ability to be with, face and deal with challenging emotions by aestheticizing them with food cravings, it conditions the mind-body system to use food as a "quick fix" rather than facing the problem head on and making the necessary changes in our life and find real solutions. We end up using food as a drug which keeps us stuck where we are! As we continue to numb ourselves to emotions, saving them for later, masking them with food, the weight of these emotions shows up on the physical body.

Doreen Virtue, PhD, an expert in emotional eating, and author of the book *Constant Cravings*, has found that the following emotional issues tend to give rise to food cravings.

- Stress, tension, anxiety, fear or agitation

- Depression, sadness, feeling down or dejected

- Fatigue and low-energy, feeling depleted emotionally or energetically

- Lack of play, joy, excitement or romance

- Anger, resentment, bitterness or frustration

- Emptiness, insecurity, loneliness or need for comforting

Dr. Virtue believes these feelings above boil down to 4 core emotions which are primary triggers for emotional eating: *fear, anger, tension* and *shame*. She uses the acronym *FATS* for these emotions, because they contribute to weight gain. These emotions are asking to be seen, heard, understood, dealt with and released, not pushed down further inside with food. It is important to be aware that these *FATS* emotions can be fed and pacified in ways other than eating.

Dr. Virtue provides a litmus test to determine whether your cravings are arising from actual hunger or emotional triggers. Once you are aware whether your cravings come from emotional triggers, you recognize that you have a choice of how to deal with them, and there are better strategies than coping with food!

Characteristics of Emotional Hunger vs. Physical Hunger: (According to Book *Constant Cravings* by Dr. Doreen Virtue)

1. Sudden- You suddenly find yourself looking in the fridge or the pantry, running to the vending machine or going through the drive-thru. You were never aware of any physical sensation of hunger. This is emotional hunger. I find myself doing this after receiving a disturbing email, or troubling phone call! Physical hunger arises as the stomach rumbles, progresses to emptiness and steadily ramps up eating cues over time to tell you it is time to eat. Physical hunger is *gradual*, emotional hunger is *sudden*.

2. Specific- Emotional hunger is for a specific food. Emotions cause cravings for sweet, salty, crunchy foods and alcohol. You want a specific food and nothing else suffices. Physical hunger on the other hand is **flexible** and **open** since it is the physical sensation of hunger that is being satisfied, rather than an emotion. If you are truly hungry, it doesn't take a specific food to satiate sensations of hungriness.

3. In the head- Emotional hunger begins in the mind and involves the mouth and the taste buds. Emotional hunger has nothing to do with hunger sensations found in the abdomen. Physical hunger is based in the abdomen. It is recognizable by growling, emptiness, burning sensations and cramping in the stomach. Emotional hunger is about distracting the mind with flavor, texture and crunch in the mouth.

4. Elicited by an experience or mood- Emotional eating is set off by something other than hunger. For me it can be an upsetting or uncomfortable encounter with a family member or acquaintance, bickering kids, an overwhelming "to do" list, or just a dreary day. I find myself standing looking in the fridge, with no idea why I am even there! Physical hunger arises from *physical* need: an empty stomach, not boredom, frustration, loneliness, or disappointment.

5. Eating unconsciously- Emotional eating is the kind of eating in which you are not even tasting the food, but just eating mindlessly. It is when you suddenly discover you ate the whole bag of chips or the whole pint of ice-cream, or when you suddenly discover food in your hand and didn't even realize you were eating at all! With physical hunger, you make a conscious choice to eat to satiate the feelings of hunger. Physical hunger causes you to consciously eat until the hunger sensations disappear. For instance, you make a conscious decision to have a second bowl of soup because you still feel hungry.

6. Guilt/shame- These emotions arise after emotional eating, usually because you over-ate, or ate the wrong things. There is no remorse when eating is for purely physical reasons, since eating is necessary.

The first step is awareness that an emotion is there, and what emotion you are feeling. Once you realize there is an emotion behind your food craving, acknowledge it. Allow yourself to witness it and to stay with the uncomfortableness for a bit. You can ask the emotion what message it is attempting to bring you, rather than trying to suppress it. Often when I ask this question, the answer arises and the emotion begins to dissipate without using food.

Which one of the 4 emotions *(fear, anger, tension* and *shame)* is really magnetizing you to the cabinet or refrigerator? Give that emotion your attention. Most of us have programmed ourselves to solve uncomfortable emotions with food. Food becomes a brief distraction, but the same emotion will continue to surface again and again until it is recognized and acknowledged. Stop procrastinating dealing with your emotions with empty calories.

Our senses become diverted by the sight, smell, taste and feel of food. Food it is pleasant and comforting, and emotions can be unpleasant and disquieting. When we place our attention on these pleasant sensations that accompany food we put off feeling our emotions. Food is heavy and grounding (*Kapha*) and emotional responses tend to un-ground us. Studies show that emotions are a chemical reaction in the brain, which last no longer than 90 seconds. Any time beyond the first 90 seconds of experiencing the emotion, it is *you* perpetuating the feeling by stirring up thoughts again and again contributing to recurring chemical reactions in the brain.

9 Ways to Pacify Uncomfortable Emotions Without Using Food

From infancy, we are taught that food solves our worry and stress . . . at least temporarily. Crying babies are immediately soothed with a bottle or a pacifier in their mouths. I remember after getting my childhood immunizations at the doctor's office, I was promptly handed a lollypop. When children are upset, they are instantly plied with cookies, candy, cake or ice cream. We are conditioned from a very young age that food makes everything better! It is no surprise that as adults we go right for the cupboards, refrigerator or even "the bottle" to make ourselves feel better during times of stress and worry. In order to break this cycle of using food to soothe the mood, it takes some powerful, intentional and conscious re-conditioning.

The healing science of *Ayurveda* offers some guilt-free new habits to counter the day-to-day tension and anxiety we experience without using food. In *Ayurveda* we use natural elements and the 5 senses as calorie-free ways to dissolve stress and ease tension and worry. We are already surrounded with ways to calm the nerves without ever using food!

1. Water: This natural element is instantly grounding. It is a heavy substance that tends to "weigh down" the heightened emotions of worry, agitation and nervousness. Try drinking a glass or two of water instead of food for grounding, and notice how food cravings seem to fade.

2. Calming Teas: I like using herbal teas to ease the tensions of the day. Teas hydrate like water, but in addition, their warmth also has a soothing effect to *vata* and *kapha* type emotions. The flavors of the teas are pleasant, so the mind is contented and distracted from worry in the same way as with food without the empty calories. The herbs in calming teas work with the mind-body system to relax the effects of stress. I find the following teas work quite well to ease the tension and stress of the day: chamomile, rose, tulsi, lavender, licorice and kava. There are also some great calming teas on the market using a combination of soothing herbs.

3. Herbs: For more acute tension and stress, naturally calming herbs are a godsend. I keep on hand tulsi, ashwaganda, gotu kola, bacopa, jatamansi, passionflower, and even some *Ayurvedic* herbal compounds when I need to bring out the "big guns" for myself or for my family. A powerful natural *Ayurvedic* nervine/sedative is simply warm organic milk, with nutmeg and saffron. It is great to ease worry, tension and stress at bedtime.

4. Time in nature: Nature immediately relieves tension and stress. The colors, sounds, scents, and textures of the natural world harmonize our mind-body system. After all, humans are a part of nature itself.

The time we spend indoors with electronics or at a desk all day removes us from our true nature and fosters tension, stress and fatigue. Try a walk in the woods, gardening, sitting by a lake, pond or stream, or even just spending time relaxing in your own back-yard to balance the effects of stress.

5. Grounding: Spending time on the earth has become all the rage. This "new" practice of "earthing" is an age-old *Ayurvedic* technique to neutralize worry and stress. This practice involves walking barefoot directly on the earth. Feel the grass, soil, or sand on the souls of your feet and in-between your toes. You can also sit directly on the ground outdoors which also has this same rebalancing effect. This practice works by stabilizing and harmonizing our own energetic field by "plugging-into" the earth's energy field. This works because the earth's natural energy cycles vibrate at the same frequency as the human bio-energetic field. The earth also gives off calming negative ions, which ground the free positive ions in our bodies.

6. Aromatherapy: *Ayurveda* also uses aromatherapy to relax the mid-body system. Try breathing your way to calm with the help of relaxing aromas! Essential oils such as sandalwood, rose, geranium, lavender, frankincense, clary sage, eucalyptus all have a naturally soothing effect on stress.

7. Soothing music: Try some sound therapy to bring about a state of relaxation. Serene, tranquil music has a profound effect on stress and worry and is even proven to affect human beings at the DNA level. Instead of turning on the evening news and heightening your levels of tension, soothe yourself with peaceful sounds. There are some great spa and yoga CDs and Internet music channels out there to calm and relax!

8. A warm bath: The water and warmth of a bath are excellent natural comforting elements helping to ease tension and relax worry away. Even better, add a few drops of essential oil to your bath, sip a cup of calming tea, listen to soothing music and gaze at a candle flame while relaxing in your bath. This works miracles for me!

9. Soft comfortable clothing: In *Ayurveda* anything feeling rough, tight, scratchy or pinchy aggravates tension and creates a subtle sense irritation in the mind-body system. Try changing into yoga clothes or your pajamas, to bring on ease and to soothe your system. Even better, do this after your warm aromatherapy bath.

These suggestions are food-free alternatives to cope with emotional stress that won't work against your health and weight goals. Employ these strategies instead of cookies, chips, ice cream or even a strong cocktail when emotional cravings arise! Your mind and body will thank you!

If you want to fly, you have to give up the things that weigh you down. ~Toni Morrison

Doreen Virtue

A prayer to help you lose unhealthful excess weight:

"One day while I was praying, the healing angel Archangel Raphael came to me and taught me this amazing method which works wonders in rapidly and healthfully releasing excess weight:

First, close your eyes in a quiet place and breathe deeply. Focus upon the excess weight and hold the intention of having a conversation with it. Silently ask the excess weight: "Why are you with me? What purpose are you serving?"

Listen to the answer, which may surprise you. Most likely, the excess weight will tell you that it's trying to protect you from something.

Ask the excess weight: "What are you trying to protect me from?"

Next, say to the excess weight:

"Thank you for your offer to protect me. I appreciate your help. From now on, though, I will protect myself without your help. You are now free to leave in a peacefully and healthfully. Thank you."

You will feel lighter after this conversation, because you'll no longer carry anger about the excess weight. You will have compassion for yourself and the weight.

Notice how your appetite shifts to more healthful foods, and how you feel more motivated to exercise afterward. Notice how you begin to have the courage and strength to stand-up for and protect yourself in assertive and healthful ways. The excess weight will gently fall away because you no longer need it for your protection."

Affirmation: I easily and effortless differentiate emotional cravings from physical hunger. I satiate hunger with food, and I satisfy emotional cravings by being soft and gentle to myself.

Today's biggest success:

Food for Thought: Emotions cause cravings. But cultivating awareness of our bodily sensations and the telltale signs of emotional cravings, we can differentiate the two, and satisfy them both in a compassionate, appropriate way.

Journal: Are you now more aware of times when you were not physically hungry, but ate to disconnect from or push down difficult emotions? What emotions tend to be triggers for you? How will you handle emotional triggers from now on?

Day 27

The Power of Letting Go

Knowledge is learning something every day. Wisdom is letting go of something every day. ~Zen Proverb

Are you putting pressure on yourself to be a perfect weight? To have a flawless body? To have the textbook family, the picture-perfect career, or to be a flawless person? Are you attached to a certain number on the scales? Are you relentlessly striving to fit into jeans with a certain size sewn on the tag? If you are, you are weighing yourself down mentally and emotionally. You are carrying too much weight in the energy body, the emotional body, as in the physical body. PRESSURE is weight! When we carry weight in our energy fields, it manifests as substance and matter, which appears as weight on the physical frame. When what you are doing is not working, it is time to try something else.

As I have said before, I know this because I was caught up in this insanity myself for a period of time. After gaining 40 pounds when pregnant with my son, I expected the weight just to come right off! It did not budge! Feeling very self-conscious, I began to exercise 3 weeks after he was born. When the weight didn't budge, I exercised harder. When it still didn't move, I exercised longer. When that still didn't work, I found myself at the gym 2-3 hours a day. I was one exhausted young mom, and still carrying around that extra weight! Finally, it dawned on me that what I was doing was not working! I realized I had to try something else! I revamped my regime to only practicing yoga, making changes in the kitchen instead of the gym, and spending more time enjoying and playing with my little one! This shift not only brought me increased joy and lightness and without pressure, but it catapulted me out of the struggle and battle I was engaged in warring with the extra weight! As I released my attachment to the weight and to results, this was the turning point at which the weight started to go! Moreover, I was enjoying being a mom more and felt more satisfied with my life! Letting go of the battle allowed me to let go of the weight!

Are you putting undue pressure on yourself to be a certain weight or size? Are you battling against yourself instead of befriending yourself? Western culture has conditioned us to believe that our weight and size must be a battle. We are taught that if we don't have the perfect bikini body or the washboard abs, that we must battle our way to a Hollywood airbrushed figure! This whole concept steals the joy from thousands even millions of lives every year! Are you clinging to Hollywood 's artificial Barbie doll ideas of how you should look? Is this really the healthiest version of yourself or anyone for that matter?

Holding on, clinging and hoarding of any-kind is a *kapha* tendency. *Kapha dosha* is the *dosha* of earth, substance and matter. The nature of *kapha* is density. When we increase *kapha* in the energy body, we manifest *kapha* or density in the physical body as well. Holding on can apply to anything! We cling to people, stuff, old ideas, beliefs and habits. We attach to comfortable ways of doing things, conditioned behaviors, and even difficult emotions.

Ayurveda specialist John Douillard puts it like this, "The most dangerous cancer-causing toxins are fat soluble – and can be stored in your fat cells for up to 20 years. In the name of survival, stress also produces molecules of toxic emotion that are stored in the fat cells." Carrying around toxic emotions like anger, resentment, bitterness, hatred, sadness, depression, worry, anxiety, grudges and unforgiveness cause you to become heavy and weighted down in the energy body. When we are carrying weight in the energy field, it materializes as weight in the physical body.

What weights are you carrying around with you? The weight of old toxic emotions is like carrying a heavy stone. Imagine if you will, that a heavy stone is strapped to your back. You are then forced to carry this stone around with you as you go about your daily activities. As you prepare meals, run errands or do chores, the stone weighs you down. As you work, the stone is with you. As you exercise, play sports, and participate in your favorite activities, the stone is still there weighing you down, even if you aren't always aware of it being there. This is exactly what it is like to carry around toxic emotions embedded in your energy body.

The pelvis is like a bowl or basket. When we swallow down our heavy emotions, they are held and accumulated in the pelvic bowl. When we carry around this heavy energy, we materialize its weight in the hips and abdomen, right where we are carrying it. Once you begin releasing these and letting them go, the emotional body becomes lighter, the spirit becomes lighter, and the physical body as a result also becomes lighter. What are you holding on to? What are you keeping that you no longer need?

Sometimes you don't realize the weight of something you've been carrying until you feel the weight of its release.

~Unknown

I vividly remember bumping into a friend, who appeared to have lost a good amount of weight in a short period of time. Being interested in weight-loss and health, I couldn't help but ask how she lost the extra weight. Her answer was surprising. She said "I have always eaten pretty healthy, that hasn't changed. What did change was that I started to let my "stuff" go. Once I let go of some old issues, the weight just came off on its own. There was no diet, there was just a "letting go."

Sometimes we get overly attached to lifestyle choices that aren't working in favor of our optimal health and weight. Are you holding on to old eating patterns and habits? Do you cling to habits and lifestyle choices that do not serve your body mind or soul? Some of us cling to the pattern of overindulging on the weekends, or binge eating at night. Perhaps you are attached to heavy drinking or partying all weekend, or even to your regular evening cocktails. Do these choices show up on you as unwanted weight?

Inspired by a post I saw recently, I have decided that during Lent I will choose at least one item each day to "let go" of, collect for the 40 Days, and then pass on to the less fortunate. I felt this was a meaningful way to practice letting-go and to observe Lent at the same time! The idea of cleaning out the closets, junk drawer, basement or garage is overwhelming to me, but just one thing per day, makes it more doable. And so far, the practice has been quite joyful! This process perfectly mirrors what I am trying to accomplish in the **40 Days to Enlightened Eating**! We make small changes *every day*, which add up over time!

Letting go is an act of spiritual growth. The more you release, the lighter your spirit. Beyond all the material stuff that overcrowds our homes and our lives, we also carry excess baggage energetically, emotionally and physically. It drains our energy to keep carrying things that no longer apply, serve or inspire us. Somehow, we forget that we can also set aside the patterns and conditioning that has been working against our highest good. By letting go, you set yourself free. You become free of unnecessary energetic weight, becoming lighter and better able to serve your soul's highest purpose with ease. But how do you know what to let go of? The following are 10 things we ALL need to set down. If you let go of just one thing, you will feel a little more freedom and lightness. If you let go of all 10, you will be liberated!

10 Things we ALL Need to Let Go of NOW:

1. Control: Release trying, striving, forcing, pushing, and struggling. What is meant to come to you will arise spontaneously, but only if you first get out of the way! Releasing control, and trusting God, the Universe or Source to move the right things at the right moments is an act of faith and a powerful step towards spiritual growth.

2. Your Past: So many folks allow their past to tarnish the present and future. They hold on to resentment, regret, guilt, anger and victimhood. They cling tightly to antiquated fears, perceptions, opinions and view-points. They cling to an old number on the scales, or their "skinny jeans!" Life takes place only in the **now**. It is time to hit the "delete" button and free yourself from the burden of your past. Do not let the past weigh you down for another day. It is gone from the reality of NOW. Start from where you are and you are free.

3. Fears: Fear causes contraction, confusion and avoidance. Fear is paralyzing. It keeps you stuck right where you are. It is said that everything you want is on the other side of fear. The only way to become liberated *from* fear is *through* fear. Fear is almost always a figment of your imagination. Fear is a thought, not a reality. Confront what scares you, and stare it down. What is your biggest fear? Mine is public speaking. Make it a point to do whatever it is you're afraid of. On the other side of fear is freedom.

4. Attachment to results: Much of what we do is in expectation of a specific outcome. We hope to get a "pay-off" or achieve something for our efforts. Herein, we are often disappointed and resentful. When we do not receive the praises, accomplishments, or achievements we think we deserve, we conclude we have failed. However, when we do the right thing without attachment to outcome, that act becomes sacred. This includes the act of healthy eating for the body, mind and soul! Letting go of results of our positive eating changes, sets our actions free from acquiring, obtaining, or any other objective. The actions become pure and light, not weighted down by expectations! "Without concern for results, perform the necessary action; surrendering all attachments, accomplish life's highest good." *~Bhagavad Gita*

5. Toxins: Detoxify your diet. Detoxify your life of people, events, situations, television shows, news media or even a career that carries toxic energy. Detoxify yourself of negative emotions such as fear, guilt, greed, anger, hatred and jealousy. Detoxify your energy field. Many of us are unaware of the energetic toxins we unintentionally pick up every day.

We accumulate and carry these heavy, negative energies around with us like dead weight. It is very important to detoxify your energy field of unhealthy vibrations, which do not serve you. No different than going on a dietary cleanse to rid the bodily organs and tissues of toxins, you can also purge your *life*. Don't just detoxify one aspect of who you are; but detoxify on *every level* as the catalyst to spiritual growth and the path to inner peace.

6. **Judging:** Let go of judging. When you judge others, you are judging and rejecting parts of yourself. What you dislike in others is simply a mirror of the parts of yourself that you refuse to see and accept. When you are unable to accept others, it signals that you do not accept your "Self." By letting go of judgment, you are saying "yes" to acceptance. Self-acceptance is embracing the dark and the light of who you are. When you let go of judgment, not only are you giving others permission to be who they are, but you are embracing all of who you are. It is only by embracing rather than rejecting all aspects of who you are, that you can move closer to your highest self.

7. **Who you're not:** What parts of you do not belong? Swami Kripalu's teacher said, "Whatever is there, throw it out, burn it out, cut it out, and that which remains is YOU." What parts of you are authentic? What parts are there to impress others? What masks do you wear to hide who you really are from yourself and from the world? What stories do you tell yourself about you? What parts of you are just sound bites from your past, replaying over and over in your mind? It is only when we learn to ignore and silence the voice of the ego, that we can hear the whispers of the authentic Self. Now is the time to throw out the costumes we've been concealing ourselves under and bare our souls unashamed. I have found that the bigger your insecurities, the greater your inner radiance really is. The ego works hard to muscle control over you to stay in charge. It does this by tearing you down with the messages "I am not good enough." and "I am not worthy." The amount of self-doubt and insecurity you have to overcome, correlates directly with your true greatness. The push and pull of these forces are even. In truth, we are all good enough and we are all worthy. Letting go of who we're not, is not a luxury; it's a birthright!

8. **Resistance:** When we reject what life brings us, we go "to war" with what **is**. We wrestle with denial and struggle against reality. Struggle and denial do not make what is there "go away," it just makes it push back harder. Imagine a game of "tug of war." Each team struggles back and forth to muscle their way to victory. If evenly matched, the struggle can go on and on. If one side simply "let's go," the other side tumbles to the ground by the sheer force of their own momentum. GAME OVER! When we intentionally choose to let go and lean in to what is there, whether it is pain,

loneliness, illness, grief, financial struggles, struggles with our weight, etc. the game is suddenly over. Acceptance is the eternal victor. Once we learn to embrace life just as it is, the struggle is gone. Pema Chodron teaches, "What we resist, stays."

9. The "glorification of busy": Are you stuck on the hamster wheel of life? "You can do anything you want, but not everything!" Inner peace is the new busy! Instead of over planning and overscheduling your family and yourself, schedule moments of inner peace. Let go of the need to be constantly occupied. The Tao Te Ching teaches, "When your cup is full; stop pouring." It is the very people who have a propensity to overload their lives, are also the ones who have the propensity to overload their plates and overfill their bellies. This is patterning in the body-mind system. Let go of the need to pile on task after task, event after event, overflowing your cup and making a mess of your life. Busy is "out" and peace is "in." Browse your daily schedule or list of "to-dos." Determine what is unnecessary. Scratch off the things that you can let go. First focus on the things you want to do, and keep those. Then focus on the things you absolutely *have* to do and leave those. What is left can be released. Use this open space to schedule rest and peace. When you lighten up on your life, you lighten up in your physical being as well. The inner always reflects the outer!

10. Going it alone: "We are all here to walk each other home." Our separation is a construct of the limited mind. Once we recognize that we are brothers and sisters on this earth, and we share in this existence together, we realize there is no need to go it alone. Help others. Serve others. Bilaterally, don't be resistant to asking for and accepting that same help when you need it. When you ask for help, the Universe, God and all that is good sweeps in at once to assist you. My favorite aspect of sharing the *40 Days to Enlightened Eating* as a class, is that we lean on the entire group for support. It has been said over and over by my students how much that group support empowers them on their 40 Day journey! The support of the group helps me as much as anyone, and I wrote the book!

Each of us is attached in some way to ancient outdated conditioning. This obsolete patterning works against us in becoming the best version of ourselves. It is time for a new paradigm. We can choose our own world, our own life, our own story and our own way. We must sift through all of who we are and discern what is conditioning and what is Truth. By letting go of things that do not serve our highest good, we change our own experience. "Letting go" invites joy, freedom, lightness and fulfillment. Let go of all 10 above, and become weightless! By giving up what no longer works, you move out of the way of the flow of grace. You open yourself up to unknown blessings. Letting go, sparks the fire of the miraculous.

By letting go, it all gets done. ~Lao Tzu

She Let Go

By Rev. Safire Rose

She let go. Without a thought or a word, she let go.

She let go of the fear. She let go of the judgments. She let go of the confluence of opinions swarming around her head. She let go of the committee of indecision within her. She let go of all the 'right' reasons. Wholly and completely, without hesitation or worry, she just let go.

She didn't ask anyone for advice. She didn't read a book on *how to let go*. She didn't search the scriptures. She just let go. She let go of all of the memories that held her back. She let go of all of the anxiety that kept her from moving forward. She let go of the planning and all of the calculations about how to do it just right.

She didn't promise to let go. She didn't journal about it. She didn't write the projected date in her Day-Timer. She made no public announcement and put no ad in the paper. She didn't check the weather report or read her daily horoscope. *She just let go.*

She didn't analyze whether she should let go. She didn't call her friends to discuss the matter. She didn't do a five-step Spiritual Mind Treatment. She didn't call the prayer line. She didn't utter one word. She just let go.

No one was around when it happened. There was no applause or congratulations. No one thanked her or praised her. No one noticed a thing. Like a leaf falling from a tree, she just let go

There was no effort. There was no struggle. It wasn't good and it wasn't bad. It was what it was, and it is just that.

In the space of letting go, she let it all be. A small smile came over her face. A light breeze blew through her. And the sun and the moon shone forevermore.

Energy Experiment: Lug a heavy stone around with you for just 10 minutes as you do household tasks. Notice how much it weighs you down and how tired you feel and how much less you are able to accomplish while carrying it around. Old habits, attachments and emotions are no different than this stone, even if you are unaware.

Letting go Jar: Take an empty jar with lid. Cut a slit in the lid with a knife. Tape a note on the jar and label it the "Letting go Jar". Take used computer paper and recycle it cut it into strips. Keep the strips of paper beside the jar. Every time you think of something you need to let go of, write it on a slip of paper and drop it into the jar.

Affirmation: Today I will stop judging myself by the number on the scale or the fit of my jeans, and instead go by the radiance of my soul and how good I feel in my own skin!

Today's biggest success:

Food for Thought: Let go of anything that has been "weighing you down," including attachment to a number on the scales. The scales do not measure the beauty of your soul or the weightlessness and freedom of your spirit. Say hello to "lighter" energies and emotions like love, acceptance and bliss by saying "goodbye" to all that no longer serves you.

Journal: What is your soul inviting you to let go of right now? Examine your attachment to outcomes, emotions, and your obligations and responsibilities. What can you release to make you feel lighter body, mind and soul? What can you take off your calendar? What can you take off your mind? What pressures are you putting on yourself that you are ready to set down?

Day 28

What Are You Feeding Your Mind?

The busier we are, the more stress on us. More stress on the mind equals more stress on the body. ~Dr. Mark Halpern

In *Ayurveda*, the stomach and intestines are not the only organs we feed and they are not the only parts of the body that digest. The mind is also a digestive organ. It feeds upon what it sees, hears, tastes, smells and touches. The mind is fed through the 5 senses, the thoughts and emotions. The mind digests and assimilates thoughts, emotions, experiences, and sensory input.

We are bombarded daily with bad news, gossip, rumors, hyped-up fear, drama, confusion, turmoil, fright and horror. It comes from news outlets, social media, Internet, radio, entertainment, video games, television, and film. Our minds are literally blasted with sensory garbage. By our constant exposure, we have become habituated to, and saturated in mental disharmony, tension and discord when our true natural state is joy, positivity and bliss. As a culture, we are unintentionally feeding our mind a "junk food" diet in the same way we have been feeding the physical body! Junk in, equals junk out!

Yoga and *Ayurveda* teach that the mind is not just inside the head or brain. The *manomaya kosha* or mental/emotional body layers right over the physical body. This is why we can actually "feel" thoughts and emotions physically. When we feed the *manomaya kosha* a diet of mental, emotional or energetic toxins, we "toxify" our whole being and poison our lives! The good news is that as easily as we can make healthy food choices for the body, we can also make healthy "food" choices for the mind. What we feed the mind, nourishes the soul!

Rather than feasting on the evening news, the latest horror film, trashy TV programs, gossip magazines, tabloids, degrading music, violent video games or a gruesome crime show, you can make healthy "food" choices for the mind. The following are some suggestions to replace unwholesome sensory "food" in ways that nourish the mind into optimal health and harmony:

1. Feast your eyes on beauty: According to the healing science of *Ayurveda*, beauty has profound healing effects on the entire mind-body system. In *Ayurveda*, we prescribe spending time with beauty because it is inherently balancing, healing and harmonizing to the mind-body system. De-clutter your home and office, and opt to make your living space neat, clean, positive and friendly. Decorate in a way that brings you JOY and uplifts your senses. Choose pictures, plants, paintings, pillows, and rugs with the intention of surrounding yourself with beauty. Use paint colors that make you feel happy and calm. Dinner always tastes better on a beautiful plate, and tea always tastes better in a beautiful cup! Make your surroundings uplifting and therapeutic!

2. Delight in nature: Being in nature is innately therapeutic. It eases and restores the mind. Through the senses, we are able to draw upon the soothing sounds, scents and colors of the water, wind, grass, birds, trees and flowers. We can soak in the healing rays of the sun (not to mention some vitamin D!) We become harmonized, grounded and tranquil when we reconnect with nature. Humans are a part of nature and humankind began immersed in nature. Only in the past 200 years, have we lost touch with this integral part of our being. It is important to return to the source from which we came, and reconnect with who we really are. Spend time in the beauty of nature: by a pond, in the woods, in the mountains, or by the ocean. You don't have to "do" anything but allow the beauty surrounding you to do its powerful healing work automatically. The healing effects from the beauty of nature are well documented and quite profound.

3. Devour harmonious sound: Sound is vibration. As vibrational beings ourselves, whatever sounds we surround ourselves with, cause our own being to vibrate at that frequency, and we become one with that vibration. There are tiny bones in the inner ear that vibrate along with the sound waves as they enter the ear canal. These vibrations are carried to the auditory cortex of the brain where the vibrations are translated into sound. These sounds are then assigned meaning, whether they are words, song lyrics, music, etc. The meaning then evokes an emotional response or even a memory. The sounds we feed our mind can either heal it or disturb it. Disharmonious sounds, loud noise or distasteful words bring about stress response. Think about being outside enjoying the sounds of the birds, when suddenly a neighbor starts up his lawnmower. Even though you are not frightened, the sound shifts your energy and mood. You mind responds instantly to whatever sound it is fed. Harmonious sounds are calming to the mind, and shift the nervous system into relaxation response. You can consciously choose a "sound diet" that will promote wellbeing. Experiment with listening to the sounds of nature such as chirping birds, a rain shower, a waterfall, rainforest sounds, or the echoes of whales. There are apps for these sounds. Also healing to the mind are soft melodious music, rhythmic drumming, mantra, chanting, singing bowls and positive affirmations.

There are studies in which a plate of sand is placed in a soundproof room with someone playing music, chanting Sanskrit mantra, or just saying a random word such as "pencil." The vibrations of melodious music, and Sanskrit mantra, cause the sand to vibrate and form beautiful, geometrically pleasing "snowflake" like mandalas. The other less pleasant sounds do not have this effect. I have placed an indoor water fountain in the main area of our home to bring the therapeutic sounds of nature indoors. Ultimately, silence is the most healing sound of all as it allows you to hear your own inner music. To reset your nervous system, experiment with turning off the TV and replacing the chatter with soothing sounds or even healing silence.

4. Ingest aromatherapy: It has been said that we "eat" with the nose before we eat with the mouth. It is no secret that realtors use the scent of baking cookies to sell houses, and it works. The mind responds powerfully to uplifting harmonious scents. Alternately, the mind is repulsed by spoiled or charred foods, or pungent smells. Aromatherapy is a powerful tool to heal and harmonize the mind body system and has been used in *Ayurvedic* treatments for millennia to balance and harmonize the *doshas*. Using essential oils, the mind can be uplifted, steadied, calmed or grounded as needed. According to Holistic Health Psychologist and Aroma-therapist Christina Wilke-Burbach PhD, "As a physical representation of the five elements (soil-earth, sun-fire, rain-water, wind-air, essence-spirit), essential oils are truly some of the most powerful healing gifts from nature. Aromatherapy is the therapeutic use of essential oils for health and wellness. Aromatherapy can quickly and effectively impact mood, emotions, mental states, and cognitions. Aromas can evoke memories, bring about happiness, joy, and peace, reduce stress and anxiety, and assist with feelings of well-being. Essential oils are easy to use and can be inhaled right out of the bottle, on tissues or cotton pads, in nasal inhalers, and in diffusers. By healing and bringing balance to the mental body, we subsequently heal the physical body and spirit."

5. Savor and balance taste: The science of *Ayurveda* acknowledges 6 tastes, and is very specific about the effects each taste has on the mind. The 6 tastes are sweet, salty, sour, bitter, pungent and astringent. Sweet taste tends to bring out the "sweet emotions" such as contentment, pleasure, joy and love. This is why we crave sweets when we are feeling stress and strain. Salty taste brings about a sense of warming and grounding since salt is an earth mineral. Emotionally, it is said to increase a "zest for life" and cultivate confidence and courage. Sour taste if overdone, is said to bring about a "sour" disposition. Bitter taste in excess can create a sense of bitterness, loneliness and grief. Pungent taste is stimulating, but in excess it can cause restlessness and agitation. Astringent taste in excess can aggravate fear and anxiety. It is important and necessary to eat each of these tastes in balance to keep the emotions in balance.

6. Healing Touch: The sense of touch directly informs our mental states. We all cringe at the thought of rough, scratchy clothing or too-tight jeans. *Ayurveda* teaches that uncomfortable clothing agitates and aggravates the mind-body system. Pain instantly affects our mood and over time can lead to depression. On the other hand, massage, hugs, caresses, and soft comfortable clothing bring about pleasant sensations and pleasant moods along with them. With nourishing touch, the body releases endorphins, *Ayurveda* employs the healing power of touch as an integral part of the healing system with practices like *snehana,* applying warm oils to the body, *abhyanga*, self-massage with oil, and *shirodhara,* the practice of pouring warm oil over the 3rd eye center of the forehead. Giving and receiving hugs is a sweet way of giving and receiving healing touch!

7. Savor sweet emotions: We have the capacity to choose on which emotions to focus, concentrate or fixate, whether positive or negative. It is up to us whether we choose to cling to fear, doubt, jealousy, anger or hatred, or release them to dissolve into the ethers. A balanced and blissful mind is fed with daily joy, love, peace, contentment, kindness, hope and humor. Often, it is the events, practices, and actions you choose to expose yourself to, which evoke these pleasant or unpleasant emotions. Before welcoming a certain situation or event into your life, assess what emotional toll or benefit will result. A strong mind is nourished and nurtured by digesting sweet emotions!

8. Baste in positivity: This world doesn't need any more negativity! What we need is to find the doorways to the positivity that is already there hidden beneath the tragedy and pessimism that we are immersed in! It is time to walk through the doors of gladness and leave the gloom behind! Here are some ways to cultivate a beautiful, harmonious, vibrant and healthy mind through the power of positivity. Read positive quotes and say positive affirmations. Do not over-indulge a negative thought. Deepak Chopra suggests saying, "Next!" when a negative thought arises, to remind yourself to move on to another thought. When you become aware of negative thinking, you can either befriend it or ignore it. As the Native Americans say, "There are two wolfs within us, a dark wolf and a white wolf. The wolf you feed, is the one you strengthen." When I notice my thoughts have drifted towards the dark wolf, I consciously redirect them to a more agreeable place.

If the mind is well-nourished and in a harmonious state, it is much better equipped to deal with unpleasant experiences when they arise with balance and resilience. A robust and healthy mind has a much greater capacity to digest disagreeable experiences that are inevitable and emerge unscathed. A mind that is regularly fed a diet of unpalatable and disharmonious sensory experiences is more likely to become disturbed, distraught or unhinged. What you feed the mind determines the strength of the mind and your state of mental health; just as what you feed your body determines your physical health.

Ayurveda also emphasizes the importance of harmonious sensory and thought intake along with your food during your meals. Remember that it is essential for the proper digestion of foods to avoid arguing, disturbing conversations, or controversy during meals. It is essential to avoid, frightening or unsettling TV programs or music. It is said that when combined with negative or disharmonious emotions or sensory input during meals, foods poorly digest and become rancid in the gastrointestinal tract, diminishing the quality and energy of even the healthiest foods. It is best to eat in silence or amidst calm, wholesome conversation to fully receive the benefits of a nourishing meal. I just recently experienced this personally. After eating dinner, I put on a historical television show on PBS. There were sordid bloody scenes I was not expecting, and I began to feel ill. My digestion felt off and my tummy began to cramp and feel bloated and uncomfortable. This uncomfortable feeling continued for 3 days every time I ate, as if my body was still trying to digest the scenes I took in along with my dinner. I won't make this mistake again! Whatever sensory input is going on around you while eating is digested along with your food.

Affirmation: Today, I "feed" my mind healthy positive thoughts, images, and sounds. What my mind digests and assimilates feeds my soul.

Today's biggest success:

Food for Thought: Begin to pay attention to how you feed you mind. Notice what your mind feeds upon, through sensory input, thoughts, moods, emotions and mental state. You are what you eat! Not unlike the physical body, you empower the mind to be strong, balanced healthy and resilient by feeding it wholesome "food."

Journal: Does your mind need to be put on a cleanse or detox? Have you been feeding your mind in disharmonious ways? What are some ways you can begin cleansing and improving your mental diet to cultivate a more wholesome, balanced and *sattvic* mind?

Day 29

High Vibrational Eating and Exercise

Eating food that is filled with preservatives is like eating a mummy! It may still look like food on the outside, but inside it contains no life-force! ~Elise Cantrell

In the modern era, eating and food have become a huge source of confusion, stress, struggle, control, judgment, profit and deception. Human beings now harbor all sorts of emotional energy and bewilderment when it comes to diet. Something as basic and simple as eating and food have become an over-complicated source of anxiety, fear and paranoia. Our most fundamental need for survival has become contaminated by these lower emotional energies we have connected with it. How do we elevate eating back up to the higher octaves of self-nourishment, nurturing, healing and sustenance it was intended to be?

Among the spiritually minded, there has been much emphasis in recent years on raising one's vibration or frequency. Raising your own vibrational frequency better attunes you to higher consciousness, your highest self, superior states of living and being and brings you in closer resonance with God or Source. At a higher vibration, you are attuned more closely to higher energies and forces such as love, joy, peace and light. At high frequencies, you are able to effortlessly and regularly experience harmony, synchronicity, miracles, balance, clarity, insight, intuition, creativity, contentment, health and ease. When we are out of sync with these higher energetic signatures, we resonate with the vibration of lower energies such as discord, difficulties, worries, malaise, illness, confusion, struggle, doubt, fear, discontentment, irritation, anger, guilt, shame and so on. These frequencies are the result of lower, denser, heavier energies.

Albert Einstein proved that everything in the universe is made up of energy and vibration, including human beings. Raising the vibration of anything can be likened to moving to a higher octave in music. Music is also vibration. Low notes are often associated with sadness, doom and gloom. These notes are heavy and dark and are used in movie and television soundtracks to project the idea and experience of darker heavier emotions. The higher notes are lighter and happier. Musically, they inspire feelings of joy and delight. These higher notes have a higher vibration and resonate at a higher frequency. Humans are energetic beings; we too are vibrational. We can choose to raise our entire life, being and consciousness up an octave . . . or two! As many of us strive towards a higher frequency, we often overlook our relationship with eating and food. Food plays a pivotal role in how low or high we resonate. After all, food is energy; energy is vibration, and food's energy directly imparts its vibration into us as we ingest it. What we eat is incorporated fully into our being. What we eat, we become. How can we come to eating and food in a way that lifts us up to greater heights?

1. Eat for contentment and satiety. When eating, avoid deprivation, hungering, denial, or dietary rigidity and harsh expectations. These create the vibration of guilt, judgment, disgust, lack and scarcity. Eating should be a joyful experience! When it becomes self-punishment, it lowers our vibration.

2. Eat with simplicity. Go back to nature. Choose simple easy recipes, using a few wholesome, real ingredients. Healthy eating does not have to be stressful or complex. Keep it simple and easy. Ease is a high vibration.

3. Decrease or eliminate alcohol. Alcohol has a low vibration. It is a *depressant* that resonates with sadness, depression, loneliness, confusion, numbness and clouded thinking. These are not higher energies. When you ingest alcohol, you become these energies.

4. Decrease or eliminate fermented foods. Fermented foods are decomposing and in the process of decay. In *Ayurvedic* science, fermented foods are considered *tamasic* (dark, dull, and heavy energetically) because they bring about this same energy of decay into the mind-body system. For a higher vibration, opt for the freshest foods possible!

5. Eliminate factory-farmed meat. The energy of poorly treated or abused animals is directly imparted into our being as we ingest them. Einstein proved, energy can neither be created nor destroyed. When you ingest these foods, you ingest these energies. For a higher vibration, opt for free-range, grass fed, cruelty-free meat. Animals who have lived a content, safe and happy life carry a much higher vibration energetically. To raise your vibration even higher, decrease or eliminate meat all-together. *Ayurvedic* science teaches that by ingesting an animal, you yourself take on a lower, animal-like nature rather than higher consciousness and high vibration.

6. Avoid processed, foods, fast foods and junk foods. These foods do not carry ANY energy, and they deplete us of ours. These foods vibrate with toxicity, heaviness, lethargy, dullness and clouded thinking. They are the quickest and surest way to lower your vibration, because they are neither real nor living. By eating junk, you are treating your body-mind system like junk. Treating your body-mind as less than the miracle that it is, lowers your entire vibration.

7. Avoid GMO foods. The genes of viruses and bacteria are inserted into the DNA of natural foods. Viruses and bacteria attack and destroy. They bring this same energy into the foods they have been spliced into. The plants these genes are inserted into, are designed to attack and destroy any insects feeding on them. These adulterated plants also attack and harm the human gut, DNA and cellular structure. When nature is allowed to exist in its purest form, the vibration is always higher. Natural foods are inherently safe for insects and humans.

8. Avoid chemicals! Artificial colors, flavors are an effort to fool the eyes and tongue into thinking what you are eating is a real food. Preservatives trick the natural biological process of decay. Deception is always a lower vibration. By interfering with the natural decomposition process with preservatives, you are eating old foods, that otherwise would have decayed if chemicals were not present. The fresher our food, the fresher we feel! Would you rather vibrate with the energy of freshness, health and vibrancy, or that of something old and preserved? Avoid foods sprayed with weed-killers, insecticides, and pesticides. These toxic chemicals vibrate with the energy of toxicity and death. Death is a state of no energy or vibration at all!

9. Eat with joy! Eating must bring joy to your kitchen and pleasure to your taste buds. Joy and pleasure are among the highest vibrations! Many people think that in order to lose weight, their food must be dull and bland! This never works in the long run! When you truly enjoy what you are eating, your vibration matches that of JOY!

10. Consume more super foods. These foods are packed with the highest level of nutrition and nourishment. These foods are Mother Nature's vitamin pill, vibrating with life, nutrients and health! These foods are potent with energy and life-force!

11. Let foods be your vitamins. Instead of taking laboratory created synthetic vitamin pills, let food be your vitamin! Do not let artificial vitamins replace the natural ones present in the optimal form, balance, combination and quantity in whole living foods. Eat nutrient dense foods, which provide a wealth of vitamins, minerals, antioxidants, micro-nutrients, plant enzymes, and phytonutrients and get much more life, health, energy and vibrancy than you can out of a bottle of laboratory created supplements.

12. Drink more pure, fresh water. Spring water is ideal. Avoid water in plastic water bottles, which is lifeless and stale, and the harmful chemicals from the bottles leach into the water. Avoid polluted, chemically treated or fluoridated water, which vibrates with toxicity. Toxins carry a low vibration. Purity and freshness is always the highest vibration. My pets intuitively avoid water that isn't pure or fresh, and so should we!

13. Reiki your meals and water. Charge you food and water with Reiki to raise your vibration. Reiki energy is high-vibrational, healing, "divine life-force energy!" Even if you are not attuned to Reiki, the intention of infusing your food and water with healing energy alone will work wonders vibrationally! Water is a conductor of energy and it will quickly and easily take on and conduct whatever kind of energy that it has been charged with!

14. Pray and bless your food before eating. Dr. Masaru Emoto made his life work the study on the effects of prayers, blessings and kind words vs. negative sentiments, expletives, curses on water and food. This difference is astounding! Food that was prayed over didn't decay or rot, and food that was cursed, became moldy and black! The entire structure of water molecules changes just from the power of words! Since antiquity, cultures and creeds from all over the world, have made praying over and blessing their food a regular practice. Blessings and prayers raise the vibration of the food which is then transmitted to you when you eat it!

15. Cook with love and JOY! The energy of the chef transmits into the food being prepared. This is why food prepared by someone who loves to cook tastes much better than food prepared by someone who thinks of cooking as a chore, even when they are following the same recipe to the letter! Never cook in a state of anger or a bad mood, and make sure you dine in restaurants in where the chefs take joy and pride in the foods they prepare. Fast-foods have a particularly low vibration as they are prepared in a hurry, by someone paid low-wages and the job is not a career path chosen for the love of cooking.

16. Eat in a harmonious setting. Is there arguing at the dinner table, or are you digesting your meal while you are digesting the daily horrors reported on the evening news? When we digest our food, we are digesting every experience that energetically accompanies it. Raise your vibration by consciously bringing harmonious energy to your snacks and meals. Meals should be accompanied by light pleasant conversation, silence or soft melodious music. Avoid harsh or negative energies anytime you eat to avoid lowering your vibration.

17. Eat organics. These foods are grown by farmers committed to using only natural methods, free of toxic chemicals and free of patented seeds that have been genetically altered by the biotech industry. Only natural growing and harvesting practices are used. These methods are in alignment with nature and with the health of the environment. Any farming methods that harm the environment, or contaminate the food vibrate at lower frequencies.

18. Pay attention to what you feed your skin. Are you slathering your skin with artificial ingredients, synthetic fragrances, petrochemicals, or a list of ingredients that reads like a chemistry set? Your skin ingests whatever you put on it by *drinking* it in through the pores. The skin is often used as transdermal delivery system of medicines and herbs because through the skin they quickly and effectively bypass the digestive tract and immediately enter the blood stream. What you are feeding your skin is feeding you. Opt for ingredients that you wouldn't mind eating. The ingredients that you feed your skin should vibrate as high as anything you swallow.

19. Pay attention to what you feed your mind. The mind also digests. It is fed through the 5 senses. Whatever sensory experience you are immersing yourself in energetically, is what is nourishing or poisoning your mind! If you would like to have joy filled, harmonious and uplifting thoughts, emotions and nighttime dreams, then you must intentionally feed the mind with harmonious images, sounds, sensations, tastes and aromas of the same high vibrational nature.

20. Avoid using the microwave. Microwave cooking has been shown to damage the DNA of the foods heated by that method. Microwaving changes the molecular structure of the foods and damages the nutrients contained in the food. Of all cooking methods, the microwave lowers the nutrient levels of the foods the most. Why buy fresh organic foods, only to destroy their highly nutritive benefits in the microwave? Microwaving changes the food energetically. It deranges, confuses and changes the food molecules. For the highest vibration, according to *Ayurvedic* science, food should be cooked over a flame (a gas flame is fine) using copper or clay cookery since this is closest to nature. Baking or cooking with electrical heat are the second-best options vibrationally.

21. Detoxify! If all else fails, it may be time for a detox! An *Ayurvedic* cleanse such as the one suggested at the beginning of the book, or as suggested in 40 Days to Enlightened Eating or the 40 Days to Enlightened Eating Cookbook, does wonders, without leaving one fatigued, depleted, or washed out. *Ayurvedic* cleanses focus on returning the body-mind system to balance and harmony while they detoxify. They recharge and re-set the whole system while bringing the *doshas* (the elements of nature within us) into their natural state of balance. When the body-mind system is in a state of balance, health and harmony, your vibration is naturally high!

By choosing even a few of these suggestions to work on, we can lift our vibration higher. It is perfectly okay to raise your vibration in baby steps. Slow and steady is always better than doing nothing at all! Watch your life transform as you lift yourself up into the higher octaves of living and being!

12 Ways to Enlighten Your Exercise
and Raise Your Vibration

Since EVERYTHING is energy, your exercise regime carries a vibration too. Whenever you spend a period of time doing something in a particular frequency, you become energetically aligned with that frequency. It is time to break some old "low-frequency" paradigms about exercise and fitness that are coming in the way between us and our highest selves and living life at the highest possible vibrations! Many of the accepted and popular points of view about exercise are anything but high vibrational and anything but healthy. Often we are doing more harm than good to our body-mind and lowering our frequency with our exercise routine. Here are 12 ways to shift your exercise regime into a higher vibration and watch your own frequency soar! I call this *"Enlightened Exercise!"*

1. Exercise in ways that brings you JOY! Find movement that you LOVE and do more of that! Ask yourself, "Am I doing this because I ought to, or am I enjoying my exercise routine? Some ways to bring more joy to your physical movement is to play your favorite tunes, exercise with friends, frequently change up your routine and engage in forms of exercise that you like! Think out of the box about fun ways to infuse exercise into your day. Here are some examples: gardening, kayaking, hiking, salsa dancing, Zumba, roller-skating, geocaching, karate, playing with your kids or grandkids and of course yoga! Choose creative ways to make your movements joyful!

2. Focus on all of the wonderful benefits of exercise. While you are exercising, remind yourself that you are boosting your energy, strengthening your heart, lowering your cholesterol, increasing your metabolism, promoting youthfulness, increasing flexibility, building muscle, and promoting weight loss or weight maintenance. Focusing on all of the payoffs sends your vibration soaring!

3. Do not exercise as "penance" or punishment out of guilt or shame for what you ate. When your fitness regime is in the vibration of punishment and guilt, then it is coming from a very low frequency. You can never punish your way to wellbeing!

4. Engage in exercise that integrates body, mind and spirit. Experiment with yoga, tai chi, Qi-gong, Nia or dance. I have great fun putting on a CD with an upbeat rhythm, and then dancing around the room when no one is home! I feel uplifted and invigorated by this form of free, uninhibited movement. My body, mind and soul thank me in unison!

5. Exercise moderately. Are you invigorating your body or depleting your energy and vitality? High vibrational exercise feels good, makes you feel good, and leaves you feeling good long after! Over-exercising or excessive exercise that leaves you exhausted, worn-out or like you were beaten with a stick, is draining your life-force energy, thus lowering your vibration. If you need energy drinks to artificially boost your energy to maintain endurance and strength during a workout, then you are ignoring and overriding the wisdom of your body. The body never lies. It knows exactly what you need and how much! When you give your body what it needs it blasts you into a higher frequency!

6. Exercise your mind via silence, meditation and prayer. Giving the mind space, stillness, relaxation and peace instantaneously increases your frequency.

7. Take a walk in nature. Nature already vibrates at a higher frequency. When we step into nature, we absorb the inherently high vibration and begin to resonate with it ourselves. This is because nature is our true nature. Spending too much time in offices, cars, buildings and houses, disconnects us from who we are and where we come from. Human beings are a part of nature. Being in nature returns our vibration to its naturally high default setting!

8. Lose the "no pain, no gain," mentality. Opt for the "no pain, no pain," mentality. Pain lowers your vibration. If you are associating the words "miserable," "uncomfortable," and "painful" with your exercise regime, then your fitness regime is lowering your vibration! Pain, misery and exercise should never meet in the same sentence, the same gym, the same routine or the same body! Feeling good raises your frequency, feeling bad diminishes it. Feeling good brings you more of the same. Feeling bad attracts more of that, and aligns you with those bad feelings vibrationally!

9. Don't "should" on yourself! Stop the long list of exercise "shoulds" you have been hammering yourself with. Your workout shouldn't be a duty, task or chore. Free yourself from the resistance and heavy energy of "should" and find ways that make exercise feel like a treat! For me walking the dog outside is a treat! I enjoy the company of my pet as we spend time together enjoying nature. I never feel that this is a chore!

10. Eliminate the "no excuses" approach to exercise. We've all heard, "dig deeper" and "push harder." This mentality breaks us down and wears us out and causes exercise to become more like self-abuse rather than self-care. Listen to your body instead. Your body doesn't lie! Perhaps you are coming down with something, feeling physically exhausted, or just need a lighter, kinder form of movement today. When you are kinder and more compassionate with yourself, you automatically raise up into the higher vibration of kindness and compassion. It is through honoring whatever our body-mind is asking for in each moment, that we lift our vibration to greater heights.

11. Take the "work" out of workout! The word "work" instantly creates a resistance around whatever you are about to do, making you feel overly serious, heavy and put upon. These are lower vibrations. Make your exercise a "playout." Fun and playfulness is a high vibration! Seek out ways to make exercise a playful and fun activity. You will naturally look forward to exercising and want to do it more often. Exercise in a way that makes the time fly by as you move your body, and you will naturally align with a higher vibration!

12. Stop striving towards perfection. If your exercise goals are to have "bikini" abs, a swimsuit model's body, look like "Magic Mike" or to morph your age 50-something body into a 20-something body, you are mostly exercising your ego! If you are striving towards the unattainable, you leave your *true self* behind and latch on to the vibration of disappointment. The basis of high-vibrational exercise should be enjoyment, wellbeing and health, rather than physical perfection. Self-acceptance is a much higher vibration than comparing, criticizing, judging, condemning and "whipping" yourself into a size zero! Begin by asking yourself, "What is already great about me that I am not yet seeing?"

Make these simple shifts in your exercise regime, and be transformed body mind AND soul into a higher vibration!

Affirmation: As I raise my own frequency, I help to raise the vibration of the world!

Today's biggest success:

Food for Thought: Today we begin to make lifestyle changes to raise our vibration, including, eating, exercise and our way of interacting with the world.

Journal: What high-frequency changes can you incorporate into your living today?

Day 30

Feeding Your Energy and Raising Your Vibration

Let your food be as nourishing to you as your breath. Let it support, sustain and increase your life-force. ~Elise Cantrell

When practiced skillfully, Yoga and *Ayurveda* are ultimately practices that raise your vibration. They alchemically align you with your inner source of energy and your best and highest self. *Prana* is the life-force energy that strengthens, invigorates and enlivens us on every level. Without *prana, chi* or *qi,* life cannot exist. When we breathe the last breath, the *prana,* or life force, that animates the body leaves and we transition from life to death. In the yoga and *Ayurveda* system of energy anatomy, it is understood that our *prana* body or "energy body" layers right over the physical body, giving it movement and life. Our *prana* body is fed by ingesting *prana* or life-force energy through the air we breathe, sunshine, pure water and the food we eat. The quality of our own *prana* or life force directly reflects the quality of the *prana* we take in. We consciously or unconsciously weaken or strengthen our own energy source with eating and food. We often unconsciously use toxic foods to block our own awareness, energy and highest potential. How can we use food to harness our highest gifts, our highest self and our own true power?

Food is energy! Einstein's formula E+ MC2 has proven that everything in the universe is energy, and everything carries its own energetic vibration. This includes the food we eat, the air we breathe and the water we drink. These impart their own energy signature and vibration to us, as the food, water and air we take in become part of our very being. You are what you eat, as you assimilate the foods, they not only build your cells, but you take on their energy and their vibration.

Whole foods grown in nature carry the energy and vibration of the cosmos, of the creator, of wholeness, freshness, and purity. The energy of these foods are uncorrupt, unadulterated, and carry the pure *sattvic* energetic intentions of creation, nature and the cosmos. When we fuel our *prana* body with these energies, we energetically align with our own creative potential, with life and with the universe. Living foods carry the vibration of health, vitality and life. These foods carry the energy of LOVE with which is the very essence of the creation, the universe and of who we really are.

Manufactured foods on the other hand carry their own intentions, their own energy and their own agenda. Manufactured foods often carry the energy of greed or profit, or even deception. These foods are often made to trick the mind-body system with artificial colors or flavors that mimic the colors and flavors found in nature. These foods can be adulterated with appetite and flavor enhancers, or they are scientifically formulated to maximize profit by adding appetite enhancers and extending the shelf-life through chemical preservatives. Preserved food has about as much *prana* as a mummy! It still looks like food on the outside, but contains no life force!

It is taught and believed that the meat of poorly treated animals carries lower forms of energy as well. When we ingest the meat of cruelly treated animals, we are not only ingesting the stress hormones stored in the tissues, but we are eating what they carried energetically in their *prana* bodies. They may have spent their entire lifetime carrying the energy of fear, hopelessness, pain, suffering and even death. As we eat these foods, we are linking ourselves with this energetically and karmically.

One of the *Ayurvedic* treatments for anxiety, depression, fear and night terrors, is to have the patient eliminate meat from the diet. There is a great deal of anecdotal evidence that this alone, raises a person's energetic vibration and lifts them up out of these heavy energies they are carrying in their *prana* body. Often people are energetically experiencing the fear of the animal with anxious thoughts, rather than their own fear! Since everything is energy, and energy cannot be created or destroyed, the energy we ingest becomes a part of us! The yoga and *Ayurveda* systems even suggests that persons who are heavy meat eaters even take on a lower "animal-like" nature, and are led by animal-like desires, urges and impulses rather than by intellect and rational thinking.

How to Raise your Energy Vibration

It is known in the yoga system that by consciously feeding the *prana* body the high-quality life-force energy found in wholesome living foods, our own energy begins to mirror that higher vibration. Changing your eating can raise your level of consciousness and bring you to higher levels of awareness and existence through energy alone!

Since the *prana* body and human energy anatomy encompass the aura, enlightened eaters will experience positive changes in the auric field just by the foods they eat. The outer aura simply reflects the energy and radiance cultivated within through our diet and lifestyle choices. Sometimes we meet a person, and we just don't know what it is about them, but they have a certain luminosity, radiance and essence about them which is very attractive. They are very likable and desirable to be around. These people have a very high vibrating energy body, and a luminous auric field. You don't recognize this consciously, but your own *prana* body picks up on this high vibrational field of energy about them.

Conversely, we have all been around people of low-vibration. We have all met chronic complainers who always have something negative to say. They may use foul language, swearing, criticism, rudeness, sarcasm and put-downs. All is wrong with the world from their perspective. They are carrying the energy of darkness, heaviness and gloom in their *prana* body, not vibrancy, enthusiasm or lightness. This can come about from a variety of emotional and lifestyle choices including diet and food. Toxic habits like smoking, excessive drinking, drugs, a poor diet has a direct impact on the energetic vibration you carry around.

It is important to note that we can also harm the energy body by what we do not eat as much as by what we DO eat! I had an anorexic roommate for a year in college, who by NOT feeding her energy body lowered her vibration. She was so difficult to be around that I was rarely in the room, spending time away as much as I possibly could. Don't we all get irritable and cranky when we are hungry? Regularly depriving the body of *prana* through food takes a huge toll on the *prana* body, the field of energy we are composed of and exist through!

What are you exposing yourself to energetically? What is the energy that your food is carrying? Energy of love? Of death? Of fear? Of greed? Of deception? Of deprivation?

I often get asked what I think about all the "healthy" bars and shakes marketed to dieters. Having them occasionally when you are pressed for time is okay, however, I fundamentally disagree with making bars and shakes a "lifestyle!" First of all, it is important to note that these ARE processed foods. Energetically, these manufactured foods are not exactly healthy! The more foods are processed, and the further they are removed from their natural form, the less life-force energy or *prana* the foods have. To make up for the missing *prana* and to create a sense of energy, they may use artificial laboratory-simulated vitamins, which are of far less quality and use to the body. Artificial vitamins have been found to block the absorption of their natural counterparts. Also, these "healthy" bars and shakes may use genetically modified ingredients which the FDA still allows to be labeled as "natural," even though there is nothing natural about them. These products are also formulated to have a "shelf life," and therefore must contain preservatives by FDA regulation. Most BARS and shakes out there do not contain organic ingredients, which again signals the possible presence of pesticides, herbicides or other chemical contaminates. When eaten on a regular basis, these same chemicals accumulate in the tissues and cells and that energy becomes a part of us. There is no substitute for REAL food. Our bodies are made to eat, digest and assimilate whole foods. We can't trick the body with laboratory created versions of food. It is always best to buy organic whole foods and cook your own way to optimal health! But certainly a "healthy" shake or bar every once in a while is better than a Big Mac!

The *prana* body governs the electrical system that promotes intelligence, clarity, clairvoyance, ideas, insights, creativity, ability to receive divine messages and signs from above. With a strong high vibrational *prana* body, you will optimize the intellect of the energy body and be able to sense the energy and intentions and vibration of what is around you. You will sense the energy of the places you visit. You will sense the energy, intentions and emotions of other people. With a vibrant, healthy energy body, you connect the circuits to your intuition, or your 6th sense! You become aware of the presence of angels, animal guides, and passed over loved ones. You will be able to easily meditate, manifest ideas, dreams and desires. You will begin to recognize that there is no need to do more and more, trying harder and harder. With a strong and vibrant *prana* body, everything that is supposed to come your way will energetically be attracted to you like a magnet. You attract the people, places, events and things to you that energetically match your own high vibration.

Sometimes we are more afraid of having a high vibration than a low one. We are afraid of the possibility of our own power and energy. We are afraid of reaching our own greatest heights. We are afraid of our own superb capacity. Many of us unconsciously fear our greatest and highest self, and so we sabotage our own energy fields and unknowingly lower our own vibration through our addictions to *low-prana* foods, and substances. Once you become aware of the energy body and its potential, owning your own personal energy and power becomes a choice. What will you do with that choice?

The power of *Hara* energy:

Hara is a Japanese word that literally translates as "belly". The *Hara* center is the energy center of the body and is located in the exact center of the *pranamaya kosha* or energy body. *Hara* refers to the "ocean of energy" within us. It is in the belly, three finger widths below the naval, about two inches beneath the skin, and is three inches in diameter. It said to be the site where our energetic "umbilical cord" connects to universal energy or cosmic life-force. It is from this place we can draw in energy and information from the world around us. It is from the *hara* center that we receive "gut" feelings based on energetic information received from the external world and processed in the center of our being. The martial arts depend on the *hara* center to contact the universal quantum energy field beyond us and draw it into the body through this portal to the outside world. It is not the power of the hand that allows a Kung Fu master to chop through cement blocks with the side of his palm. He has been taught to access cosmic energy through the *hara* center. The *hara* center is also used in yoga practice and in meditation as a point of focus, strength and transformation.

People who are sensitive to energy in the areas around them are typically picking up on this external energy through an open and active *hara* center. With an open *hara* center you may be able to pick up on energy residue in an old home, or place of business. You may also pick up on energy from other people, sensing their emotions, attitudes or intentions via the *hara* center. From this invisible cord, we have an energetic doorway between our internal selves and the external world. The *hara* center has an intelligence all its own in order to protect us and also to provide us access to the strength we need to do the seemingly impossible. There are more neurons in the gut than in the brain!

When we over-eat, we are suffocating the *hara* center and anesthetizing the brain. We have all heard of a "food coma." Too much food creates a smothering effect here dampening the strength of *hara*. Habitually overeating creates a thick "barrier" of fat between the *hara* center and the outside world. It is not too big a stretch to presume that overeating may be an unconscious way to close up the *hara* center. It is difficult to receive and process more energy and emotion along with today's fast paced, stressful way of life. Perhaps we are overloading our energetic sensory system with input. Maybe on the unconscious level, we notice when we over-eat, that this information temporarily quiets. When we hide the *hara* beneath layers of belly fat, we remain closed off from access to this source of strength and awareness for better or for worse.

Hara energy can be utilized for many things. It builds heat in the body. *Hara* energy strengthens the metabolism, and boosts the immune system. It is known to improve sexual relations. It purifies, cleanses and opens the energy channels, removing blockages. *Hara* energy recharges our own energetic battery. If we access it and tap into it, great things can be accomplished. We can draw on power from beyond us to persevere and to do things in life beyond our own capacity. When a mom lifts a six-ton car off a child, she is dipping into her *hara* center, gathering the energy of the universe to aid her strength! It is important to be aware of this power portal within us and know how to dip into the deep well of life-force there within our reach anytime we need a boost of strength, confidence, endurance, courage or power. This tiny little space inside of us is a great source of energy and vitality. Discovering and accessing the power of *hara* can be transformative.

We are energy beings. Human beings are much like batteries! Our own bodies contain a proper ratio of saline and acid. What you do to recharge your battery all the way to its fullest capacity makes a profound difference as to who you are and what you become. Your capacity is as vast as the energy you allow yourself to access. How you are feeding your energy or *prana* is the most powerful form of alchemy. This is the most well-guarded secret that the yoga and *Ayurveda* tradition has carried with it for millennia. Are you ready to own your own power and feed your *prana*?

Affirmation: "I am healthy and filled with energy. I know and affirm that my body is a friendly place to live. I have respect for my body and I treat it well. I connect with the energy of the Universe, and allow it to flow through me. I have wonderful energy. I am radiant, vital and alive!" ~Louise L. Hay

Today's biggest success:

Food for Thought: By choosing LIVING foods, we automatically boost life-force! Living foods come from trees, plants, vines, and stalks, not from boxes, bags or cans. Challenge yourself to incorporate as many *living* foods into your snacks and meals as you can into your day! You will FEEL the difference!

Journal: Have you ever experienced low energy? Have you felt tired, sluggish or lethargic after eating certain foods? One of the best ways you can improve your energy level is to focus on eating more foods containing vital "life-force energy." You can help your own body tap into the infinite well of life-force. How can you tweak your diet and lifestyle to better feed the *prana* body?

Day 31

Does Your Food Have an IQ?

I discovered that the new reality of the world is that chemical companies are feeding us. ~Jeremy Seifert

You are your own guru. All the answers, truths and wisdom you will ever need already lie within you. However, if your mind is dulled with tainted foods, the insights you are seeking are difficult to uncover, remaining shrouded behind a clouded, sluggish and heavy mind. Intelligence is vibrational. Intelligence is a high frequency thought vibration. In order to live intelligently and think intelligently, we must eat intelligently. Foods actually carry their own intelligence! Living foods vibrate with divine life-force energy or *prana*. *Prana* is understood to be intelligent and evolutionary. Eating intelligent food raises our own IQ. *Ayurvedic* science teaches that the subtle energetic essence of the foods we eat, becomes the substance of the mind. Eating food with little or no vital essence and intelligence, or "dead" foods, imparts that very nature to us. The more intelligent life-force energy your foods contain, the more of that essence will be imparted into your mind-body system. According to *Ayurveda, sattvic* eating (pure, harmonious, enlightened) equals a *sattvic* mind. As we raise our vibration, our bodies require more high quality vitamins and nutrients to support and sustain us at that frequency.

Recent studies show that the human race as a whole is experiencing a cognitive decline, specifically a decline in intelligence. Among the many theories behind this, is that it is due at least in part, to the modern diet. Twenty percent of our food intake is used to feed and nourish the brain! Instead of ingesting the intelligence of nature as we have for millennia, our diet has shifted in recent decades to soft drinks, processed foods, fast foods, convenience foods, GMOs, instant foods, and frozen microwaveable meals. These foods lack vital life-force energy or *prana*. They lack the inherent intelligence found in natural, whole, living foods. The "fall-out" is quite predictable! Eating foods devoid of *prana,* or life-force is akin to eating "dumb" food. The Sanskrit word for the physical body, *annamaya kosha,* directly translates as "food body" because it is composed entirely of the foods we eat. Since the brain is a part of the physical body, then the adage "you are what you eat" holds true. In the words of Forrest Gump, "Stupid is as stupid does."

Eating foods that lack intelligence, impacts our own evolutionary intelligence. At this stage of human development, we are working against the advancement of our own intelligence as a species. Humankind is choosing convenience and cost cutting over brainpower and intellect.

The modern diet has brought us to a dangerous crossroads in the evolution of human intelligence and consciousness. A University of London study done on 4000 children reported that children fed a fast food diet, develop lower IQ's than children fed freshly prepared home cooked meals. Higher fast food consumption was statistically linked to lower intelligence!

An Oxford University study on rats revealed that after just 10 days on a junk food diet, the rats performed significantly poorer, making more mistakes and taking longer to complete a maze. Almost half of today's children are diagnosed with ADD, ADHD, dyslexia, learning disabilities, Autism, Asperger's, cognitive impairment or mental illness. Humans are genetically designed to be born healthy, whole, and intelligent, yet we are being duped into forfeiting our own intellectual birthright by our very food system!

Presently, baby formula contains a high percentage of GMO corn and soy. Over 80% of corn and soy crops are genetically modified and sprayed heavily with glyphosate herbicide (Roundup®). Glyphosate is a known neurotoxin, carcinogen, hormone disruptor, and a genotoxin, known to damage human DNA. The long-term growth and development of the human brain under the effects of this chemical is unknown. Whether it is intentional or not, how can a neurotoxin belong in infant nutrition? What lasting effects will this have on human intelligence and why are infants being subjected to this experiment? Trusting parents are not to blame for this shocking lapse in judgment, but formula manufacturers and the biotech industry are!

By microwaving, chemically spraying, genetically engineering and irradiating foods, we are damaging our food's DNA and the basis of its underlying intelligence. Studies show that the neurotoxins found in chemical pesticides and herbicides sprayed on conventional produce, harm brain development and lower IQ. A Harvard analysis of 27 studies revealed that fluoride fortified drinking water reduces children's IQ by an average of 7 points and warned that fluoride is more damaging to the brain than lead or mercury. Fluoride is chemically classified as more toxic than lead, but there is approximately 20 times more fluoride than lead in the average glass of tap water.

It is time to wake up and start questioning the foods you are eating! Food containing intelligent life-force energy has the capacity to impart its own intelligence into you, while contaminated foods have the power to destroy the potential of our human intelligence, our birthright! What we are feeding ourselves, will affect future generations. Their DNA will come from our DNA, our seeds will be their seeds, and our crops are their crops. The blueprint we leave behind is the one they will inherit. What we are doing to ourselves now will have evolutionary effects for generations to follow. Does your food have a low IQ? Choose well!

Many cultures and countries live in a state of tyranny. For westerners, it is a tyranny of the food industry, as they pedal their chemically and genetically tainted food on an unsuspecting populace while the government at best looks the other way, and at worst is complicit. There are some conspiracy theorists who suspect that tainted food is part of a more sinister plan than to line the pockets of the food industry. There are some who believe that there are ulterior motives behind the toxic chemicals so freely allowed in the food supply. One such theory is that foods are deliberately contaminated as a means of abating the increasing over-population of the planet by promoting disease, diminishing human reproduction and shortening life span. It is also seen as a way to combat the progressively high cost of senior health care, (Medicare and Medicaid) of an aging population of baby boomers by also deliberately decreasing the life span due to dietary related disease. Whether or not this is true, one thing is for certain; the modern diet is robbing human beings of quality of life. It has been widely speculated that the present generation will have a shorter average life expectancy than that of their parents' or grandparents' generation due to dietary linked health concerns such as obesity, heart disease, diabetes and cancer.

Other conspiracy theorists believe that the food industry is in cahoots with the health care industry. While the food industry is fattening, and sickening the population with highly processed, preserved, overly sweetened, artificially flavored and colored foods, which are deliberately designed to tempt our eyes and fool our taste buds; the health care industry is cashing in with record profits. Cancer, diabetes and heart-disease are multi-billion dollars a year industries. There are numerous other "manageable" but incurable diseases, illnesses and syndromes which are also diet related, and similarly fattening the bank accounts of the pharmaceutical industry. The *Ayurvedic* proverb "Without proper diet, medicine is of no use and with proper diet, medicine is of no need." immediately comes to mind.

Corrupt governments such as North Korea and Cuba have intentionally infected their country's water supply and contaminated or limited food sources. This is done to deliberately inflate the cost of food and water while limiting the availability of these basic needs to keep the population poor, needy and in a state of weakness and deprivation, so the government can maintain tyrannical control. By controlling the supply of the most basic human needs, these oppressive governments maintain rule because desperation and survival override the need for personal freedoms. It is easy to enslave a population when the ruling force directly controls access to the most basic needs.

Another theory proposed by "conspiracy theorists" is that we are deliberately being fed foods that "dumb us down" in order to keep us too oblivious and ignorant to what is going on. This was reportedly the case in Nazi Germany where Fluoride was deliberately put into the water supply to "dull and sedate" the public. Hitler was quoted to have said, *"How fortunate for the leaders, that men do not think."* IQ lowering, brain-altering neurotoxins (which have also been linked to ADD, ADHD, Alzheimer's, Dementia, Autism and other forms of brain disease) such as aspartame, fluoride, pesticides, preservatives and weed-killers are freely allowed into our own food and water supply here in the United States. The seemingly benign conventionally grown potato contains seven neurotoxins, six developmental or reproductive toxins, 12 suspected hormone disruptors and seven known carcinogens. Our very food supply has become a potent biological weapon!

Whether there is any credence, the fact that these theories are floating around, indicates something is suspicious about the present state of our food. Our collective consciousness and intelligence is in the hands of the food industry! What we do at a DNA level now affects the entire future of humankind!

Dumb foods: GMO, Processed, fast foods, convenience food, packaged foods, commercial candy and snacks are "dumb foods!" Genetically modified foods for example have had their fundamental intelligence altered. The genes of bacteria, viruses and animals are inserted into the genes of plants in a laboratory to create a new man-made species of plant. As we all know genetic abnormalities and aberrations in the human genome can affect human intelligence. By consciously tampering with the genetic makeup of foods, we are inflicting genetic defects and disorders into our foods. That same intelligence is being transmitted into our bodies, our cells and our own DNA. We are what we eat. Food does have the capacity to impart its own intelligence . . . and also wields the power to damage human intellect! Fortunately, in this country with a bit of detective work and some pre-planning the choice is still yours! Choose carefully!

Foods which contain nature's intelligence: Fresh, wholesome, minimally processed, organic living foods. This includes plant foods such as leafy greens, nuts and seeds, whole grains, legumes, eggs, fresh fruits and berries. Fatty fish and seafood also support a healthy human brain. Always choose foods naturally grown without chemical sprays or residues!

How Can I make sure I am feeding my family "Intelligent foods?"

- **Grow your own!** I have an indoor and outdoor herb garden, apple and lemon trees, raspberry plants, and a garden during the summer months. Freeze, dehydrate and can whole foods for winter.

- **Avoid GMO foods.** Common sources are non-organic corn and soy, canola, cereals and snack foods, corn chips, papaya, sugar beet, summer squash, non-organic tofu. Look for non-GMO verified label.

- **Opt for Organic:** Organic foods cannot be GMO and they cannot be chemically sprayed. Look for USDA organic label. For organic produce, look for a PLU code that start with 9.

- **Eat Real food:** Intelligent food is naturally grown on a vine, tree, bush or plant. It does not typically come in a bag, box or can! (Nuts and seeds may be sold in a bag or can.)

- **Avoid processed or laboratory created food.** Avoid fast food, junk food and convenience food.

One cannot think well, love well, sleep well, if one has not dined well. ~Virginia Woolf

Affirmation: Eating foods that contain intelligent life-force energy (prana) impart that same vibration of cosmic intelligence to me. I eat wisely and I am wise.

Today's biggest success:

Focus for thought: Our food choices powerfully affect our intelligence, our DNA and our evolution! Choose wisely, for what we do now will affect generations to come!

Journal: Have you ever experienced feeling mentally dull, confused, cloudy, headachy and muddled as a result of eating certain foods? Have you had the experience when you have felt sharp, clear and fast thinking as a result of a clean diet? Note how food has a direct impact on the quality of your intellect!

Part 3

Eating for the Spirit

Day 32

Soul Food

Whole food is soul food. ~Elise Cantrell

Perfect health and weight is our true nature. We were created in health and for wellness. Wellbeing is who we are. Anytime we stray from these, it is because we have deviated from the perfect divine plan for eating and caring for our wellbeing, which is in alignment with the rhythms of nature and living in harmony with our own biology! When we deviate from our natural state of health and wellness, our soul cannot do the sacred work it came here to do.

Our relationship with food has become distorted, broken and fatal. We have left the safety, harmony and wisdom found in the "sacred garden" from which humanity originated. We have removed ourselves from the innate healing power of nature and abandoned our own true nature just as we have abandoned the "sacred garden." We no longer eat the fruits of the trees, plants and vines. Are we trading our soul for the sake of food convenience? Have we sacrificed our spiritual destiny as the human race for something as trivial as tempting food?

Parable or prophecy? Was the very downfall of humankind prophesized in the book of Genesis thousands of years ago? The Biblical "fall of humankind" began with food! The trouble all began when Adam and Eve found it impossible to resist food they had been warned about! In this parable, Eve or "woman" offers tempting food to Adam or "man," which precipitates their exodus from the garden. Since it is often women who shop for and prepare the meals in our culture, then it can be reasoned that women, who are often juggling home and careers, have fallen for the allure of fast, convenient, flavor intensified, lower-cost foods with long shelf lives and offered it to their families.

Perhaps this story predicts that the fall of humanity will hinge on food. Not just any food, but tempting food-forbidden food of our times. The food industry itself is tempted by huge profits. It uses deceptive advertising, commercials and slick photography to lure us, and further tempts us by enhanced flavors, artificial colors and brightly colored packaging. We are tempted by the long shelf life that chemical preservatives create. We are *tempted* by the convenience of processed food and fast food. We are tempted by highly sweetened and salted commercial food. Sugar and salt tend to anesthetize the brain and stimulate feel good hormones.

We live in an age when we are tempted by our capability to create genetically engineered foods, designed in a laboratory so they can withstand being sprayed with man-made chemicals. Could this precipitate our decline as a species? Adam and Eve were said to have eaten "forbidden fruit" from the "tree of knowledge" after being tempted. As we all know a little knowledge can be dangerous when we don't see the big picture! Perhaps mankind had to leave "the garden" not because God exiled them, but because they destroyed it with their own knowledge!

Is it possible that the story of the "forbidden fruit" God warned about in the book of Genesis is a parable, which foretells of our modern-day struggle with genetically modified and chemically tainted foods? The modern apple is even more dangerous than the one that tempted Adam and Eve! The FDA has recently approved genetically modified apples that will never turn brown. Now in addition to an exaggerated shelf life, this will add to the six known or probable carcinogens, sixteen suspected hormone disruptors, five neurotoxins and six developmental or reproductive toxins found in a non-organic apple.

I believe the sufferings of the modern diet were eerily predicted in Genesis, the first book of the Bible. It is in eating forbidden foods where our separation from nature began. Mankind left behind the safety, health and harmony of the "garden" in exchange for tempting foods! Eve represents womankind who is traditionally and typically the one to gather and prepare food for the family table. In the modern age, womankind has been tempted and tricked by "the great serpent," which is the commercial food and biotech industries. The book of Genesis even predicted the "fallout" from this separation from nature and leaving "the garden" behind: suffering, illness, disease and eventually death. I cannot believe this Biblical metaphor is merely coincidental. We should take heed of Adam and Eve's plight as a dire warning for the modern age!

The change in how agriculture is produced has brought, frankly, a change in the profile of diseases. We've gone from a pretty healthy population to one with a high rate of cancer, birth defects and illnesses seldom seen before. The tobacco companies denied the link between smoking and cancer, and took decades to recognize the truth. The biotech and agrochemical corporations are the same as the tobacco industry; they lie and favor business over the health of the population. ~Dr. Medardo Avila Vazquez, a pediatrician specializing in environmental health

Ironically, the modern biotech company, Monsanto, responsible for pioneering genetically modified seeds engineered to tolerate Roundup® spray (glyphosate, a known neurotoxin and carcinogen) has been referred to tongue-in-cheek, as "Mon-Satan" by its non-GMO opponents and environmentalists alike. Our culture has consciously exiled itself from the garden where we were provided by nature alone with everything we needed to eat. It is possible to rewrite this parable, but we must rewrite it NOW before it is too late!

How could we have ever believed that it was a good idea to grow our food with poisons? . . . As part of the process, they portrayed the various concerns as merely the ignorant opinions of misinformed individuals —and derided them as not only unscientific, but anti-science. They then set to work to convince the public and government officials, through the dissemination of false information, that there was an overwhelming expert consensus, based on solid evidence, that GMOs were safe. ~Jane Goodall

It is possible to refuse to eat the fruits we were warned about thousands of years ago! By refusing to be confused or tricked into eating that which goes against our very nature, we metaphorically "return to the garden." Now is the time to return to our true place, our birthright, which is a part of nature, a part of the sacred garden. It is within the garden where harmony, health, intelligence, peace, prosperity and ease exist. Is it worth giving up our intellect, clarity and health for the convenience of genetically engineered, preserved, processed food? By consciously growing and eating real foods the way we were designed to eat, we return to that natural harmony that is our inheritance.

I am not a preacher or even a textbook perfect Catholic by any measure, however I am inspired to get mankind to return to the garden of our birth for the sake of the future of our species. When we realize that nature IS our true nature, only then can we return home.

How far we have strayed from the metaphorical "garden?" How have we been duped and tricked into eating tainted foods? Somehow we have mistakenly chosen to trust the for-profit biotech and commercial food industry, over Mother Nature, over God-made foods. The end result is separation and disharmony. I believe these ancient Biblical stories are meant to lead us back to the garden, to the retrieval of our soul, back to a place of ease and harmony. But first we have to WAKE-UP to what is happening right before our eyes! When we realize that nature IS our birthright and our true nature, only then can we return home to that place of health and wellbeing.

Food and Guilt

Perhaps this story is also an allegory behind the guilt we are conditioned to have surrounding food. Removing "guilt" from eating is eliminating a huge obstacle and a heavy weight from the eating process. The need to eat is a natural physiological process. It is we humans who have brought guilt into the eating process with "sinful foods." When we eat the foods that we are designed to eat, there should be no guilt involved! It is time we humans release the guilt we attach to eating, and rediscover the pleasure and the delight that is present in the foods that we are created to eat guiltlessly! It is time for mankind to restore our spiritual relationship with food and trust the magnificence, intelligence and balance of nature to nourish, replenish and restore us.

Another Biblical allegory for purifying our bodies is the Cleansing of the Temple in Luke 19. Jesus enters the temple and finds cheating, deceit and swindling going on. In a fury, he threw out those who were engaged in duplicitous behavior along with their trappings. Since the body is considered OUR temple, it is logical that we need to cleanse away the things that do not align with our own highest good, body mind and soul! If the physical body is our temple, then we must be mindful of what we house and host in our temple-FOODS. Here are the foods we need to purge from our own physical temples!

1. **Chemically tainted foods**–foods sprayed with chemical pesticides, herbicides and insecticides which contain hormone disruptors, carcinogens, and neuro-toxins.

2. **Laboratory created foods "Franken foods"**–artificially flavored, colored and preserved. For these foods, shelf-life is dated in years, not in days or weeks!

Natural foods ripen and decay. Artificial colors and flavors have confused our instincts as to the foods that serve our body, mind and spirit. Returning to natural whole foods restores our natural instincts towards eating and health.

3. **Fast Foods**–Although these items may be edible, they barely resemble food. I remember eating flavorful chap-stick in first grade. It tasted really good and even smelled like food, however in hindsight, I now realize that was not a good idea! It was not really food!

Microwave cooking: 5 Top Reasons to Avoid Heating Foods in the Microwave:

1. It destroys more nutrients than any other form of cooking. You will receive fewer nutrients from your food.
2. It damages and destroys the inherent life-force or "prana" of the food.
3. It causes the degradation of the proteins in the food.
4. It alters foods at the molecular level, creating free-radicals and carcinogenic bi-products.
5. It dehydrates the food, drying out its healthy moisture content, which helps to nourish and hydrate us. This also makes the food more difficult to digest.

Affirmation: I honor my body by feeding it the way it was designed to eat, which provides the health and energy to do what I came here to do! I am living the life I was meant to live and fulfilling my soul's highest purpose! I was made in perfect health for a life of wellness.

Today's biggest success:

Food for thought: Cancer and disease is not a natural part of human existence. We fell out of alignment with the wellness that is our birthright, that is our true nature, when we departed from the proverbial garden. We can come back to the garden any time, as long as we take it upon ourselves to return while it is still here.

Journal: Journal about your meditation experience.

Day 33

Meditation to Feed the Mind

Meditation practice isn't about trying to throw ourselves away or become something better. It's about befriending who we are already. ~Pema Chodron

Meditation delivers potent alchemy along any journey you undertake. It is the space of quiet openness, which gives rise to all possibilities. It is the fertile ground on which transformation grows. Today is the day we add this powerful tool to our toolkit on this 40 Day journey! Meditation is the best way to feed the mind and cultivate consciousness and choice in all aspects of living and being including eating and food! Meditation is a time-tested way to feed and nourish the mind and intellect, broadening and expanding awareness in every direction!

I think one of the reasons that I really enjoy cooking is its inherent meditative quality. I love the process of chopping vegetables. I become completely absorbed, and as I do, I find myself becoming increasingly calm, focused and relaxed. When stirring a batter, beating an egg or kneading dough, in that moment, the food and I become one. It is as if before it becomes one with my physical body by eating it, we first become one in the mental body or *manomaya kosha*, the field of the mind. Cooking is almost foreplay to the eating process, which is a precursor to digestion and assimilation. Following a recipe requires *mindfulness*. Without watchful awareness, step-by-step, the outcome could be disastrous! Cooking is a practice of being present, being in the now.

The whole foods diet promoted by yoga and *Ayurveda* is formulated to naturally promote awareness, focus, concentration and mindfulness. Now that we have cultivated this way of eating for 32 days it is time to put it to the test by adding the practice of meditation.

Meditation is a practice of silent stillness. When the mind is still and quiet, we begin to have the awareness that we have the opportunity to carefully choose what thoughts, ideas, emotions, music, television shows, books, media sources we wish to focus upon and feed it with. The same holds true in the body. We practice the 3-4 hour rule between eating experiences, giving our belly time to empty. It is at this point of emptiness, that we then have the opportunity to choose what we will refill it with. This empty space gives us the opportunity to "check-in" with the body and the mind to find out what it wants or needs to be fueled with in order to function optimally. When we learn to quiet the mind through meditation, we cultivate the ability to be able to listen to and hear the subtle messages of the body. When you ask your body, "Body, what food would most satisfy and nourish you in this moment?" With a quiet still mind we can hear it speak up and tell us what foods it truly desires.

Meditation cultivates attention and awareness in all aspects of the body, mind and soul. With this newfound awareness, choice and possibility begin to present themselves! When conscious awareness is invited into your reality, it permeates all aspects of your living and being. You begin to operate from deliberate choice rather than from pattern or habit. This alone has the power to transform your relationship with eating and food, and *enlighten* your eating!

> Ordinarily we are swept away by habitual momentum and don't interrupt our patterns slightly. ~Pema Chodron

The ultimate destination of yoga practice and of yogic eating is to reach higher states of consciousness, greater concentration and enhanced awareness. It is through reaching these states of consciousness that we connect to Self-knowledge, Universal wisdom, Source, God, absorption, *Samadhi* and enlightenment. It is in these higher states of consciousness where we achieve "*yoga*" or "oneness" a reunion with our true nature, our creator and our True Self.

Jesus said, "The kingdom of God is within." It is only by going within that we visit that kingdom. I tell my students that prayer is talking to God, but meditation is listening to God and to your higher self. You will be astonished by the messages there waiting for you in a state of silent stillness, absorption, union, yoga, *Samadhi*.

> If you want to find God, hang out in the space between your thoughts. ~Alan Cohen

The benefits of meditation are manifold! However, it is important to recognize how well meditation enhances and supports healthy eating. A regular meditation practice can increase attention and awareness to what why and how you eat. Meditation is shown to dramatically lower stress levels, so its relationship with reducing stress-based eating is quite apparent. The practice naturally increases presence, consciousness and awareness, which can ultimately lead to more conscious, mindful eating. By absorbing the right foods for the body-mind system, we reach a state of health, harmony and unity. This is *yoga*.

When walking walk, when eating eat. ~Zen proverb

What is meditation???

Meditation is a mental practice, which began in antiquity. Ancient carvings, 5000 years old depict figures seated in meditation. The earliest mention of meditation was in the Vedas 15th Century BCE.

Meditation has been practiced over millennia across various traditions, cultures and beliefs. It has been around thousands of years because it is a practice and a discipline, which is extraordinarily effective. In fact, studies show that you don't even have to like meditation for it to work! It has been shown to be powerful and successful in stress and pain reduction. Meditation helps the mind to disconnect from the body in states of discomfort, pain and stress. In *Ayurveda*, meditation is the main tool (or medicine) for healing the mind.

Meditation is the yoga path to inner freedom. Meditation is the royal road to freedom, a mysterious ladder reaching from earth to heaven, from error to truth, from darkness to light, from pain to bliss, from restlessness to abiding peace, from ignorance to knowledge, from mortality to immortality.

~Swami Srinivasananda

Meditation has been described as:

Doing less; being more	Pondering
Focused attention	Mental technique to quiet mental chatter
Relaxed openness	Inward looking personal practice
Introspection	Voluntary thought control
Concentration	Sitting with a steadfast mind
Concentrated focus	Clear seeing
Contemplation	To see within
Reflection	Awakening the inner witness
Returning to the "now"	Higher self
Awareness	Observing what is present
Being	Witness consciousness
Silence	Being in the present moment
Spaciousness	Inner retreat
Insightfulness	Chanting
Stillness	Mantra
Altered state of consciousness	Resting in your true nature
Relaxed consciousness	Expanded consciousness
Just being rather than doing	Surrender to what is
Mindfulness	Absorption

What meditation is NOT:

Silencing ALL thoughts	An escape from reality
Sleeping	A religious practice
A trance	A "new age" practice
Self-hypnosis	A "hippie" trend

Recognized Benefits of Meditation: (Here are a few of the over 100 known benefits of a regular meditation practice)

- Reduces stress hormones and calms the Central Nervous system
- Increases the mood improving neurotransmitters, serotonin and dopamine

- Increases memory, ability to learn, intelligence and even boosts IQ
- Improves focus, concentration, self-control, cognizance and awareness
- Boosts immune system
- Lowers blood pressure and heart rate
- Improves conditions of anxiety and depression
- Heightens feelings of calm and other positive emotions
- Increases emotional stability and resilience
- Said to bring about self-knowledge and self-awareness
- Enhances longevity and can slow the aging of the body and mind

Contraindications for Meditation:

Epilepsy, trauma, PTSD (post-traumatic stress disorder), psychosis.

Seats for meditation:

Finding a comfortable seat is of paramount importance when developing a meditation practice. If you are not comfortable, you are less likely to meditate, and more likely to struggle. Originally, there were only four yoga poses and seats for meditation. The word *asana*, which means "seat" in Sanskrit, the language of yoga, eventually became the word for yoga posture. You will notice every yoga pose name ends with the word *asana*. Eventually there were 9 seats for yogic meditation. These first 9 seated meditation options are the original 9 yoga poses. Experiment with the following seated meditation positions, and find which ones work best for you.

1. **Easy pose–** *sukhasana*-sitting on the earth, place one shin in front of the other, forming a triangle shape with the knees and thighs.

2. *Siddhasana*– Said to be the meditation seat of choice for the Buddha. Sitting on the earth or a chair, stack ankles, forming a triangle with the thighs, shins and knees.

3. *Swastikasana*– Seated on the earth/floor, place feet behind "cave" of the knees, forming a triangle shape with the legs and hips.

4. *Gomukhasana*– Knees stacked, heels rest beside opposite hips. Both sit bones contact the floor. Allow spine to stack.

5. *Bharadvajasana*– seat of the warrior sage. Begin in kneeling position shift sit bones to one side onto the floor. 1 heel rests beside the hip, the sole of the other foot is placed in the inner thigh of the other leg. Both sit bones should contact the earth.

6. *Padmasana*– (Lotus Pose) – ankles rest on opposite thighs.

7. *Ardha Padmasana*– (Half Lotus) – one ankle rests on the other thigh.

8. *Vajrasana*– hero pose-kneeling position sitting on heels. Modify by placing bolster between knees under sit bones, or placing yoga block or blocks between heels. A blanket can also be placed behind the knees between the calves and the thighs. If feet are uncomfortable, a rolled-up blanket or towel can be placed underneath the front of the foot/ankle.

9. *Mandukasana*– seated frog pose-Big toes touch, knees wide apart, sitting back on your heels. To modify, place a yoga block under your sitz-bones.

10. **Seated against wall**– Sit comfortably on a bolster or cushion, with a cushion behind back, blanket under knees and feet.

11. **Chair**– with folded blanket or small roll to support sacral-lumbar spine. Place blocks or books under feet to keep the knees at hip level. Place the folded blanket behind the sacrum.

12. **Reclining**– (Constructive rest or lying release) On back, knees bent. Place feet wide apart and allow knees to fall together. Place one hand on belly, one hand on chest.

13. **Restorative**– prop a bolster at a 45-degree angle. Place a folded blanket near the top of the bolster to act as a pillow. Sitting in front of the tilted bolster, recline back and rest your head on the blanket. Place a blanket beneath each forearm as it rests at the sides for extra support.

14. **Legs up the wall**– Reclining on the floor on a blanket or yoga mat with legs extended up the wall. You can place a folded blanket under the head and neck for added support.

*Careful in the reclining positions if you are sleepy. Our bodies are conditioned to sleep when reclining. This position should be a position of relaxed wakefulness. If you are especially sleepy, you may need to choose a seated position. The seated positions are designed to promote a relaxed yet alert state of awareness. The reclining positions are perfect for persons suffering from back, neck or shoulder discomfort. They are also helpful in states of physical fatigue.

*In all positions the sitz-bones need to be firmly grounded on floor or on cushion. If knees "float" when reclining, support with blanket or pillow. Arms and hands can be supported with pillows or blankets. A blanket across the lap or hips can have a calming and "grounding" effect.

Hand positions:

Mudras are yoga poses for the hands. Hand *mudras* are said to be even more powerful than *asanas* or yoga poses. It is important to hold *mudras* with energy and intent and not let the hands become careless or sloppy. This changes the energy of the *mudra*.

Chin mudra/jnana mudra – The *mudra* of wisdom. Index finger and thumb touch in both *mudras*. In *jnana mudra* the palm is turned up and in *chin mudra*, the palm is turned down.

Bhumisparsha mudra – *"mudra of enlightenment"* Place fingertips of the left hand on the floor beside the left hip, let the right-hand rest on the right knee, palm up, fingers open. This symbolizes being grounded to earth, but being open to grace. Also, represents the fact that we must fulfill our earthly obligations first in order to achieve enlightenment. (Hirschi, p.156, c. 2000)

Vishnu mudra – Always use right hand. Right hand is symbolic of giving, and left hand is symbolic of receiving. If the right hand is injured, then the left hand may be used. Bend in index finger and ring finger, resting them against palm. The other fingers extend out with intention. (Used for *nadi shodhana pranayama)*

Prana mudra – Use *prana mudra* when feeling sleepy, and only for a short duration. Do not use in evening or at night. This can cause restlessness and sleeplessness. This one looks just like "the girl scout's honor sign." Bend pinky and ring finger towards palm, and hold down with thumb. The middle and index fingers extend together as one unit.

Apana mudra – The tip of the middle and ring fingers touch tip of the thumb. This *mudra* is said to be balancing to the mind as it imparts patience, serenity, harmony, and inner balance. In *Ayurveda*, this *mudra* stimulates detoxification through the kidneys and the liver. (Hirschi, p.78, c.2000)

Dhyani mudra – Diamond *mudra* – *Mudra* of concentration. Classical meditation hand position. The two hands together form an empty "bowl" symbolizing how emptying ourselves of expectations, preconceptions, judgments, and other things which do not serve us, we become open and receptive to receiving what it is we do need. (Hirschi, p. 146)

Ushas mudra – fingers are interlaced so that right thumb is above left for men. Women should place the left thumb over the right. Hands form a bowl. This is a great *mudra* to help wake yourself up in the morning if you are still sleepy. This is the *mudra* of new beginnings. It heightens mental alertness, and is said to harmonize the endocrine system. (Hirschi, p.62)

How to make time for meditation and make it a consistent practice:

You should sit in meditation for 20 minutes every day-unless you are too busy; then you should sit for an hour.

~Zen proverb

1. **Create a meditation space.** Make it comfortable, pleasant and eliminate distractions. Make it special and sacred. Try to fill it with positive thoughts and images. Keep negativity away from this sacred space. Allow it to be charged with the energy of peace, love and light.

2. **Find a comfortable seat.** (Refer to the previous suggestions.)

3. **It is not recommended to meditate on a full stomach.** An empty stomach or eating very lightly is the most conducive to meditation. It helps the mind stay focused. Blood and *prana* are directed away from the brain and mind to the digestive system, making concentration difficult.

4. **Create a specific and conducive time**. Early morning as soon as you awaken is said to be the most "auspicious" time for meditation. This is because the "veil" between the conscious and unconscious mind has not completely lifted, and the noise and the clutter of the day have not yet scattered the mind. That being said, what is most important is to find the time of day that works in your life and is the most "auspicious" for you. Schedule it in. Don't just wait for it to "happen". UCLA research suggests that a minimum of 12 minutes a day of meditation has measurable benefits. Set a timer for whatever length of time you choose. 20 minutes is often recommended. Set an intention. Interestingly, research also shows that you don't have to like meditation for it to have benefits. I have found the best time of day for me personally is right after my yoga practice.

5. **Make a commitment. I** _____, commit to practicing some

    form of meditation _____ minutes a day _____ times a day _____ days a

    week for the next 40 days.

6. **Set a timer.** Usually I do not need or want a timer. I prefer not to be interrupted by a bell. However, I notice on days when I am pressed for time, that I have more difficulty settling in, fearing I may run over and end up late for an engagement. This creates anxiety for me. On these days I set a timer, so I can relax and know this space of time has a safe container. There are numerous phone apps with meditation timers and pleasant sounding chimes. Experiment and see if this is right for you.

Deepak Chopra suggests that one should ideally meditate for 30 minutes in the morning and 30 minutes in the afternoon or evening. However, this is not practical for everyone. However, what is important is that you make a commitment to a time, place and duration then stick to it! Self-discipline is a key to making meditation a regular lifelong "practice."

Yoga poses to prepare body/mind for meditation:

- Hip, shoulder and heart openers.
- Arm across chest shoulder stretch
- Elbow up shoulder stretch, holding elbow with opposite hand.
- Hindi squat
- Standing forward fold-ragdoll
- Cowface with eagle arms
- Frog-*mandukhasana*
- *Bharadvajasana*

Close both eyes to see with the other eye. ~Rumi

Easy ways of Tuning Inward:

1. Close the eyes and scan the body and mental activity and just asses your level of stress on a scale of 1-10.

2. Close your eyes and begin to notice your sit-bones contacting the chair, cushion or floor. Notice the breath without trying to change it. Just become aware of the movement of the breath in and out.

3. With the eyes closed, do a brief mental scan of the body beginning at the head and moving down. Noticing what is present in each area as the mind moves into the presence of each location.

In the words of Paramahansa Yogananda, "When by meditation, we withdraw restless thoughts from the lake of the mind, we behold our soul, a perfect reflection of the spirit."

Meditation Techniques:

Meditation is integral to yoga. Because people are different, various approaches to meditation have evolved to suit their needs. Seekers should experiment with a variety of techniques until they find one of their liking. But if there is no meditation practice, it cannot be called yoga. Experiment and find what ever ways are effective to achieve the state of meditation. ~Swami Kripalu

Breath Centered Meditations- Called *ajapa japa,* in breath-centered meditation, the meditator closely observes the breath. Breath meditation techniques or *pranayamas* are designed to bring about the altered states of consciousness which best support meditation. Breath techniques *"pranafy"* the body vitalizing the life-force. The life-force or *prana* is said to contain its own intelligence. By inviting the life-force to open and expand, we bring about higher states of consciousness. *Pranayama,* conscious breathing is the highest form of meditation.

The following breath meditation techniques are based on concentration on the breath and the movement of the breath in and out. When the concentration wanders, *and it will,* the mind is patiently and steadily redirected to back the breath. Time and time again awareness is returned to the breath without judgment. With a focus on the breath, the mind flows patiently with the ebb and flow of breath just as a ship bobs up and down in the waves. The breath is a wave too with peaks and crests, just as is life itself. Breath centered meditation is said to allow the meditator to quiet the chattering mind, while riding on the wave of the breath.

Focusing breath on:

- Rim of nostrils
- Septum
- Rise and fall of navel-If there is excessive mental chatter, drop the focal point to the naval. Typically, this will assist in quieting the *chitta vrittis* or restless thoughts.
- Rise and fall of hands resting on naval or chest

Ujjayi – ocean sounding breath – Constrict the back of the throat softly to slow down the flow of breath in and out. As the breath passes through the constricted area, it creates a hissing sound. Some people liken the sound to Darth Vader's breath, or the sound of ocean waves. The mouth remains closed in this breath. *Ujjayi* means "victorious". This breath builds heat and warms the body. It slows down the inhalations and exhalations allowing more oxygen to enter the blood stream as opposed to gulping in air. The sound of the breath is very calming and meditative.

Nadi shodhana – Alternate nostril breathing. *Ujjayi* can be added to this breath to build heat and heighten focus on calming sound. Place the right hand in *Vishnu mudra*. Press the right thumb against the right nostril to gently press it closed. Always begin breathing in through the *left* nostril, or lunar side. This stimulates a relaxation response. After the inhalation, release the thumb, and press the ring finger against the left nostril, closing it off to exhale on the right side. Inhale right, close with the thumb, and exhale left. Inhale left; exhale right. Continue breathing by alternating nostrils on the inhalation and exhalation. Feel free to support the elbow by resting it on a pillow, cushion or block placed on the right thigh.

If *Vishnu mudra* is not comfortable for your hands, another option is to rest the index finger and the middle finger of the right hand in the area between the eyebrows and use the thumb and ring finger alternately to press the nostrils closed. The area between the eyebrows is commonly referred to as the 3rd eye or the eye of insight, intuition, and inner seeing. In *ayurveda*, this area is referred to as the *sthapani marma*, a point of awareness that is said to bring about insight, clarity and calm the chatter of the mind.

Annuloma Viloma – *Annuloma viloma* means *with the* hair and *against the* hair, referring to the movement of nostril hairs back and forth with the inhalation and exhalation. This breath is simply alternate nostril breathing with internal breath retentions (*Antera kumbhaka*) (Elbow can rest on a pillow, cushion or block.) Always begin breathing in through the left nostril, or lunar side. This stimulates a relaxation response. After you breathe in hold the breath until you intuitively sense the need to exhale. Breathe out the right side. Inhale on the right side. Hold. Exhale left. Continue breathing through alternate nostrils holding the breath on the inhalation. Elbow can rest on a pillow, cushion or block. Ujjayi can be layered onto this breath.

Dirgha – 3-part breathing – inhale into abdomen, lower lung, upper chest right under collar bone. Exhale, release first from under collar bone, then from lower lung, finally from belly. *Ujjai* can be layered onto this breath. Add visualization of air swirling into each part, like a wave curling into each part of the lung right and left.

Hands-free *nadi shodhana* – Begin mentally breathing in through the left nostril. As you inhale imagine your breath rising up the left side of the body, from the sole of the foot through the leg and hip, up the left side body to the 3rd eye. As you exhale imagine breathing out of the right nostril and picture the breath traveling down the right side of the body from the 3rd eye down to the sole of the foot. As you inhale again draw the breath up through the right side of the body to the 3rd eye, and then down the left. Continue imagining the breath or *prana* (life-force) moving up and down each side of the body along with the breath. Always begin and end this technique on the left side.

Breathe up front of body, and down back of body – In general females should energetically draw the breath up the front of the body and down the back of the body. Males should draw the breath up the back of the body and down the front of the body. The breath can also be alternated up the front and down the back and up the back and down the front. Energetically, the front of the body is considered masculine and has a more solar and confrontational aspect to it, and the back of the body is more lunar and feminine, and vulnerable. It represents the unseen and the unknown. The front side of the body is perceptive (the eyes, ears, mouth and nose are all facing forwards.) The back of the body is more intuitive. (Eyes in the back of the head, or hair being raised on the back of the neck.) Experiment with the movement of breath or *prana* up and down the spine.

Breath up and down the spine – Inhale up the front of the spine from tailbone to the crown of the head. Then exhale the breath down the back of the spine, softening slightly and filling the back body with breath. You can play with reversing the energetic direction of the breath by Inhaling down the spine, and exhaling up.

*After practicing the breathing technique of your choice for a chosen duration, simply drop the technique and sit in that space, resting in the present moment . . .

After dropping the technique, you may want to experiment with selecting an internal focal point or *drishti*. Begin with the coccyx, move to the navel, then the solar plexus, the heart, the throat, the third eye and the crown. Notice what changes as you move your awareness to a different energy point. Notice that the tailbone and the naval create a sense of grounding. Notice how different the energies of the solar plexus, heart and throat are. Finally notice the sense of expansiveness of consciousness as you place the focus on the third eye or crown.

Affirmation: My eating invites increased focus, concentration, insight, understanding and awareness. My meditation practice encourages more consciousness and mindfulness in my eating practice.

Today's biggest success:

Food for thought: Our food choices powerfully affect our ability to meditate, concentrate, focus and relax. A meditation practice feeds and empowers our eating practice by easing away stress based eating and supporting conscious eating! Begin a daily meditation practice using one of the techniques suggested in this chapter, or choose a different technique that resonates with you. Even just 7-10 minutes a day can have profound benefits!

Journal: Journal about your meditation experience.

Day 34

Maitri: Unconditional Friendship
. . . with Yourself

See the goodness that you are. Do not fight the dark, just turn on the light, let go, and breathe into the goodness that you are. ~Swami Kripalu

Most of us are our own harshest critics and our worst enemies. We beat our-selves down with unforgiving words and unkind thoughts. Day after day, we break our own heart. In the healing system of yoga and *Ayurveda*, and many other Eastern sciences and philosophies, the heart is the seat of the soul. If the heart is broken, the soul is wounded. We can't always control all the twists and turns life has in store for us, however, we literally hold our heart in our own hands. In order to heal our heart and advance our soul, we must embrace the practice of *maitri*.

Maitri is the Sanskrit word for the practice of offering unconditional kind-ness, compassion, forgiveness, acceptance, nourishment, care, and love . . . .to ourselves! *Maitri* is the practice of "befriending" yourself. Are you your own worst enemy or your dearest friend? It is only through befriending yourself, that deep healing begins. You cannot punish yourself into your optimal weight and health! Becoming the ideal version of you begins and ends with loving yourself just as you are! When you love yourself, you then begin to nourish and nurture yourself as if you were your own precious child. It is through this "self-care" that the best version of you can emerge! When you heal your heart and lighten you soul, the real transformation takes place. *Maitri* begins with self-acceptance.

Self-acceptance

Self-acceptance doesn't mean you don't want to change. Quite the contrary, it often leads to dramatic change as you give up the limiting beliefs and self-sabotaging behaviors that you'd adopted trying to be someone you're not. The secret to finding the happiness and peace you seek in your life is not in trying to figure out what's wrong with you; instead, your aim is to explore the truth of who you really are.

~J. Marie Novak

Somewhere inside of many of us, seeds have been planted that make us believe that we aren't worthy. We are conditioned to believe that we aren't good enough, smart enough, pretty enough, and we don't work hard enough. We have been conditioned to believe that we don't even deserve to look and feel our best! We've accepted the belief that this is for other people, not us! We have bought into the idea that it is selfish to take time for ourselves! As long as you believe you are not worthy, you will continue to sabotage your own success and wellbeing consciously or unconsciously. Your Enlightened Eating journey is ultimately one of self-acceptance, which is the real doorway to success! The irony is that it is only when you accept who you are, and what you are right now, without resisting or rejecting it; only then, are you free to transform. When you believe you are undeserving of your own approval, this very belief blocks your success. Self-acceptance is the path to transformation!

I've spent way too many years resisting, neglecting, and negating my body. Wanting Diana Ross' hips instead of my own. Those days are over. Every morning when I wake up, I stand in front of the mirror in my PJ's and bless my body. All the years I dieted, complained and was less than satisfied with my shape have yielded to a different perspective and appreciation for a body that's brought me this far.

~Oprah Winfrey

Hollywood has given us the idea that our bodies should look the same at 52 as they did at 22. This is unrealistic, and puts the body-mind system at odds with itself and at odds with nature. This unrealistic ideal steals our peace and robs us of our true power, which is in owning exactly who we are at any age. It is essential that we accept the natural process of aging in a kind, compassionate way with ourselves! What **is** realistic is to be the best 52 year-old version of yourself, by making eating and lifestyle choices that align with wellbeing and health! The worst enemy of self-acceptance is perfection. Perfection is impossible to attain, and harrowing to try and sustain. Every time you fail to live up to perfection, you judge yourself as unworthy, as a failure, as worthless . . . Striving for perfection is an act of fear and self-hatred. Ironically, perfection is an obstacle between you and your highest self, not the pathway to it! Voltaire put it well in his aphorism, "Perfection is the enemy of the good."

> Perfection is shallow, unreal, and fatally uninteresting.
>
> ~Anne Lamott

Self-acceptance is about *not* rejecting yourself for any perceived flaws, faults, mistakes, limitations or weaknesses. It is befriending yourself just as you are, and becoming your own best ally, supporter and cheerleader. Self-acceptance is about starting right where you are. It is about letting go of the idea that you are a "project" or that you need to be "fixed."

Self-acceptance means letting go of the idea that you have to be super-mom or super-dad or M.V.P. V.I.P., Summa-Cum-Laude, valedictorian, or employee-of-the-year to be worthy. It is about releasing the notion that you must strive for the perfect silhouette, look flawlessly coiffed and ageless, all while driving the right car, having the most well-behaved and talented kids, and the most successful career! You are already worthy just as you are, how you are, just because you are. By virtue of just being born into this existence, worthiness is our birthright. There is nothing to fix or improve before you are "up to snuff." Some people measure their worthiness by the number on the scales, the number on their bank account, or their IQ number. Numbers can never encompass the potency of who we are! Numbers cannot measure our worthiness!

> The curious Paradox is that when I accept myself just as I am, then I can change. ~Carl Rogers

I have a confession to make. After years of maintaining my "ideal" weight, suddenly when I hit my mid-40s, I gained a few pounds. As my hormones began to change, my body shifted as well. I have done nothing different. I continue to eat very well and practice yoga daily. At first, this weight gain was an especially bitter pill to swallow, after-all, I wrote and published, *40 Days to Enlightened Eating*, a book designed to achieve optimal weight, health, energy and vitality. However, even I am not immune to the effects of middle age. My dad likes to joke, "aging is not for sissies."

It dawned on me recently as I practiced yoga in a room with mirrors, that I now have some curves, a more feminine look. How can that be a bad thing? After all, I AM a woman! The excessively toned, ultra-lean physique women are culturally pressured to attain is not who women really are! It is not how we were created; it is not our natural composition. As I consciously work towards deepening my own authenticity and embracing my True Self, I realize looking and being feminine IS my True Self. To beat myself up by chaining myself to a treadmill or becoming a fanatic about eating to try to look any different, would be to enslave myself to a false way of being, using force to achieve a body at-odds with who I really am. I am by no means overweight. I am healthy; I enjoy preparing healthy, flavorful food and eating these delicious meals. I deeply love my yoga practice. I LOVE sharing these practices with others. What I am doing is authentic.

Yoga is not about self-improvement, it's about self-acceptance. ~Gurmukh Kaur Khalsa

"Enlightened Eating" is not about a number on the scales. Your optimal weight, health, energy and vitality can only be what is healthy and realistic in the NOW. In my first book, I state that *"self-acceptance is the new skinny."* Yoga IS the path of self-acceptance, a path of love that includes loving yourself just as you are. With that in mind, I choose to love and accept my softer, curvier middle-aged body without judgment. In fact, the softer edges on the outside also mirror the inner softening that has happened. With practice and awareness, over time, I have learned to soften my own struggling, straining and judging. The sharp edges of me are gone. By softening into what is there, body, mind and soul soften. The softness there within me has created a comfortable space for my soul to settle cozily into this being that is me. Some would say that this alone is enlightenment!

The highest spiritual practice is self-observation without judgment. ~Swami Kripalu

Self-Love

Love is the capacity to take care, to protect, to nourish. If you are not capable of generating that kind of energy toward yourself- if you are not capable of taking care of yourself, of nourishing yourself, of protecting yourself- it is very difficult to take care of another person. To love oneself is the foundation of the love of other people. Love is a practice. Love is truly a practice. ~Thich Nhat Hahn

Self-love is a critical component of *maitri*. When practicing self-love, you begin to treat yourself with love. You begin to stop forcing your body to exercise in a way you hate which is a form of self-hatred and self-punishment. Do not force yourself to exercise on days when you are not feeling well or are recovering from an illness. Let your body tell you what it truly feels like doing! Begin to trust your body's inner wisdom and do what you LOVE and that feels right in that moment! This is a form of self-love.

Don't eat foods you dislike just because they are deemed healthy. This does not benefit the body-mind system in the slightest. Find healthy foods that you love, and enjoy your way to looking and feeling your best. You can't starve yourself or beat yourself up at the gym and expect to uncover the ideal you! You can only love, accept and nurture yourself into the best version of you!

Life is too short for self-hatred and celery sticks.

~Marilyn Wann

Exercise: Set your intention for optimal self-love by finishing this sentence: "I love myself enough to _____" and fill in blank. Practice this intention as you go about the rest of your day!

As I Began to Love Myself – Poem

By unknown author, often attributed to Kim and Allison McMillen, but also to Charlie Chaplin.

As I began to love myself I found that anguish and emotional suffering are only warning signs that I was living against my own truth. Today, I know, this is "AUTHENTICITY.

As I began to love myself I understood how much it can offend somebody if I try to force my desires on this person, even though I knew the time was not right and the person was not ready for it, and even though this person was me. Today I call it "RESPECT".

As I began to love myself I stopped craving for a different life, and I could see that everything that surrounded me was inviting me to grow. Today I call it "MATURITY".

As I began to love myself I understood that at any circumstance, I am in the right place at the right time, and everything happens at the exactly right moment. So I could be calm. Today I call it "SELF-CONFIDENCE".

As I began to love myself I quit stealing my own time, and I stopped designing huge projects for the future. Today, I only do what brings me joy and happiness, things I love to do and that make my heart cheer, and I do them in my own way and in my own rhythm. Today I call it "SIMPLICITY".

As I began to love myself I freed myself of anything that is no good for my health – food, people, things, situations, and everything that drew me down and away from myself. At first I called this attitude a healthy egoism. Today I know it is "LOVE OF ONESELF".

As I began to love myself I quit trying to always be right, and ever since I was wrong less of the time. Today I discovered that is "MODESTY".

As I began to love myself I refused to go on living in the past and worrying about the future. Now, I only live for the moment, where everything is happening. Today I live each day, day by day, and I call it "FULFILLMENT".

As I began to love myself I recognized that my mind can disturb me and it can make me sick. But as I connected it to my heart, my mind became a valuable ally. Today I call this connection "WISDOM OF THE HEART".

We no longer need to fear arguments, confrontations or any kind of problems with ourselves or others. Even stars collide, and out of their crashing new worlds are born. Today I know "THAT IS LIFE"!

Self-Care

As an *Ayurveda* practitioner, if I could write a universal prescription that would prevent every known disease of the body and the mind, then I would write a prescription for "self-care." All disease, mental or physical arises from an imbalance in the mind-body system. The ancient healing science of *Ayurveda* teaches that it is impossible to catch any "bug' or pathogen if your body-mind system is in a state of balance. It is only when we have a "chink in the armor" of our immune system that pathogens can slip in and illness is able to arise. Why are so many people sick today? The truth is if we got enough sleep, ate right, rested, set adequate boundaries for ourselves and lived a harmonious existence, health would prevail. Often, overeating is a misguided attempt at self-care. It has a quick "Band-Aid" effect, "covering-up" the areas when you are lacking in care for yourself.

I have observed that there are only 2 times when women begin to acknowledge and practice the need for self-care: illness and pregnancy. Most illness would be preventable if we began to refuse to wait until we are sick to begin to administer care for ourselves. Illness is our soul's way of directing us towards the vital business of self-care! Think of self-care not only as self-healing but as a practice of health maintenance.

During pregnancy, women make sure to get proper rest and sleep, focus on nutrition, partake in moderate exercise, avoid pharmaceutical medications and chemical food additives, and steer clear of toxins. Women are willing to do for their babies, what they have been previously unwilling to do for themselves! If only we would choose to become our own best mother, the wellness and vitality that is our birthright would be ours once again! If we cared for ourselves as the precious child that we are, our wells would be full to care even more fully for our loved ones.

Most of us are familiar with the oxygen mask analogy. If there is a loss of cabin pressure on a flight, you are instructed to put the oxygen mask on yourself first before placing it on anyone else. This is to ensure that you will not run out of oxygen while you are trying to help those around you, rendering you helpless yourself. In order to serve others, we must first serve ourselves. We can't hold space for others if we are unable to hold space for it in ourselves. If we give away all our time and energy to everyone else around us, we become depleted, and are no longer able to be of service to anyone else. How demanding are you being of yourself? Do you require more of yourself than you would ever expect of anyone else? Are you guarding your energy, so that you have adequate "oxygen" for yourself so you can be there for others or are you leaving yourself depleted?

Exercise: The following process recommended by author Esther Hicks, has made a profound difference for me! Try making a list with 2 columns. In the first column, list what **you** will do this week. In the second column, write what you would like God or the Universe to do this week. When the list is complete, see how many of the things on your "to do" list you can shift over to the second column and let the universe accomplish them. How much you soften and lean into the support that is already there is directly proportional to how much you are supported. Move the ego out of the way, and be supportive of yourself, asking and receiving the assistance your body, mind and soul are begging for!

Open Your Arms to Receive: The universe is constantly giving to you in ways both small and large. When someone offers to assist you, buys you lunch, or hands you a gift, open your arms to receive. The more that you say yes to blessings, the more the universal energy freely flows to and through you. When you push away proffered help, you close the door to this abundance.

Today, open your arms to welcome any gifts that come your way, and say yes to the universal flow. Allow yourself to be helped, loved, and pampered . . . let yourself receive . . .

~Doreen Virtue

Self Compassion

If your compassion does not include yourself, it is incomplete.

~The Buddha

Have you chastised yourself for eating a "bad" food? According to *Ayurveda*, the negative self-talk is worse for the body than the food itself! If you make a "food flub" be compassionate with yourself and gently move back in the right direction! Self-compassion is lacking without there being space for self-forgiveness whether it is about a dietary indiscretion, causing a fender bender, forgetting to pay a bill, making a mistake in your checkbook, or even something far more serious. Something restorative yoga guru, Judith Hansen Lasater said that has stuck with me is that when she makes a mistake, she says to herself, *"How human of me!"* We are harder on ourselves than we would ever be on another human being. Sometimes we need to remind ourselves that we, too, are only human!

Self-compassion is the practice of being **kind** to yourself without any requirements, prerequisites, guilt or judgment, but just because... It is about giving yourself permission to make you a priority. It is about always giving yourself the "benefit of the doubt." There is an axiom that "The more deeply you rest, the livelier you work and play." Our culture has conditioned us to believe if we do anything kind for ourselves, we are selfish. However, it is selfish NOT to do for yourself. For the less you do for yourself, the less you are able to do for others. If we don't fill our own tank, we have nothing to give out.

Each and every day, practice a gesture of kindness towards yourself. Losing weight is not about self-denial, self-bashing, self-rejection or comparison with others. It is about self-acceptance, self-care, and self-compassion.

> We should not succumb to the tyranny of our own self-judgment. ~Rolf Gates

Here are some suggestions for offering yourself small acts of compassion:

1. **Offer yourself small sweetnesses-** (This doesn't mean a Hershey's kiss!) It can mean bringing home a bouquet of flowers for the kitchen table, making your favorite meal for dinner, curling up by the fire or indulging in a lighthearted or inspirational read!

2. **Allow yourself little luxuries-** A soak in an aromatherapy bath, a chair massage, a splurge on something you've been really wanting, a long nap.

3. **Give yourself the gift of unstructured time-** Block off space in your calendar to do whatever you want or even NOTHING at all! Give yourself the space to see what arises.

4. **Take "time-outs" in your busy day-** Give yourself a "time-out." Take a cup of tea, a few minutes outdoors, a relaxing walk, a few minutes of alternate nostril breathing, some "chair sun salutations" at your desk, etc. Take a break to give yourself a brief reprieve from the daily grind.

5. **Meditation**- Give yourself the gift of silent stillness. See chapter 33 for inspiration.

6. **Rest**- Stop and give yourself down-time! Take a break from your electronic devices and get away for a weekend, or just an evening out! Laze on the sofa for an afternoon. Take an extended *savasana* on your yoga mat! Remember rest is sacred!

7. **Self-nurturing**- Be your own best mother. Cook warm nourishing meals, wear warm cozy comfortable clothing, stop demanding more and more from yourself and praise yourself for all the good you have already done. Let that be enough for today!

Affirmation: "I love and accept myself just as I am." ~Tara Brock

Today's biggest success:

Food for Thought: Befriend yourself! Be kind, loving and compassionate with yourself. When your well is full, you feel full and don't need food to fill the void.

Journal: Are you making yourself a top priority? Instead of loving yourself, could you be substituting food for love? In what ways can you love and befriend yourself more today?

Day 35

Are You Feeding Your Body but Starving Your Soul?

One of the reasons people consume anything too much is because they don't consume other things enough. You tend to take in too much material substance when you are starving yourself of spiritual substance. ~Marianne Williamson

Often we stuff ourselves with food when what we really desire is to fill a deeper emptiness. After an afternoon of my own self-guided yoga practice, meditation, *Ayurvedic* self-massage, followed by *yoga nidra*, I realized late into the day, that I hadn't eaten since breakfast. Strangely, I wasn't even hungry, and continued to feel satiated as the day turned into night. Then it dawned on me, that there are many ways to feed ourselves, and I had just fed my soul in a way that deeply nourished my being. My soul was no longer hungering to be fed. It made me ponder how many times we feed our body when it is the soul, which is in need of nourishment.

Are you feeding your soul? When your soul is "full-filled" you won't try to compensate by filling the body with food! Are we feeding the body only to starve the soul? I believe the number one disease of today is overfeeding the body in neglect of the soul. Our tummies are full but our souls are hungering to be tended, nurtured and loved. What if we began to feed the soul in the way it is longing? Would we still be overeating or longing for the short-term sweetness from candy, cookies and cakes? An undernourished soul creates a sense of hungering. We most often mistake this hungering as a need for food, when what we need is to care for the most timeless and eternal part of ourselves, which is neglected due to the day-to-day demands we put upon ourselves. We forget to refill our tank, and leave ourselves running on empty. We perceive this emptiness to be an empty belly when in fact; it is our souls that are deprived. How do we "refill the tank of our soul" when it is depleted?

Feeling a sense of weariness, fatigue or "jet-lag" along with unresolved hunger is a side effect of a soul running on empty! Feeling exhausted, worn-out, or depleted is a sure sign that your soul tank is running low. Summer "vacation" was once a time to laze in the sun, but in the age of electronics, it has become busier than ever, leaving many of us worn out. In *Ayurveda*, fatigue is considered a sign of an imbalance. When we find ourselves imbalanced, if we keep doing what it is that is causing the imbalance, things continue to escalate and the result is eventually disease. A way of regaining balance is as simple as "refilling your tank." Cars can't run on empty, and neither can we! We do not have anything to give when we have neglected filling our tank.

> Why are we here? We exist not to pursue happiness, which is fleeting, or outer accomplishment, which can always be bettered. We are here to nourish the self. ~Deepak Chopra

There is a parable told by the Buddha in which 2 acrobats are discussing how best to remain safe when performing together. If either of the acrobats is in harm's way, then chances are that the other acrobat is also unsafe. The first acrobat suggests that they each focus on keeping the other acrobat safe, and then they will both be safe. The second acrobat suggests they both concentrate on keeping themselves safe and then they will both be safe. Finally, they conclude that the only way to ensure the well-being of both is if they concentrate on keeping themselves as well as the other one safe. It is only then that they can be assured of being free from harm. When we forget to focus on ourselves, and only focus on others, we are forgoing a "safety net" for our own wellbeing as well as that for those who depend on us. In order to take care of others best, we must also practice taking care of ourselves.

It is important to eat well and to spend time keeping your body healthy; but it is critical to spend time feeding and nourishing your soul. Our bodies are temporary; our soul is eternal. It is essential to remember our soul needs feeding and tending too. We cannot continue to over-nourish the physical body while starving the soul.

The following are the "foods" the soul craves!

1. **Creativity-**The soul has a natural yearning to create. Our souls are extensions of the Creator in physical form. When we deny our soul creative outlets, we are denying our innate drive to become a co-creator with the Divine. Creativity is how we share and emanate the very Source that is within us!

2. **Downtime-** Rest is just as necessary for the soul as mental rest is for the mind, and physical rest is for the body. Take breaks often and as necessary, to give the soul a rest! A rested soul is a fruitful soul!

3. **Playtime-** The soul is playful at heart! We are all children of God, and playfulness is how we celebrate our aliveness. According to Brian Sutton Smith, "The opposite of play is not work; the opposite of play is depression."

4. **Joy-** Joy, bliss and ecstasy is at the basis of who we are and the essence of that from which we came. Without joy, our soul begins to wither like a plant that thirsts for water. When you are in a pocket of joy, you are experiencing your very essence while here in human flesh.

5. **Beauty-** When we connect with sources of beauty such as melodious music, works of art or poetry, bouquets of flowers, a well-decorated space we reconnect to the beauty of who we really are at our core.

6. **Acceptance-** Your soul longs to be accepted, not only by others, but most importantly by YOU! When you practice self-acceptance without judgment, you are able to see yourself through the eyes of God! Swami Kripalu referred to self-acceptance without judgment, as *"the highest spiritual practice."*

7. **Love –** Love is our true nature, the essence of the soul. To give and receive love is an essential part of who we are. There is medical evidence that babies who are well-fed, but do not receive love, fail to thrive and can even die from lack of love. We cannot stuff ourselves full of food and expect to thrive without nourishing ourselves with love of self and love of others.

8. **Connection –** It is essential to have a connection to other souls, whether human or animal. The human soul also yearns for a connection to something greater. Some call it God, the universe, Source, the Creator, Great spirit, whatever you call it, make time to connect through prayer, gratitude and meditation.

9. **Ongoing learning –** Life is often referred to as "soul school." We are here to learn and grow. To be denied the right to learn is to suppress the soul's reason for incarnation and existence. It is no wonder that the young Pakistani girl, Malala Yousafzai was willing to risk her life for the right to an education as a female, when the Taliban banned girls from attending school. The need to learn went beyond human need; for it is a basic requirement for the expansion of the soul.

10. **Silence and stillness –** It is in silence and stillness where the soul can go be with itself and get to know its own likes and dislikes, its own purpose and its own gifts. In silent stillness, the soul reconnects to Source and recharges its own spiritual battery. It is in silent stillness that we recognize that we are in the Creator and the Creator is in us. It is here we understand that we are in the Universe, and the Universe is in us.

11. **Empathy –** The soul is innately empathic. It feels what others feel and vicariously experiences what others experience. The soul is validated by understanding that others can experience a sense of what it is experiencing. When the soul is suffering, it can rest assured that others sympathize with the experience of suffering, and this in itself is healing. The soul also desires to validate, support and have compassion for others as well, knowing it too plays a role in others healing. Empathy is experiencing compassion on a very visceral and intuitive level.

12. **Service** – The soul longs to share with others. It loves to be of help or service! The soul derives a deep sense of confidence, self-esteem and self-worth for the act of giving back. Service gives the soul a sense that its existence truly needed, and is not just of a selfish nature. Swami Kripalu taught, "Serve with a full heart. By making others happy, you make yourself happy. The key to your heart lies in the heart of another."

13. **Freedom** – The soul was not made to be confined by rigid principles, unyielding dogma, or rigid constructs or forced conformity. The soul is inherently designed to think and live "outside of the box." It is difficult enough for a soul to live within the limitations and confines of a human body with the physical limitations and realities of human existence. To give your soul some "breathing room" and a sense of freedom, allow it to experience unstructured time, freedom to make mistakes, blunders, and foibles. Take vacations, mini-breaks, daydream, meditate, and engage in any form of physical movement that provides a sense of liberation, such as free-form dance, intuitive flow yoga or walking in nature. (Sorry a stair-climber or treadmill does not count!)

A Zen master was asked by one of his students, "What is the secret to enlightenment?" His answer was simple, "When I am hungry, I eat; when I'm tired, I rest, when I am sleepy, I sleep. This is the secret to enlightenment." It is my hope that you are now enlightened about feeding your soul.

Self-nourishment is ultimately a spiritual practice. Feeding the spirit is the doorway to an enlightened soul! ~Elise Cantrell

Affirmation: Today I love myself just as I am. I am as kind and loving to myself as I am to others. I am worthy of my own love.

Today's biggest success:

Food for Thought: Are you OVER-NOURISHING yourself with food because you are UNDER-NOURISHING yourself with play, fun, rest, sleep or simply saying "no?" Your body, mind and spirit are always seeking balance. If there is an imbalance in one area, it will show up somewhere else!

Journal: Is your "tank" running on empty? What are some ways you plan to refill your well?

Day 36

Ojas: Cultivating Radiance and Bliss

Beauty is health, and health is beauty.
Bliss is beauty, and beauty is bliss. *~Ayurvedic* proverb

Radiance and bliss is a lifestyle choice. These qualities shine from the inside out! Dr. Robert Svoboda describes the *Ayurvedic* picture of health like this, "They have smooth, soft, lustrous skin, shining eyes, and resonant, mellow strong voices. They walk with a firm tread." These characteristics are a result of a person having the optimal amount of *ojas,* or "vital sap of life." *Ojas* is the underlying "vital juice", responsible for the body's energy, vitality, youthfulness and exuberance. *Ojas* also fuels the fire of the immune system like oil fuels the radiance of a lamp. *Ojas* is the very basis of health and longevity. The Sanskrit word *ojas* literally translates as "vigor."

This life juice is said to be the most basic essence of all bodily tissues, the foundation of the immune system, and the essential innermost source of energy and vitality. *Ojas* is contained in the heart and is circulated throughout the body. Having a continuous ample amount of *ojas* is critical to our state of health, longevity and potency. Optimal *ojas* shows up in the "bliss body" or the *anandamaya kosha*, the subtlest of the five *koshas* or sheaths of human existence, as radiance and luminosity. Ample *ojas* gives off a glow and brilliance that is obvious outwardly by its presence in the aura, similar to the glow of a well-fueled lamp. This essence is what is experienced as that *je ne sais quoi* that is attractive and appealing in certain individuals. It nourishes a beauty that shines from the inside out. People with ample *ojas* are attractive to other people physically, mentally and energetically, without even trying. Plentiful *ojas* amplifies beauty in all layers of being, from the inner to the outer. Ample *Ojas* is responsible for health, beauty and bliss!

To be beautiful is to fully nourish who you are body, mind and soul! ~Elise Cantrell

Characteristics of optimal *ojas*:

- Cheerful disposition
- Feeling enlivened and enthusiastic
- Positivity
- Blissful
- Clear, balanced mind
- Kind and compassionate
- Lustrous skin
- A gleam in the eye
- Eye whites are clear and bright
- Tongue is clear and pink
- Strong shiny hair
- Strong immunity
- Mental and physical resilience
- Stamina and endurance
- Calm, peaceful demeanor
- Feeling grounded and centered
- Feeling well-rested
- Bright glowing aura

Characteristics of low *Ojas:*

- Confusion
- Poor memory
- Feeling mentally scattered
- Dull eyes
- Weak voice
- Fatigue
- low immunity
- Dimness
- Poor stamina
- Lack of resilience
- Anxiety, fear
- Stiffness and join pain
- Lackluster, pale skin
- Lack of enthusiasm for life

In an era of disposable everything, we've been treating our health as if it were disposable too. It is as if we believe we can throw it away, and then retrieve it again by paying for a simple doctor's visit or popping the latest miracle pill. The truth is health is not disposable! It is not easy to come by renewed health as if buying a new pair of shoes! Once our health has been destroyed, it is very difficult if to bring it back. We're all going to grow old, but we don't have to grow old *and* sick. Early on, diet and lifestyle choices create the momentum for long-term health or for eventual disease.

As an *Ayurvedic* health counselor working with various clients with a variety of health conditions, I have seen for myself the profound effects diet and lifestyle have on any and every disease! In fact, I have yet to see anyone's health not improve once diet and lifestyle are improved! Diet and life style are the main difference between wellness and suffering, heath and disease! Knowing the distinctive properties of different foods allows us to tweak the diet even further, using food itself to shift the body's momentum back towards a state of health, harmony, radiance and bliss.

When *ojas* is abundant, the soul can shine through brightly into all aspects of our being! The only way to build *ojas* is to nourish the body, mind and soul. Yoga's goal of union is not complete until you have found union in every corner of your life. Yoga is about joining all aspects of your life with who you truly are. You are joy, love and light. The way you eat and exercise should reflect the light of who you truly are to nurture and sustain your highest self. Who you truly are is bliss!

> **The "Bliss" Factor:** *Ojas* stabilizes and optimizes life-force. *Ojas* is also responsible for mental health and stability. Without sufficient *ojas,* the mind becomes unstable. Sufficient *ojas* protects the mind, keeping it grounded and harmonious and promotes positive emotions such as love, joy, pleasure, creativity and bliss! Adequate *ojas* promotes an overall sense of satisfaction, pleasure and wellbeing.

Ojas vs. *Ama*:

Ancient *Aurvedic* physicians believed the body was given 8 drops of *Ojas* from the time of birth. *Ojas* is stored in the heart center, and if depleted, death occurs. For this reason, *Ayurveda* puts a strong emphasis on proper digestion. The end product of proper, healthy digestion is the formation of *Ojas,* the vital life giving nectar, which nourishes, builds and supports all tissues in the body, and is ultimately responsible for the vitality of all bodily fluids, including reproductive fluids.

The end product of improper digestion, is the formation of *ama,* a thick, channel clogging toxic sludge. (See Day 1 for more information on *ama.*) If the body is not producing *ojas,* it is producing *ama.* The first signs of low *ojas* are weakness, fatigue, and frequent illness. As the condition worsens the result is chronic disease. For example, AIDS is considered a condition of low *ojas* in the *Ayurveda* system. *Ama* and *ojas* are both products of digestion, but opposite in nature. *Ojas* makes the body hospitable to health, and *ama* makes the body hospitable to disease! Excess *dosha* (*vata*, *pitta* or *kapha*) tends to attach itself to *ama*, traveling with it through the channels, causing disease symptoms to arise in the weak sites of the body. Varying symptoms will arise characteristic of the particular *dosha* attached to the *ama*. In order to build radiance, health and vitality, it is essential to focus on supporting the production of *ojas* and avoiding the production of *ama*, all while keeping the *doshas* in balance and harmony.

Lifestyle causes of low-*Ojas:*

- Poor quality diet
- Lack of nourishment
- Extreme or crash dieting
- Working (or studying) long hours
- Excessive exercise
- Excessive worry/stress
- Repressed emotions
- Extended Fever
- Excessive sex
- Overly strenuous physical labor
- Chronic pain
- Poor sleep or staying up too late
- Living a "rock star" lifestyle
- Dehydration
- Exposure to toxins
- Negativity
- Over-imbibing in alcohol or coffee
- Volatile home life

Lifestyle Practices that Build *Ojas*

- Meditation
- Time in nature
- Ample rest and sleep
- Keeping good company (time with loved ones and pets)
- Laughter

- Hugs
- Finding fulfillment, doing what brings you joy
- Yoga (gentle to moderate, not strenuous)

Foods that build *Ojas*:

- *Chavanprash*, an *Ayurvedic* medicinal jelly/jam formulated with fruits and herbs to deliberately build *ojas* in times frailness, convalescence and weakness.
- Moist, cooked foods
- Sweet, fresh, juicy fruits
- Raw milk
- Raw honey
- Figs
- Dates
- Almonds
- Sesame seeds, sesame oil
- Ghee, clarified butter
- Nuts and seeds, nut-butters
- Avocado
- Sweet potato
- Whole grains

Dietary causes of disease/*ama* according to *Ayurveda* expert Dr. Vasant Lad:

1. Eating inappropriately for one's *dosha*
2. Under-eating
3. Overeating
4. Emotional eating
5. Incompatible food combining
6. Eating too many raw foods
7. Eating in a stressful environment
8. Gulping down foods too quickly

What is extremely empowering about *Ayurveda* is that is places our health back in our own hands where it belongs. Diet and lifestyle are choices, and we can choose for ourselves the lifestyle and diet most compatible with health, or with disease. We can build and support our health or deplete it! Healthy *Ojas* is a product of how we treat our body, mind and soul. The present status of *ojas* is easily assessed by the criteria listed in this chapter. What is the status of your *ojas* currently? What diet and lifestyle patterns are coming between you and your innate radiance and bliss?

Important tips about honey from the healing science of *Ayurveda*:

1. Honey is an *ojas* nourishing food.
2. Honey is medicinal, used both internally and externally.
3. Honey is considered the most "*sattvic*" or pure form of sweetness.
4. Honey should only be taken raw and unfiltered.
5. Never bake with honey. Heating honey above 140F changes the properties of honey and reduces the health benefits. *Ayurveda* teaches that honey becomes toxic, clogging the channels when heated above 140F.
6. Let your tea cool a bit before adding honey.
7. Honey is used in combination with herbs and spices because it helps to transport them into the tissues.
8. Honey is said to build "*ojas*", the "sap of life" which is the basis of energy, vitality, youthfulness and immunity.

Every meal is a chance to heal. ~Dr. Mark Hyman

Affirmation: I cultivate good health by "being health". My lifestyle is in alignment with health. I get adequate rest and moderate exercise. I choose foods that vibrate with energy and vitality. I deliberately choose to make balance and well-being who I am.

Today's biggest success:

Food for thought: Are you building *ojas* or *ama*? Are you filled with radiance and bliss, or do you feel weak and fatigued? Pay attention to diet and lifestyle factors that work against optimal *ojas*.

Journal: How can you tweak your eating and lifestyle to cultivate more radiance and bliss?

Day 37

I AM

I am: two of the most powerful words; for what you put after them shapes your reality. ~unknown

The words "I am" set a powerful intention about who and what we are and what we shall become. As we have come to learn, intentions are the seeds of manifestation. They create your reality! In the English language, we abuse the words "I am" by asserting, "I am hungry." I am tired." "I am starving." "I am full." Our unconscious language sets the intention for how we really feel. Your body believes every word you say. In most other languages, these statements are spoken differently: "I have hunger." "I have fatigue." "I have starvation." These situations are temporary. However, when you repeat the mantra "I am hungry." I am starving." You are making these sensations into a permanent state of being. Are the sensations of hunger, starvation, fatigue or fullness how you want to define yourself? I believe words alone have tremendous power over our behavior. What if we began to say, "I feel hungry." Knowing feelings are temporary, and feelings will pass.

We are not our feelings and our feelings do not define us. The French who are not suffering from an obesity epidemic, are also not linguistically conditioned to identify "I am" with a feeling they are having like we do in the English language. They use the words "I have" in connection with feelings. The French simply say, "I have hunger." "I have fatigue." Their very language alone allows them to recognize that they are separate from their feelings. Through wording they set the intention that they are not their feelings. Feelings are temporary, and they will pass. Perhaps now is the time to become more aware of the words we put after "I am."

I constantly hear people say, "I am sick and tired of this or that." Coming from the south, I've even heard people say, "I am sick to death of . . ." By using these words, they are affirming sickness, tiredness and even death in the mind-body system. The body hears and believes everything we tell it. When these words are repeated enough it becomes like a mantra, vibrationally recalibrating who we are. Repeated phrases work like intentions or spells, rewiring neural-pathways in the brain. What we tell ourselves is who we are to become. The words "I am" are powerful words, so pay attention and be mindful of the words that follow it!

I notice our culture places so much focus on illness and disease. Too many times I have observed people say "my diabetes", "my high blood pressure", "my cancer," etc. What if we began to place our focus on the parts of us that are healthy? Our thoughts amplify the energy of health or of disease. Where our thoughts go, energy flows.

Who am I?

"Who am I?" Is a question, which has been asked since the dawn of mankind. The answer: *Who are you not?* When we start to peel away the layers of who we are not, underneath it all at the very core, exists the truth behind **I am.** "I am" is who remains. As you deepen the practices of yoga and meditation, you begin to separate "me" from "not me." You begin to unveil the Truth of who you are. Sometimes this process is met with apprehension as the parts of us we thought were real begin to fall away.

We sometimes fear reaching down deep to find our own True Self. This journey takes courage. I have observed in myself and in others how we unconsciously sabotage ourselves as we come closer to the truth of who we really are. We become afraid of reaching our highest self out of the fear of discovering how truly glorious we really are. Our eating and lifestyle choices can help us bring about our greatest harmony and our highest good, or they can slowly destroy us a little more every day. Intuitively we know this, but we make choices that work against us. We stand in our own way. We ourselves are our greatest obstacles. Why is it that we resist practicing what we know is best for us? Why do we fight revealing the truest, purest most harmonious version of who we are? Perhaps we fear our own true power.

One thing I know for sure . . . You are not the number on your bathroom scales, you are not the size of your jeans, you are not what you look like in a swimsuit. You are not the car you drive or the house you live in, or the name brand of your sunglasses or dress.

The Power of I am . . .

I experienced a huge personal awakening during an unpleasant encounter with someone who made it quite a challenge to be the loving person that I attempt to be. How do you love someone who is very difficult to love, someone who is being nasty and insulting? It came to me: I don't have to strive to love that person, I just have to **BE LOVE** and then the loving happens all by itself. **I am** LOVE. Once I recognized the power of I am, I no longer had to struggle and strive to do that which I already am at the core of my being! I was able to apply it to all areas of my life! In my yoga practice, I noticed, I don't have to do the pose, if I just embody the pose. When I am in tree pose, I become that tree. When I am in hero pose, I am a hero. When I am in warrior pose, I become the warrior. When I am in child pose, I am a child.

The word "yoga" means wholeness and unity. Yoga is **oneness**. Yoga is embodying "**I am**." It is complete integration. Ultimately the purpose of yoga is to bring about oneness with God, but to become one with God, you first must have the courage to become one with yourself.

It is said that "the kingdom of God is within," and that "We are created in the image and likeness of God." That is our journey, wholeness and oneness. Jesus said, "I am in the father and he is in me; I and the father are one." This oneness is available to all of us. At our very core, we already are peace, love, harmony and health, because that is who the creator is and we were created in that image and likeness.

Today, I don't have to be peaceful, if **I am** peace. I don't have to take it easy, when **I am** ease. I don't have be healthy, if I personify health and wellbeing. I don't have to be loving, when **I AM** love. When **I AM** love, the creator and I are one. I would like to thank that difficult person for *teaching* me who **I AM.**

The poem entitled "Zazen on Ching't'ing Mountain" brings this point home:

> The birds have vanished down the sky.
>
> Now the last cloud drains away.
>
> We sit together, the mountain and me,
>
> Until only the mountain remains.

Short "I AM" meditation:

This first meditation inquiry reminds me of a "Google" search. As you eliminate extraneous words, you are able to narrow the search. See what happens as you begin to narrow your own search into what meditation is. Find a comfortable seat with your eyes closed. Take a moment to make any micro-movements or adjustments to your seat to deepen you sense of comfort and relaxation. Bring your hands into a comfortable hand position or *mudra*. Trust the hand position that feels right in this moment.

1. Say the words to yourself: "I am sitting here meditating."
2. Remove the last word: (Narrowing the search) "I am sitting here."
3. Remove the last word: "I am sitting."
4. Remove the last word: "I am."
5. Remove the last word: "I"
6. Remove the "I" . . .
7. Now rest in the spaciousness of the true self...without the "I", without the ego.

What did you sense when the "I" dropped away?

Without "I" or "my" we are free . . . This is an ego awareness meditation. Thoughts are like ripples on the lake of the mind. When we still the ripples, we are able to see the clear reflection of our true selves. When we begin to see the true self, we become more adept at distinguishing self from non-self. That which is not real begins to fall away.

2nd Short "I AM" Meditation:

"Be still and know that I am God." Psalm 46:10

Say this verse to yourself: *"Be still and know that I am God."*

Remove the last word: *"Be still and know that I am."*

Remove the last word: "Be still and know that I."

Remove the last word: "Be still and know that."

Remove the last word: "Be still and know."

Remove the last words: "Be still."

Remove the last word: "Be"

For the next few minutes of the meditation, simply rest in stillness and just "be".

Inquiry: What is standing in the way between you and "being"? Really go in and look and allow that which stands in the way between you and being to surface. Reflect upon how and why these stand in the way, and how you encourage or enable it. Awareness is potent. What does it mean to you just to "be"?

Knowing yourself is the beginning of all wisdom. ~Aristotle

Affirmation: This "I am" affirmation was pieced together from several different sources. It should be done in front of a mirror gazing into your own eyes, and repeated 3 times

I am fearless.

I am beneath no one.

I am independent of other's opinions.

I love myself.

I accept my uniqueness.

I have nothing to prove.

I am grace of God.

Today's biggest success:

Food for thought: The cells in your body respond to everything you think and say. Choose your thoughts and words as carefully as you choose the foods you eat! Be selective of the words you put after the statement, **I am.**

Journal: Complete this statement: "I am . . . " What stands in the way between me and being? How and why? How am I enabling this to occur? What parts of me are *"not me"* and are ready to go.

Day 38

The Power of Momentum

We are what we repeatedly do. Excellence therefore is not an act, but a habit. ~Aristotle

As these 40 Days near their conclusion, know that you have an extraordinarily powerful force moving in your favor. The power of momentum! With momentum alone, we have the potential to shift our lives towards the outcomes we desire!

Momentum is energy. It is the force of movement and its velocity. In the martial arts, the master uses his opponent's own momentum to defeat him. By pulling him in the direction he is already moving, he can be easily taken to the ground. Even a smaller opponent has the potential to overcome someone much larger if he masters the skill of using momentum. We, too, can become masters of momentum, by moving forward in the direction in which we have already started to evolve and grow!

The Merriam-Webster Dictionary defines Momentum with the following:

—the strength or force that something has when it is moving.

—the strength or force that allows something to continue or to grow stronger or faster as time passes

—the property that a moving object has due to its mass and its motion.

Clearly, momentum is a force that has the power to carry us far in life if we tap into it. This 40 Days is designed to provide you momentum toward optimal weight and health. Once momentum gets going, transformation begins to happen all by itself!

Action + Grace = Momentum. Action and grace brought together create a powerful force. Fusion of these two things is magical. Put together they can accomplish anything!

Action + Grace + Momentum = Manifestation. This is the alchemic formula for making the impossible possible! You can't just make a grocery list of things you need at the store and expect those things to appear in your refrigerator without going to get them. You must decide what it is that you want and then go get it and bring it home. By taking right action, you can manifest everything you wanted on the grocery list. All things work this way including the healthiest, most radiant version of you.

*Take a moment to make a "grocery list" of the actions steps, desires and outcomes you intend to continue to come along with you beyond the 40 days. These intentions will fuel your progress moving forward. If you go to the grocery store without a list, all sorts of things end up in the cart including foods you'll later wish you hadn't bought! At the same time, you might get home and find ingredients you were hoping to have on hand, never made it into your cart! The same holds true when choosing what it is you want for yourself! It is important to consciously curate what belongs in your transformational journey and what needs to be left behind. If you get into a taxi, and don't tell the driver where you want to go, you may move forward, but you could wind up anywhere! If you give the driver your desired destination, he may take an unfamiliar route or even the "round-about way," but there is a very good chance that you will arrive at your chosen destination!

At the beginning of the 40 Days you set your intentions. (You told the driver, YOU, where you wanted to go.) Then you began moving in that direction. Actions bring intentions into being. By taking conscious actions you were able to move stagnation, and break up old patterns. Conscious action began with the mind as the catalyst, but then moved into the physical realm as a concrete "doing." You deliberately took an action that formally broke with the past, and brought about the energy of a new beginning, and new momentum. Conscious action is kinetic energy, which is the energy of being in motion. Moving forward! Combining skill with being in motion creates the right action behind our intention and desires, which is powerful momentum. You have already been taking this action, and there is no point in turning back!

Positivity carries powerful momentum. According to quantum physics and the law of attraction, "like" attracts "like." Knowing this truth, over the 40 days we used this law in our favor. We used affirmations; focused on successes and the cultivation of *sattva*, harmony and purity to empower our journey. If you want positive things to happen in your life, "positive" energy will attract it to you. Positivity is a choice. It does not happen by its self. By choosing to focus on the positive you generate great force behind your efforts. Positivity will be drawn into your life almost magnetically, increasing the momentum for your life to shift and transform in a positive direction.

Letting go enhanced our momentum on this 40 Day journey. As we set down the foods, habits, thoughts and emotions which no longer served us, we became lighter, and freer. By letting go, we got excess baggage, resistance and friction out of our way, and intensified our forward moving momentum.

I urge you to continue with the powerful winds of momentum that are now behind your sails. This momentum alone will keep you moving in the right direction and headed towards your destination, which is ultimately your greatest and highest self. This world needs that self to show up! If not now, with all the momentum behind you, then when?

> You cannot change your future, but you can change your habits, and surely your habits will change your future.
>
> ~Dr. Abdul Kalam

Affirmation: I have the power of momentum working in my favor now. There is no going back! I am on my way to the best version of myself!

Today's biggest success:

Food for thought: You can harness the power of your own momentum to keep moving forward in the right direction almost effortlessly!

Journal: What changes have brought me the most momentum towards achieving my optimal weight and health? What changes will I continue to embrace as I am backed by the power of momentum? Make a "grocery list" of the actions steps, desires and outcomes you intend to continue to come along with you beyond the 40 days. These intentions will fuel your progress moving forward.

Day 39

Transformation

From proper diet arises longevity, good memory, wisdom, health, youth, lustrous complexion, excellence of voice, strength of the body and senses of the highest order, power of speech, respect and beauty. ~Ancient *Ayurvedic* Text – The Charaka Samhita

I once thought that transformation happened only once and then you are done. Now I understand that, transformation is an ongoing process, like peeling away the layers of an onion, one layer at a time. Life is full of mini-transformations. It is through the many cycles of transformation that we evolve and progress body, mind and soul.

Transforming your eating can't help but be a catalyst for personal transformation. What we eat transforms us from the inside out. When we change one thing in life, like a ripple effect, it begins a chain reaction. When just one person changes for the better, the whole world feels the effects and moves towards a better future. As more and more people reach for and achieve the highest version of themselves, a tipping point is reached, and the whole world transforms.

Could You Be the Hundredth Monkey?

Allegedly, Japanese scientists observed a very surprising phenomenon occur with monkeys during the 1970's. There were monkey populations living on deserted islands in the pacific. As the monkeys increased in population, they depleted their food supply. In a humanitarian effort, crates of food were air-dropped on the islands to feed the primates. When the crates were dropped, they would break open upon hitting the ground, making it easy for the monkeys to recover the items, but the food would get dirty in the process. Because they were so hungry, the monkeys would eat the food, dirt and all. Finally, on one island, one of the monkeys began washing his food in the water. One-by-one, the other monkeys on the island observed this behavior and began to wash their food too. What was most astonishing though, was that when the hundredth monkey on the same island began to wash his food, it triggered an effect in which the monkeys on the other islands suddenly spontaneously began washing their food too, without ever having observed it! The scientists called this the *Hundredth Monkey effect*.

The hundredth monkey effect happens when a behavior reaches a "critical mass." It can be inferred that when a "tipping point" is reached, it suddenly activates behaviors in the general population without any direct observation or influence. With awareness, this effect could be used for the greatest and highest good! Are you the hundredth monkey?

Transformation is defined as, "A marked change, as in appearance or character, usually for the better."

An art history lover, I remember studying the sculpting methods of Michelangelo. As he gazed at a slab of marble stone, he envisioned the image concealed within. With patience, he simply removed what didn't belong to reveal the beauty that was already there, only hidden. In this way, a massive piece of stone was transformed into a work of art. Perhaps, that is what transformation is about for human beings . . . removing what doesn't belong to uncover the brilliance that is already there waiting to be revealed.

One thing I have discovered over my own many *40 Days to Enlightened Eating* experiences is that each time I make the journey, the right changes at that place in time come to light for me. Transformation is never "one-size fits all!" I notice that my students each focus on different positive changes. They each intuitively know which changes are right for them at this point in their lives. We all have different things to work on. Our own souls know what we need to do and they are leading us towards our own highest good and the most positive expression of ourselves! This is what transformation is really about! Our souls already know the work we need to do, it is just our minds that sometimes second guess or get attached to things that do not serve our soul's highest good! Once we get ourselves out of the way, transformation is not only possible, but probable. It is by following the voice of the soul that we meet our best and highest self! If we all unleashed a superior version of ourselves in the world, can you imagine what this world would become?

The journey of becoming who we were born to be never ends. It's limitless, eternal. We don't arrive—we grow. And to grow requires presence and practice. ~Mark Nepo

Transformation is about change and evolution toward a better way of living and being. The word transformation always implies a positive advancement, but never promises to be easy or without challenge. Sometimes change can happen suddenly and quickly, as in a shift in perspective, discovering a new truth or opening the mind to new possibilities. Frequently change is as difficult a process as chiseling away at marble, piece by piece. Most often transformation requires perseverance. It takes thousands of years for charcoal under pressure to become a diamond. It is not instantaneous; it is a process. Sometimes, transformation involves struggle. Muddy clay cannot become beautiful pottery until it has been put through the fire. Refinement is a part of transformation. Heating the metal and burning away impurities produces the purest, high quality gold.

Yoga itself is a catalyst for transformation. I tell my students that I am a miracle of yoga! When I started out I was one of the stiffest, clumsiest most uncoordinated people you have ever met, but also one of the most determined! I kept showing up, consistently and almost undetectably, the transformation happened class-by-class, week-by-week, year-by-year.

You start wherever you are, mentally, physically and spiritually and just by "showing up" regularly and consistently, transformation is inevitable. Yoga is a process of refining the body, mind and spirit. The practice begins working on the physical level, as the postures and breath begin to move toxins out of the tissues, channels, lymph nodes and glands. "stuck" energy begins to release from areas of tightness and tension and flow freely. As toxins and tension release out of the physical body, toxins and stiffness of the mind begin to clear away as well. Old rigid thought patterns, fears and obstacles slowly begin to lose their hold. As we gradually release old stuck patterns and limitations, our spirit is slowly freed. As we stretch the physical body, we also begin to expand towards our highest self, our true nature.

To journey without being changed is to be a nomad. To change without journeying is to be a chameleon. To journey and be transformed by the journey is to be a pilgrim. ~Mark Nepo

Transformation is not a one-time deal. Life is a series of transformations. Transformation is cyclical, not unlike the seasons in nature: spring, summer, winter and fall. Each one of us is regularly experiencing a mini birth, life, death and rebirth as parts of us die away to reveal something new and more valuable underneath. Little by little, we chisel away at the rough-hewn stone exterior to reveal more and more beauty of our true self, our splendor and our greatness waiting underneath to be revealed as the masterpiece we truly are.

According to Deepak Chopra, "The most creative act you will ever undertake is the act of creating yourself." It is through our own transformations that the world itself begins to transform. Paramahansa Yogananda taught, "The person who can transform himself, can transform the world."

Some of the most powerful transformers are self- acceptance, self-nourishment, self-compassion, self-love and self-care. We MUST transform because this world needs to transform. This transformation begins and ends with you!

Ayurvedic Mealtime Prayer

The food which we are about to eat,

Is earth, water and sun, compounded through the alchemy of many plants.

Therefore earth, water and sun will become a part of us.

Food is also the fruit of the labor of many beings and creatures.

For all of this we are thankful.

May it give us strength, health and joy.

May it increase our love.

Affirmation: I am a powerful being! I have the power to transform myself, my life and my world! I am doing it by simply "showing up" and doing the right thing again and again and again!

Today's biggest success:

Food for Thought: By harnessing the alchemy of yoga, *Ayurveda*, healthy eating and meditation, you cannot help but transform and peel away what doesn't belong! Embrace the exquisite work of art that you are!

Journal: Where have you transformed on the 40-day journey? What parts of you still need to be chiseled away to reveal the beauty that is already there? What parts are the radiant true you that need to stay and shine? What have you uncovered underneath all the layers that you have removed so far?

Day 40

Moksha: Liberation

Your body is not your masterpiece – your life is. It is suggested to us a million times a day that our BODIES are PROJECTS. They aren't. Our lives are. Our spirituality is. Our relationships are. Our work is. ~Glennon Doyle Melton

The Sanskrit word *moksha* literally translates as emancipation, liberation or release. Enlightenment is just that. It is liberation from that which has restrained you, trained you, controlled you and held you down. Liberation is about breaking the confines of your "small self" so that your highest and greatest self can shine through! It is impossible to achieve a higher state of being when you are treating yourself with inadequate nutrition, rigid diets, self-limiting habits, little rest, a deficit of self-love, inferior self-care and depleting or abusive exercise regimes. It is equally freeing to release yourself from perfection and rigid cultural stereotypes of how *everyone's* body should look regardless of age or body type. *Moksha* is ultimately freeing yourself from false expectations, culturally conditioned ideas, habitual behaviors or fitting into a preconceived mold physically, mentally or spiritually. *Moksha* is the freedom to be you . . . all of you . . . the best of you!

Respect yourself enough to care about your dreams. Respect others enough to allow them the freedom to be who they are. ~unknown

Over this 40 Day journey, you have walked the path of liberation. You have freed yourself from old patterns, habits and *samskaras*. You are liberated from the cravings, aches and pains and sluggish energy that arises from eating in unsupportive ways. You may even be liberated from unwanted pounds if that was your intention. Most importantly, you have begun the process of becoming liberated from unrealistic or harsh expectations about how you should look, emotional baggage that weighed you down, and poor self-care paradigms that held you back from connecting to the best and highest part of yourself. You are not your True Self when the effects of poor eating and lifestyle habits cloud your mind and moods.

Over the 40-Day journey, we have been cultivating *sattva* in our body, mind and soul. *Sattva* is the state of no longer being bound by toxic energy, thoughts, emotions or habits. *Sattva* is the quality of harmony and purity towards which yogis strive, making liberation possible.

You are what your deep, driving desire is. As your desire is,
so is your will. As your will is, so is your deed.

~Brihadaranyaka Upanishad

The struggle with temptation to eat unhealthy foods is your soul giving you the opportunity to break free! The soul is teaching you the discipline and self-control necessary to promote self-liberation, *moksha*. It is that discipline that ultimately leads to freedom . . . freedom from disease, excess weight, low-energy, poor moods and premature aging. This freedom opens you up to new possibility . . . the possibility, to own your health, own your weight and own your life!

Moksha is also liberation from the control food or substances have over you. You are in control of your eating choices. With new awareness, the food industry does not control you with tempting ads, marketing tactics, flavor and appetite enhancers, or profit boosting solutions like artificial colors, flavors and preservatives. You are no longer helpless against food cravings. You have new tools in place, so you are no longer at their whim. You are no longer controlled by addictions to sugar, caffeine, or alcohol. With awareness, you are no longer choiceless. You are liberated. You are free.

May I have the courage today
to live the life I would love,
To postpone my dream no longer
But to do at last what I came here for
and waste my life on fear no more.~John O'Donohue

Affirmation: I am free to choose the life I want to live! It is already mine, and my choices are bringing me closer to it every day! I am an infinite being, beyond measure! I am free!

Today's biggest success:

Food for thought: You are no longer a choiceless participant when it comes eating and food. With awareness, discipline, compassion and self-acceptance, you are liberated to become that which you came here for.

Journal: What have you freed yourself of over the 40 day journey? What changes have set you free?

Day 41

Jai: Victory

It is through the alignment of the body that I discovered the alignment of my mind, self, and intelligence. ~BKS Iyengar

Jai is the Sanskrit word for "victory!" Today marks a day of victory for you! You have successfully completed 40 Days of Enlightened Eating! When you give the body, mind and soul what nourishes, supports and nurtures you at every level, the end product is the best and highest version of you! When you align your life with optimal health, energy and vitality then the result cannot be anything other! This 40 Day journey is ultimately one of self-empowerment, soul-growth and self-enlightenment!

Take a few moments to savor your victory! Notice how you look and feel today! Pay close attention to your thoughts and mood. How do you feel you fit into your own skin? Do you feel a new radiance, an inner glow?

Your victory should be measurable by now! Perhaps you have witnessed the inches come off, a more comfortable fit of your clothes or a smaller number on the scales. Perhaps, your blood sugar, cholesterol or blood pressure has lowered. Perhaps you have observed better sleep, greater energy and mellower moods! If you checked and recorded your BMI index at the beginning of the 40 Days, it is now time to check it again.

Check BMI Index again:

U.S.	Metric
$\dfrac{703 \times \text{weight (lb)}}{\text{height (in)}}$	$\dfrac{\text{weight (kg)}}{\text{height (m)}}$

Body Mass Index:

Underweight = <18.5

Healthy weight = 18.5–24.9

Overweight = 25–29.9

Obesity = BMI of 30 or greater

Self-advancement and improvement is empowering! You have walked every step of the way, one day at a time, to a victory! In the words of one of my most treasured Kripalu teachers, Sudha Carolyn Lundeen:

Don't undo who you just undid.

Carry with you the victory of transformation, body, mind and soul, and share your knowledge with others. Can you imagine a society in which we all felt as happy, healthy, vibrant and empowered as you do right now?

As we have discussed, the downfall of human kind begins and ends with food. The original "fall of mankind" was precipitated by eating tempting food . . . which ultimately led to separation, disease, suffering and death. All these years later, humankind is still being tempted by foods that are leading to our demise . . . Victory can happen one person at a time, and it begins with you! The day we all have awareness and make the vital changes, is the day we all awaken victorious! In consciously choosing to eat the way we were designed to eat, in harmony with nature, we collectively return to "the garden", to paradise and to *moksha* or liberation. We all begin again to live in harmony with the intention of our creator. We become who we were always destined to be, healthy, beautiful, powerful, intelligent, enlivened, and joyful! By owning the greatness of our human potential, body, mind and soul, we all emerge victorious!

The rhythm of the body, the melody of the mind, and the harmony of the soul create the symphony of life.

~BKS Iyengar

Jai!

Bearing Gifts

    by Robert Holden

You are gift-wrapped.

Unwrap yourself now.

Let your gifts spill to the floor and all over the world.

Watch how your kindness transform this cruel world.

See how your love heals fear.

Notice how your courage inspires us all.

Let your smile release this old sad world.

Give everyone you meet the star in your eye.

Shine your light.

Open your heart.

Notice how your peace of mind

makes any war more meaningless and harder to fight.

Your happiness is a gift.

It attracts angels from afar.

Your smile is like champagne.

Your laughter is like love.

Your healing inspires us.

Your presence is a miracle.

Unwrap yourself now.

Today's Affirmation: Today I am victorious! Let us all enjoy the victory of optimal health, energy, longevity and vitality, for it is our birthright!

Today's biggest success:

Food for thought: Now it is your turn to lead the way to victory! Share what you have learned and lived over the 40 Days with others! Let us all return to the garden!

Journal: List your own personal victories over the 40 Days. Create a resolve as you now move forward on your own! Live your victory!

Appendix 1

Dosha Quiz

The following *Ayurvedic* constitutional self-quiz was developed by Dr. David Frawley, director of the American Institute of Vedic Studies. Dr. Frawley is the foremost *Ayurvedic* expert in the western world. This quiz can be found in his book *Ayurvedic Healing* page 31-34. There are many versions of *Ayurvedic dosha* quizzes, but I think this one is very thorough. Simply circle the best answer in each row. If you feel that two answers in the same row are completely equal, then it is fine to circle both answers. At the end, total up the number of circled answers in each column. The column in which you have the highest total is your dominant *dosha*. It is not uncommon for a person to be *bi-doshic*, having two *doshas* with about the same number of answers. Being *tri-doshic*, balanced in all three categories is somewhat rarer, but is also a possibility.

AYURVEDIC CONSTITUTIONAL TEST

BODILY STRUCTURE AND APPEARANCE

	Vata	*Pitta*	*Kapha*
FRAME	Tall or short, thin; poorly developed physique	Medium; moderately developed physique	Stout, stocky, short, big; well-developed physique
WEIGHT	Low, hard to hold weight, prominent veins and bones	Moderate, good muscles	Heavy, tends towards obesity
COMPLEXION	Dull, brown, dark-ish	Red, ruddy, flushed, glow-ing	White, pale
SKIN TEXTURE AND TEMPERATURE	Thin, dry, cold, rough, cracked, prominent veins	Warm, moist, pink, with moles, freck-les, acne	Thick, white, moist, cold, soft, smooth
HAIR	Scanty, coarse, dry, brown, slight-ly wavy	Moderate, fine, soft, ear-ly gray or bald	Abundant, oily, thick, very wavy, lustrous
HEAD	Small, thin, long, unsteady	Moderate	Large, stocky, steady
FOREHEAD	Small, wrinkled	Moderate, with folds	Large, broad
FACE	Thin, small, long, wrinkled, dusky, dull	Moderate, ruddy, sharp contours	Large, round, fat, white or pale, soft contours
NECK	Thin, long	Medium	Large, thick
EYEBROWS	Small, thin, un-steady	Moderate, fine	Thick, bushy, many hairs
EYELASHES	Small, dry, firm	Small, thin, fine	Large, thick, oily, firm
EYES	Small, dry, thin, brown, dull, un-steady	Medium, thin, red (inflamed easily), green, piercing	Wide, prominent, thick, oily, white, at-tractive
NOSE	Thin, small, long, dry, crooked	Medium	Thick, big, firm, oily

	Vata	*Pitta*	*Kapha*
LIPS	Thin, small, dark-ish, dry, unsteady	Medium, soft, red	Thick, large, oily, smooth, firm
TEETH AND GUMS	Thin, dry, small, rough, crooked, receding gums	Medium, soft, pink, gums bleed easily	Large, thick, soft, pink, oily
SHOULDERS	Thin, small, flat, hunched	Medium	Broad, thick, firm, oily
CHEST	Thin, small, nar-row, poorly devel-oped	Medium	Broad, large, well or overly developed
ARMS	Thin, overly small or long, poorly devel-oped	Medium	Large, thick, round, well developed
HANDS	Small, thin, dry, cold, rough, fis-sured, unsteady	Medium, warm, pink	Large, thick, oily, cool, firm
THIGHS	Thin, narrow	Medium	Well-developed, round, fat
LEGS	Thin, excessively long or short, prominent knees	Medium	Large, stocky
CALVES	Small, hard, tight	Loose, soft	Shapely, firm
FEET	Small, thin, long, dry, rough, fis-sured, unsteady	Medium, soft, pink	Large, thick, hard, firm
JOINTS	Small, thin, dry, un-steady, cracking	Medium, soft, loose	Large, thick, well built
NAILS	Small, thin, dry, rough, fissured, cracked, darkish	Medium, soft, pink	Large, thick, smooth, white, firm, oily

WASTE MATERIALS / METABOLISM

	Vata	*Pitta*	*Kapha*
URINE	Scanty, difficult, colorless	Profuse, yellow, red, burning	Moderate, whitish, milky
FECES	Scanty, dry, hard, difficult or painful, gas, constipation	Abundant, loose, yellowish, diarrhea, with burning sensation	Moderate, solid, sometimes pale in color, mucus in stool
SWEAT / BODY ODOR	Scanty, no smell	Profuse, hot, strong smell	Moderate, cold, pleasant smell
APPETITE	Variable, erratic	Strong, sharp	Constant, low
TASTE PREFERENCES	Prefers sweet, sour or salty food, cooked with oil and spices	Prefers sweet, bitter or astringent food, raw, lightly cooked, no spices	Prefers pungent, bitter or astringent food, cooked with spices but not oil
CIRCULATION	Poor variable, erratic	Good, warm	Good, warm, slow, steady

GENERAL CHARACTERISTICS

	Vata	*Pitta*	*Kapha*
ACTIVITY	Quick, fast, un-steady, erratic, hyperactive	Medium, mo-tivated, pur-poseful, goal seeking	Slow, steady, stately
STRENGTH / ENDURANCE	Low, poor endurance, starts and stops quickly	Medium, in-tolerant of heat	Strong, good endurance, but slow in starting
SEXUAL NATURE	Variable, erratic, deviant, strong desire but low en-ergy, few children	Moderate, passionate, quarrelsome, dominating	Low but constant sexual desire, good sexual energy, devoted, many children
SENSITIVITY	Fear of cold, wind, sensitive to dry-ness	Fear of heat, dislike of sun, fire	Fear of cold, damp, likes wind and sun

	Vata	*Pitta*	*Kapha*
RESISTANCE TO DISEASE	Poor, variable, weak immune sys-tem	Medium, prone to in-fection	Good, prone to con-gestive disorders
DISEASE TENDENCY	Nervous system dis-eases, pain, arthritis, mental disorder	Fevers, infec-tions, inflam-matory dis-eases	Respiratory system diseases, mucus, edema
REACTION TO MEDICATIONS	Quick, low dosage needed, unex-pected side ef-fects or ner-vous reactions	Medium, av-erage dosage	Slow, high dosage required, effects slow to manifest
PULSE	Thready, rapid, super-ficial, irregu-lar, weak / like a snake	Wiry, bound-ing, moderate / like a frog	Deep, slow, steady, deep, rolling, slippery / like a swan

MENTAL FACTORS AND EXPRESSION

	Vata	*Pitta*	*Kapha*
VOICE	Low, weak, hoarse	High pitch, sharp, mod-erate, good tone	Pleasant, deep, good tone
SPEECH	Quick, incon-sistent, erratic, talkative	Moderate, argumen-ta-tive, con-vincing	Slow, definite, not talkative
MENTAL NATURE	Quick, adaptable, indecisive	Intelligent, penetrat-ing, critical	Slow, steady, dull
MEMORY	Poor, notices things easily but easily forgets	Sharp, clear	Slow to take notice but will not forget
FINANCES	Earns and spends quickly, erratically	Spends on specific goals, caus-es or pro-jects	Holds on to what one earns, particularly property
EMOTIONAL TENDENCIES	Fearful, anxious, nervous	Angry, irrita-ble, conten-tious	Calm, content, at-tached, sentimental
NEUROTIC TENDENCIES	Hysteria, trem-bling, anxiety at-tacks	Extreme temper, rage, tan-trums	Depression, unre-sponsiveness, sorrow

	Vata	Pitta	Kapha
FAITH	Erratic, changea-ble, rebel	Determined, fanatic, lead-er	Constant, loyal, con-servative
SLEEP	Light, tends to-wards insomnia	Moderate, may wake up but will fall asleep again	Heavy, difficulty in waking up
DREAMS	Flying, moving, rest-less, night-mares	Colorful, passionate, conflict	Romantic, senti-mental, watery, few dreams
HABITS	Likes speed, trav-eling, parks, plays, jokes, stories, triv-ia, artistic activi-ties, dancing	Likes com-petitive sports, de-bates, poli-tics, hunting, research	Likes water, sailing, flowers, cosmetics, business ventures, cooking

Totals	Vata	Pitta	Kapha

The column with the most items circled indicates your dominant *dosha*. The more dominant a *dosha* is, meaning the higher the total in one column, and the larger the discrepancy there is between the dominant *dosha* and the other *doshas*, the more attributes of that *dosha* a person will have. Remember some people are a near balance of two *doshas*, and a few people are balanced between all three. *Ayurveda* recognizes seven different constitutional types: *vata, pitta, kapha, vata-pitta, vata-kapha, pitta-kapha,* and *vata-pitta-kapha* (V-P-K) or *tri-doshic*.

Appendix 2

Suggested Grocery List:
There is absolutely nothing you must buy for the 40 Days, but this list gives you some ideas and a starting point as you begin to restock your shelves.

Breads: Organic is preferable, preservative-free, free of chemical ingredients
Ezekiel bread
Whole grain breads
Sprouted breads

Grains: Organic is preferable.
Barley
Black rice
Brown rice
Bulgar wheat
Chia
Faro
Millet
Organic oatmeal
Quinoa
Pop-corn (organic, non-GMO)
Steel cut oats
Whole wheat Couscous

Legumes: preferably frozen or dried, not in can, organic when available. (When in a hurry, I use organic beans in BPA-free cans.)
Black beans
Black-eye peas
Cannellini beans
Chickpeas
Edamame
Lentils
Mung beans-most balancing
Peas
Pinto beans
Sugar snap peas

Dairy: organic when possible, if available. Reduced-fat is not recommended.
Butter (*Ghee*, if available, is considered medicinal in *Ayurveda*)
Cheeses (Do not buy pre-shredded cheese. It is treated with mold-inhibitors and anti-coagulants.)

Cottage cheese
Eggs organic, cage free
Milk or goat's milk
Ricotta cheese
Yogurt (Greek yogurt has double the protein of regular yogurt.)

Nuts and seeds:
Almond butter
Almonds
Cashews (organic if possible)
Coconut
Macadamia nuts
Peanuts (organic if possible)
Pecans
Pine nuts
Pistachios (organic if possible)
Poppy seeds
Pumpkin seeds
Sesame seeds
Sunflower seeds
Tahini
Walnuts

Oils:
Canola oil (Only if expeller pressed, otherwise chemical solvents are used to extract oil from the seed)
Coconut oil
Coconut oil
Extra-virgin olive oil
Grape seed oil
Hempseed oil
Sesame oil
Walnut oil

Condiments:
Apple cider vinegar
Coconut aminos
Grated coconut
Olives
Organic Mayonnaise
Rice vinegar
Tamari
Veganaise

Herbs:
    Basil
    Bay leaf
    Chives
    Dill
    Lemongrass
    Mint
    Oregano
    Parsley
    Rosemary
    Sage
    Tarragon
    Thyme

Spices: (Use fresh high quality organic. Spices turn rancid/toxic after about 1 year.)
    Black Peppercorns, whole, grind as needed
    Cinnamon
    Chili powder
    Cilantro
    Cloves
    Coriander
    Fennel
    Garlic powder
    Ginger
    Mustard
    Nutmeg
    Red pepper flakes
    Pink Himalayan salt
    Turmeric

Superfoods:
1. Almonds
2. Apples
3. Bananas
4. Beans/legumes
5. Beets
6. Berries
7. Broccoli
8. Butternut squash
9. Dark chocolate
10. Extra-virgin olive oil
11. Flaxseed
12. Garlic
13. Ginger

14. Green tea
15. Kale
16. Organic grapes
17. Pomegranates
18. Pumpkin
19. Pumpkin seeds
20. Spinach
21. Sweet potatoes
22. Swiss chard
23. Tomatoes
24. Walnuts
25. Wheat grass
26. Yogurt (preferably organic Greek yogurt)

Sweeteners:
Agave
Brown rice syrup
Coconut palm sugar
Maple syrup
Molasses
Raw Honey
Raw sugar
Stevia

The **"Dirty Dozen"™** (provided by EWG, Environmental Working Group, Shopper's Guide to Pesticides in Produce)-fruits and vegetables you should always buy organic: (in alphabetic order)
1. Apples
2. Bell peppers
3. blueberries
4. Celery
5. Grapes
6. lettuce
7. Nectarines
8. Peaches
9. Pears
10. Potatoes
11. Spinach
12. Strawberries

The **"Clean Fifteen™"** (According to EWG-the Environmental Working Group Shopper's Guide to Pesticides in Produce) fruits and vegetables safe to buy non-organic:

1. Asparagus
2. Avocado
3. Cabbage
4. Cantaloupe
5. Corn
6. Eggplant
7. Grapefruit
8. Kiwi
9. Mangoes
10. Mushrooms
11. Onions
12. Pineapple
13. Sweet peas
14. Sweet potatoes
15. Watermelon

The following fruits and vegetables are preferably organic if available and affordable. These items are not the worst offenders, but have been shown to have pesticide contamination:

1. Bananas
2. Broccoli
3. Blueberries
4. Carrots
5. Corn
6. Cucumbers
7. Green beans
8. Honeydew melon
9. Hot peppers
10. Lemon
11. Mushrooms
12. Oranges
13. Papaya
14. Plums
15. Tangerines
16. Tomatoes
17. Winter squash

Juices:
Buy fresh citrus and juice yourself with a citrus juicer.
Organic juices
Use a Vitamix or Blendtec to create your own juice concoctions.

Meats:
Free-range grass-fed mutton
Free-range poultry
Grass-fed beef
Lunch meats (Most of these are preserved with nitrates and nitrites. Many of these are very processed. Look for those preservative free all-natural lunch meats if lunch meat is a necessity.)
Pork (The least clean of all meat-I recommend avoiding pork products over the next 40 days.)
Venison

Some great substitutions:
1. Tortillas- preservative-free whole wheat tortillas
2. For alcoholic beverages- calming teas such Kava tea, or other calming infusions.
3. For wine-pomegranate juice or grape juice mixed with purified water or sparkling mineral water.
4. For sodas- try sparkling mineral water with a squeeze of lime or lemon.
5. For white pasta- whole grain pasta, quinoa pasta, mung bean pasta, organic pasta.
6. For white rice or minute rice-Organic brown- black or wild rice.

Foods that Should be Eaten No More than Once a Week
1. Pasta
2. Red meat
3. Alcohol
4. Potatoes
5. Dessert
6. Bread

BIBLIOGRAPHY

5 Powerful Reasons to Eat A Plant-Based Diet: A Cardiologist Explains. (2013). Retrieved March 05, 2016, from http://www.mindbodygreen.com/0-11465/5-powerful-reasons-to-eat-a-plant-based-diet-a-cardiologist-explains.html

A. (1999). *Ayurvedic healing for women: Herbal gynecology.* York Beach, ME: Samuel Weiser.

Batmanghelidj, F. (1995). *Your body's many cries for water: You are not sick, you are thirsty! Don't treat thirst with medications.* Falls Church, VA: Global Health Solutions.

Chopra, D. (1991). *Perfect health: The complete mind/body guide.* New York: Harmony Books.

Chopra, D. (1994). *Perfect weight: The complete mind-body program for achieving and maintaining your ideal weight.* New York, NY: Harmony Books.

Dale, C., & Wehrman, R. (2009). *The subtle body: An encyclopedia of your energetic anatomy.* Boulder, CO: Sounds True.

Emoto, M. (2004). *The hidden messages in water.* Hillsboro, Or.: Beyond Words Pub.

Emoto, M. (2004). *Love thyself: The message from Water III.* Carlsbad, CA: Hay House.

Food Cravings Engineered by Industry – Cornucopia Institute. (2014). Retrieved March 05, 2016, from http://www.cornucopia.org/2014/08/food-cravings-engineered-industry/

Frawley, D. (1997). *Ayurveda and the mind: The healing of consciousness.* Twin Lakes, WI: Lotus Press.

Frawley, D. (1999). *Yoga and Ayurveda: Self-healing and self-realization.* Twin Lakes, WI: Lotus Light Pub.

Frawley, D. (2000). *Ayurvedic healing: A comprehensive guide.* Twin Lakes, Wisc.: Lotus Press.

Frawley, D., & Ranade, S. (2001). *Ayurveda, nature's medicine.* Twin Lakes, WI: Lotus.

Frawley, D. (2003). *Frawley Ayurveda course.* Monoblet (BP 4, 30170): Éd. Turiya.

Frawley, D. (2012). *Soma in yoga and ayurveda: The power of rejuvenation and immortality.* Twin Lakes, Wisc.: Lotus.

Govinda, K. (2002). *A handbook of chakra healing: Spiritual practice for health, harmony, and inner peace.* Old Saybrook, CT: Konecky & Konecky.

Halpern, M. (2011). *Healing your life: Lessons on the path of ayurveda.* Twin Lakes, WI: Lotus Press.

Judith, A. (1987). *Wheels of life: A user's guide to the Chakra system.* St. Paul, MN, U.S.A.: Llewellyn Publications.

Kacera, W. (2006). *Ayurvedic tongue diagnosis.* Twin Lakes, WI: Lotus Press.

Krishan, S. (2003). *Essential Ayurveda: What it is & What it Can Do for You.* Novato, CA: New World Library.

Lad, V., & Frawley, D. (1986). *The Yoga of Herbs: An Ayurvedic Guide to Herbal Medicine.* Santa Fe, NM: Lotus Press.

Lad, V. (2002). *Textbook of Ayurveda.* Albuquerque, NM: *Ayurvedic* Press.

Lonsdorf, N., Butler, V., & Brown, M. (1993). *A woman's best medicine: Health, happiness, and long life through Ayur-Veda.* New York: Putnam.

Pushpanath, S., V., & Philip, J. (2005). *Essential Ayurveda.* Kerala, India: Dee Bee Info Publications.

Raichur, P., & Cohn, M. (1998). *Absolute beauty.* London: Bantam Books.

Sachs, M. (1994). *Ayurvedic beauty care: Ageless techniques to invoke natural beauty.* Twin Lakes, WI: Lotus Press.

Svoboda, R. (1999). *Ayurveda for Women:* Devon: David & Charles.

Tirtha, S. S. (1998). *The Ayurveda encyclopedia: Natural secrets to healing, prevention & longevity.* Bayville, NY: *Ayurveda* Holistic Center Press.

Tiwari, M. (1995). *Ayurveda: A life of balance.* Rochester, Vt: Healing Arts Press.

Villoldo, A. (2000). *Shaman, healer, sage: How to heal yourself and others with the energy medicine of the Americas.* New York: Harmony Books.

Virtue, D. (1999). *Constant craving A-Z: A simple guide to understanding and healing your food cravings.* Carlsbad, CA: Hay House.

Yarema, T., Rhoda, D., Brannigan, J., & Ouellette, E. (2006). *Eat-taste-heal: An Ayurvedic guidebook and cookbook for modern living.* Kapaa, HI: Five Elements Press.

40 Days to Enlightened Eating

Daily Food Journal

No deprivation allowed! Focus on **nutrients** not calories.

Pay attention to your portions. You should feel **satiated** not full.

Date: _____ Intention for the day: _____

Time	Meal/ Snack	Food/ Drink	Veggies (no limit)	Whole Grains (1-2)	Protein (3 or more)	~~Junk food~~ ~~White Sugar Flour~~

Essential Hydration: X off each beverage as you consume

Lemon Water	Detox Tea	Detox Tea	Detox Tea	Water	Water	Water	Water	Water

Today's Reflections:

Biggest Success:	
Biggest Obstacle:	
What I will do differently:	
What I learned today:	
Yoga or Moderate Exercise:	

*Yogi Plate: 1/4 Protein, 1/4 Whole Grain, 1/2 Veggies

40 Days to Enlightened Eating

Daily Food Journal

No deprivation allowed! Focus on **nutrients** not calories.

Pay attention to your portions. You should feel **satiated** not full.

Date: _____ Intention for the day: _____

Time	Meal/ Snack	Food/ Drink	Veggies (no limit)	Whole Grains (1-2)	Protein (3 or more)	~~Junk food~~ ~~White Sugar Flour~~

Essential Hydration: X off each beverage as you consume

Lemon Water	Detox Tea	Detox Tea	Detox Tea	Water	Water	Water	Water	Water

Today's Reflections:

Biggest Success:	
Biggest Obstacle:	
What I will do differently:	
What I learned today:	
Yoga or Moderate Exercise:	

*Yogi Plate: 1/4 Protein, 1/4 Whole Grain, 1/2 Veggies

Made in the USA
Lexington, KY
24 April 2019